US and WORLDWIDE GUIDE
to
RETREAT CENTER
GUEST HOUSES

John and Mary Jensen

CTS Publications, Newport Beach, California

PROVISO

This book is designed to provide accurate information in regard to the subject matter covered. It is sold with the understanding that the author and publisher are not engaged in rendering legal or other professional services. If legal advice or other expert assistance is required, the services of a competent professional should be sought.

While every effort has been made to assure the information in this guide is correct, it may contain errors both typographical and in content, and the information provided may change.

The authors and CTS Publications shall have neither responsibility nor liability with respect to any inconvenience, loss or damage caused, or alleged to be caused, by the information in the book.

Library of Congress Catalog Card Number: 92-71162

©MCMXCV John and Mary Jensen

Typeface: Cover/title page — New Brunswick, Switzerland; main text — Toronto

Layout, Design, Typesetting: David Underwood

Printer: Webcraft

CTS Publications, P.O. Box 8355, Newport Beach, CA 92660

ISBN: 0-9640313-0-2

Table of Contents

Welcome To
Retreat Center Guest Houses

Do you yearn for a few days away from the frantic, dizzying pace of daily life, from the jarring noise of jets, traffic snarls, and other day-to-day pressures?

Retreat Center Guest Houses open their doors for you to enter quite another world: one of serenity, friendliness, rest and exploration. Here you divest yourself of everyday burdens in an environment where you can sit back, relax, and take the time to discover yourself and your relationship to a complicated world. The volume is turned down, and during those quiet hours you will experience a sense of self-renewal and purpose. You may see your problems with a clearer eye and they become less threatening. You relax physically, mentally, and spiritually.

Through meditation and solitude in the beautiful and tranquil settings of Guest House Centers, you find spiritual refreshment and the added strength to continue life's journey.

Whether you choose your retreat to be at the foot of the majestic Rocky Mountains, in the picturesque high desert of New Mexico, or in an elegant English manor house, this is a quest that should not be missed.

What Are Retreat Center Guest Houses?

Retreat Center Guest Houses are functioning monasteries, abbeys, priories, convents and religious centers that provide room and board for individuals and groups. Those who live there permanently devote themselves spiritually to an understanding of their humanity and their place in the infinity of the universe. They strive to be as self-sufficient as possible, often operating their own farms, gardens, gift stores, food enterprises, and fabric outlets.

Mission of the Guest Centers

The abiding philosophy of the Guest Centers is to let all guests be welcomed as if they were the Saviour *(Rule of St. Benedict)*. People of all faiths, of all or no religious persuasions, are treated as welcomed guests. You may request a *private retreat* where you manage your own time, or a *directed retreat* whereby you meet once a day with a spiritual director. The *open retreat* is for groups who usually spend a weekend with their own director or leader.

The Centers do not offer psychological counseling, nor should they be considered a commercial bed-and-breakfast service. They do provide a peaceful environment for personal renewal and enrichment.

Accommodations and Costs

Accommodations range from mountain cabins to imposing mansions, some modern buildings with spacious rooms, private baths and ocean views, to simple dormitories with shared bathrooms. All are clean, safe, and have basic amenities. The rooms do not have radios, telephones, or television sets.

The cost for Guest Houses is very inexpensive — much lower than a comparable hotel. Prices range from $30 to $40 per person. This includes three meals daily and overnight accommodation. Some Houses rely on your generosity, asking only for a free-will donation of what you can afford. Tax-deductible supplemental donations do help to maintain the Guest Houses and provide extra services. Some Centers have a minimal linen charge.

Guest Center Provisions

Guests are requested not to bring pets. The Guide lists those Houses that restrict smoking and the use of alcohol. Guests appreciate consideration for each other in maintaining a quiet and peaceful atmosphere. Making your bed with fresh linens provided by the House before you leave is accepted practice in some of the Houses.

How To Make Arrangements

If you desire to find out more about a particular House before making a reservation, write requesting a brochure, and be sure to include a self-addressed stamped envelope.

To request a reservation, simply call or write and specify the date you wish to arrive and the approximate length of your stay. Stays of one to three days are not uncommon. Many Guest Houses do not request an advance deposit. In any event, do not arrive without first calling ahead for reservations. Retreatants have a better chance for accommodations on weekdays rather than weekends, but that fact shouldn't deter you from requesting the time that best suits you. Some Centers will even pick you up at the airport or train station if you are not driving. When making a reservation, be sure to ask for specific directions to reach the guest house center.

What to Expect When You Attend
A Retreat Center Guest House

First, you will be welcomed, met with understanding, and assured of a homely, warm, friendly atmosphere. The Guest Master or Guest Sister will orient you to the grounds, the courtesies to be observed, and the time for meals. You may want to take part in the liturgical life of the community or not, as you please.

Retreat Centers provide different amenities: some have nature trails through wooded forests, swimming pool facilities, libraries and lounges for study and relaxation, chapels for solitude and reflection, walking paths along ocean-front, tennis and jogging trails, or opportunities to participate in workshops or seminars.

You may want to spend time alone, or if you choose, in the company of others. Some guests enjoy helping with light chores — in the dining room, in the gardens harvesting fresh produce, or setting up arrangements for conference rooms — such volunteer work is sincerely appreciated by the community.

All in all, your personal retreat is just what you want to make of it.

Guidebook Note

The Guide describes some of the highlights of the area where each House is located. These descriptions give a sampling of the historical landmarks, cultural centers, or natural wonders of the region that you would not want to miss, either before or after residing at a Retreat Center Guest House. The self-fulfilling and uplifting experience of the Retreat Center along with your travel sojourn combine to create the perfect vacation.

Every effort has been made to ensure the accuracy of our listings. However, we cannot be responsible for any changes in policy or pricing that may take place.

We would be pleased to learn of your retreat experience and any other comments or information you may have about other Retreat Center Guest Houses. Send your comments to: Publisher, Retreat Center Guest Houses, P.O. Box 8355, Newport Beach, CA 92660.

United States

ALABAMA

1. Blessed Trinity Shrine Retreat, Holy Trinity, AL 36859
(205) 855-4474 ❖ **Contact:** Sister Judith Jones
✓**Single Rooms** ✓**Twin Rooms** ✓**Other:** Hermitage apartment
Individual Guest Rate: $25.00 to $35.00
✓**Includes 3 Meals Daily** ✓**Self-Catering Kitchenette**
✓**Reservations Required** ✓**Advance Deposit:** $15.00
Guest Rules: No tobacco or alcohol in bedrooms; no pets.
On Site Attractions/Nearby Points of Interest: Located 25 miles SW of Columbus, GA on 1,200 acres of woodlands; trails, pond, river, shrines, etc. Nearby are the Eufoula Wildlife Refuge, Fort Gaines Lock and Dam, Frontier Village, Kolomoki Indian Mounds and visitor center.
Additional Information: Primary purpose is to provide space and programs for prayer, spiritual growth and development. Groups are welcomed — must be non-profit and church-affiliated. Children OK.

2. Monastery of the Visitation, 2300 Spring Hill Ave., Mobile, AL 36607
(205) 473-2321 ❖ **Contact:** Sr. Rose Marie
✓**Single Rooms** ✓**Twin Rooms**
Individual Guest Rate: Voluntary offering; meals can be
provided at an additional charge.
Guest Rules: No smoking in buildings; no alcohol. Doors close at 8:30 p.m.
On Site Attractions/Nearby Points of Interest: Mobile, in the far southwestern corner of the state on Mobile Bay, is sandwiched between Florida and Mississippi. The retreat house is completely modernized with air-conditioned rooms, tiled baths and a restaurant-equipped kitchen. Lovely gardens surround the gracious old mansions and iron-grillwork balconies. Ft. Condé (c. 1711) has been restored. Close at hand, Gulf Coast beaches, Bellingrath Gardens — 60,000 chrysanthemums and 250,000 azaleas ablaze with bloom.
Additional Information: Children OK with families. Groups welcomed. Suggested offering for board and room: $30.00 per person per day.

ALASKA

1. Holy Spirit Retreat House, 10980 Hillside Dr., Anchorage, AK 99516
(907) 346-2343 ❖ **Contact:** Peggy Bergsrud
✓**Single Rooms** ✓**Twin Rooms** **Individual Guest Rate:** $35.00
Guest Rules: Silence observed in sleeping areas.
On Site Attractions/Nearby Points of Interest: Twenty-two acres of wooded forest; resident moose population; 24 hours of daylight in the summer. Center overlooks city of Anchorage; view of Mt. McKinley; northern lights view in winter; 1½ miles from Alaska State Park and ski area; 2 miles from the Alaska Zoo. Eskimo handiworks are sold at the Alaska Native Arts and Crafts Showroom in Anchorage.
Additional Information: All religious persuasions welcomed; children accommodated; groups can book up to 2 years in advance, with a 6-week advance cancellation policy. Meal service provided to groups. For groups of 33 or more, no lodging charged.

1

2. Shrine of St. Therese, 5933 Lund St., Juneau, AK 99801
   (907) 780-6112 ✤ Contact: Thomas P. Fitterer, Dir.
✓**Single Rooms** ✓**Twin Rooms** ✓**Other:** Twin cabins
Individual Guest Rate: Varies ✓**Self-Catering Kitchenette**
✓**Reservations Required** ✓**Advance Deposit:** Call ahead for rates
Guest Rules: The center provides the ultimate as a locale for peace and serenity — individuals return again and again because of the striking natural beauty.
On Site Attractions/Nearby Points of Interest: Located 23 miles north of Juneau in an exceptional area of beauty and solitude. Nearby walks reveal soaring eagles, sea lions, whales, pink salmon spawning in August. Chilkat Mountains are a backdrop to the shores of the surrounding Lynn Canal. Juneau, Alaska's capital, the "Little San Francisco," displays log cabins, Russian Orthodox churches eye-to-eye with Victorian mansions.
Additional Information: Small charge for linens. Groups welcomed, rental agreement sent upon request. Children OK in cabin accommodations. Food service available.

ARIZONA

1. Our Lady of Solitude House of Prayer
   Box 1140, Black Canyon City, AZ 85324
   (602) 374-9204 ✤ Contact: Sister Therese Sedlock
✓**Single Rooms** **Individual Guest Rate:** Donation
✓**Self-Catering Kitchenette**
✓**Reservations Required** ✓**Advance Deposit:** $20.00
Guest Rules: Guests bring their own food, bedding, towels. Lodging is in self-contained retreat rooms; there is a beautiful chapel, a spacious library room with fireplace, a kitchen and dining room. An atmosphere of silence and solitude prevails.
On Site Attractions/Nearby Points of Interest: 5 miles north of Phoenix, surrounded by mountains and the Sonoran Desert; main structure on a desert mesa overlooking Black Canyon City. Nearby are all of the Phoenix area attractions.
Additional Information: No children. No groups.

2. Servants of Christ Monastery, 28 W. Pasadena Ave., Phoenix, AZ 85013
   (602) 248-9321 ✤ Contact: Guestmaster
✓**Single Rooms** ✓**Twin Rooms** **Individual Guest Rate:** $35.00
✓**Includes 3 Meals Daily** ✓**Self-Catering Kitchenette**
✓**Reservations Required** ✓**Advance Deposit:** None
On Site Attractions/Nearby Points of Interest: Heard Museum of Anthropology and Primitive Art; desert botanical gardens, Gila River Indian crafts center, Frank Lloyd Wright's Taliesin West; Phoenix Zoo; South Mountain Park, major league baseball's training camp.
Additional Information: Pamphlet provided to each guest on arrival. Cannot accept retreat groups. No children.

3. Franciscan Renewal Center, 5802 E. Lincoln Dr., Scottsdale, AZ 85252
   (602) 948-7460 ✤ Contact: Sponsored Retreat Office
✓**Single Rooms** ✓**Twin Rooms** ✓**Other:** Triple rooms
Individual Guest Rate: $45.00 first night; $35.00 additional nights
✓**Includes 3 Meals Daily**
✓**Reservations Required** ✓**Advance Deposit:** $25.00

Guest Rules: Check in prior to 8 p.m.; bed to be made up before departing.
On Site Attractions/Nearby Points of Interest: The center is a desert oasis with extensive lawns and gardens, swimming pool and jacuzzi on the premises. Mountain hikes within walking distance, desert walks; nearby Phoenix with the Heard Museum of Anthropology, Gila Indian Crafts Center, South Mountain Park, etc.
Additional Information: All rooms include private bath and thermostat controlled heat and air conditioning. Children OK with adult supervision at all times. Groups welcomed at special rates.

4. Redemptorist Picture Rocks Retreat House
   7101 W. Picture Rocks Rd., Tucson, AZ 85743
   (602) 744-3400 ✤ Contact: Betty Preininger, Ret. Coordinator
✓**Single Rooms** ✓**Twin Rooms** **Individual Guest Rate: $35.00**
✓**Includes 3 Meals Daily**
✓**Reservations Required** ✓**Advance Deposit: 30%**
Guest Rules: Guests requested not to climb petroglyph rocks, light candles, have bonfires, or to occupy kitchen area. Quiet atmosphere is to be observed.
On Site Attractions/Nearby Points of Interest: Tucson Desert Museum; jagged Tucson mountains and Sonora desert; petroglyph Indian etchings of humans, animals, flora; old Tucson studios, ghost towns. Home of the University of Arizona with its galleries, research center and performing arts theater.
Additional Information: All retreatants will be sent a policy and agreement to sign and return. No children. Groups welcomed.

5. Desert House of Prayer, Box 574, Cortaro, AZ 85652
   (602) 744-3825 *(9-12 a.m. Mon.-Fri. Mountain time)*
✓**Single Rooms** ✓**Other:** Self-contained cottages — full bath, kitchenette
Individual Guest Rate: $27, 1-3 days; $24 extra stay; $32 hermitage
✓**Includes 3 Meals Daily** ✓**Self-Catering Kitchenette**
✓**Reservations Required** ✓**Advance Deposit: $25.00**
Guest Rules: Respect the silence desired by others. It is requested that guests devote a major part of their time to becoming a part of the "community;" Desert House philosophy is grounded in social justice, with the attempt to expand knowledge about spirituality, art, theology, film, literature, government, and ecumenism.
On Site Attractions/Nearby Points of Interest: The House is located just outside Tucson on 31 acres of primitive high desert land at the foot of Stafford Peak, profusely covered with desert plants, flowers, and trees. Nearby are the San Xavier and Papago Indian Reservations. Three mountain ranges with peaks rising to 10,000 feet surround the rugged grandeur of the area. Picture Rocks is within easy walking distance. A nearby magnet attraction is the Desert Museum of Saguaro National Monument.
Additional Information: No children. No groups. What guests prize most is solitude, the freedom to hike in the green desert, and to enjoy the time to read from the 6000 volumes in the House library.

6. Living Water Worship & Teaching Center
   P.O. Box 529, Cornville, AZ 86325
   (602) 951-9494 ✤ Contact: Lee Brownson
✓**Twin Rooms** ✓**Other:** Dorm facilities
Individual Guest Rate: $50.00 twin; dorm $45.00 ✓**Includes 3 Meals Daily**
✓**Reservations Required** ✓**Advance Deposit: None**
Guest Rules: No smoking in buildings, guns, or alcohol.
On Site Attractions/Nearby Points of Interest: Cornville is an easy 2 hour drive

Living Water Worship & Teaching Center, Cornville, Arizona

north of Phoenix, about 35 miles south of Flagstaff. Living Water is a lush oasis in the heart of the vast, beautiful desert mountains of Arizona. Active recreation on the grounds: fishing, swimming, volleyball, jogging along Oak Creek, hiking, horse-shoes, softball. Nearby: Sedona's canyons, creeks, Indian ruins, dreamscape of gnarled red rocks; Montezuma Canyon National Monument; Tlaquepaque colony, where scores of artists sell paintings and sculptures.
Additional Information: Children OK. Groups welcomed, up to 100. The Center, dedicated to unity and healing, encourages visits to inspect the facility and be a guest for a weekday lunch.

7. Sunglow Mission Ranch, HCR 385, Pearce, AZ 85625
   (602) 824-3334 ❖ **Contact:** C. Truett Baker
✓**Single Rooms**   ✓**Twin Rooms**   ✓**Other:** Apartment (sleeps 8)
Individual Guest Rate: $18-$25 efficiency; $24-$37 1-bedroom; group and weekly rates available
✓**Cooking Facilities Available**
✓**Reservations Required**   **Advance Deposit:** 25%
Guest Rules: Listed in ranch brochure.
On Site Attractions/Nearby Points of Interest: Sunglow Ranch is located 1½ hours east of Tucson, at an altitude of 5,200 feet in the foothills of the Dragoon Mountains. Close by are several ghost towns, and Pearce itself shows the remnants of its role as a gold mining boom town at the turn of the century. Recreational activities include: hiking, fishing, wildlife observations, excursions to Fort Bowie and the Chiricahua National Monument. At nearby Tombstone ("The Town Too Tough To Die") are the O.K. Corral, Birdcage Theatre, Rose Tree Inn Museum, and Boothill Graveyard. Celebrations in Tombstone include: Territorial Days, Wyatt Earp Days, Revue of Gunfighters, and Helldorado Days.
Additional Information: Children and groups welcomed.

ARKANSAS

1. Little Portion Retreat Center
   Route 4, Box 430, Eureka Springs, AR 72632
   (501) 253-7379 ❖ **Contact:** Bill Reuter, Assoc. Director
✓**Twin Rooms**   **Individual Guest Rate:** $15.00   ✓**Self-Catering Kitchenette**
✓**Reservations Required**   ✓**Advance Deposit:** $10.00

Guest Rules: No smoking in building or bedrooms.
On Site Attractions/Nearby Points of Interest: Located in the NW corner of Arkansas near the Missouri border. Eureka Springs Victorian Town, the Great Passion Play; the town has been described as the most unique and beautiful small town in the country. Area surrounded by mountains, trees, lakes, rivers. Native crafts, bicycling, canoeing, hiking; near to Pea Ridge National Park and the acclaimed Ozarks.
Additional Information: Groups welcomed with meals provided for weekend retreats. No children.

2. The Abbey Retreat, Coury House, Subiaco, AR 72865
(501) 934-4411 ✣ Contact: Fr. Aaron, Coury House
✓**Single Rooms** ✓**Twin Rooms** **Individual Guest Rate:** $35.00
✓**Includes 3 Meals Daily**
✓**Reservations Required** ✓**Advance Deposit:** $10.00
On Site Attractions/Nearby Points of Interest: Located 105 miles west of Little Rock. Outdoor swimming pool, gift shop and book store; located in pleasant wooded area, near the abbey is Mount Magazine; the "wine country" at Altus is about an hour away by car, as is the world-famous Hot Springs National Park with 47 thermal springs.
Additional Information: Children OK with adult supervision. Groups welcomed.

CALIFORNIA

---

1. Incarnation Priory, 1601 Oxford St., Berkeley, CA 94709
(510) 548-3406 *(Holy Cross)* ✣ (510) 548-0965 *(Camalodlese)*
Contact: Guestmaster
✓**Single Rooms** ✓**Twin Rooms** **Individual Guest Rate:** $30.00
✓**Self-Catering Kitchenette**
✓**Reservations Required** ✓**Advance Deposit:** None
Guest Rules: The Priory is a joint partnership of Episcopal and Catholic orders. Guests are welcome to join the host community for the evening meal. Spiritual counselling is available.
On Site Attractions/Nearby Points of Interest: The cultural performances at the University of California, Berkeley. Half-hour by commuter rail to San Francisco: Golden Gate Park, Fisherman's Wharf, boats to Alcatraz, bay cruises. In Berkeley, stylish boutiques, political cadres, ethnic restaurants, the imposing UC's Bancroft Library.
Additional Information: No children. Cannot accept groups.

2. San Damiano Retreat House, Highland Dr., Danville, CA 94526
(510) 837-9141 ✣ Contact: Mary Paella
✓**Single Rooms** ✓**Twin Rooms**
Individual Guest Rate: $45.00 ✓**Includes 3 Meals Daily**
✓**Reservations Required** ✓**Advance Deposit:** 20%
Guest Rules: No smoking in bedrooms. Quiet atmosphere.
On Site Attractions/Nearby Points of Interest: Located 12 mi. E. of Oakland. Natural paths, hills, fountains, gardens and scenic views on the grounds; on-site gift shop and book store. Nearby: Napa Valley wine country, Russian River, Sausalito craft shops and restaurants, Berkeley, Marin County, San Francisco.
Additional Information: Groups welcomed at special rates. No private retreats on weekends. Priority bookings go to stays that are spiritual and educational. No children.

3. **Jesuit Retreat House**
300 Manresa Way
Los Altos, CA 94023
(415) 948-4491
Contact: Sandy Carveiro
✓Single Rooms
✓Twin Rooms
Individual Guest
Rate: $50.00
✓Includes 3 Meals Daily
✓Reservations Required
✓Advance Deposit: $35.00
On Site Attractions/Nearby
Points of Interest: Stanford
University with its art gallery,
theater, sports complex is 10
minutes away; within an
hour's drive, Monterey's fish-
ing village and art boutiques,
Pacific beaches, University of

San Damiano Retreat House, Danville, California

California at Santa Cruz and San Francisco.
Additional Information: Retreat groups welcomed. No children.

4. **Presentation Center, 19480 Bear Creek Rd., Los Gatos, CA 95030**
(408) 354-2346 ✤ **Contact:** Virginia Leach
✓Single Rooms   ✓Twin Rooms   ✓Other: Cottages
Individual Guest Rate: $45.00   **✓Includes 3 Meals Daily**
✓Self-Catering Kitchenette
✓Reservations Required   ✓Advance Deposit: $15.00
Guest Rules: Quiet requested on the grounds, particularly after 10 p.m. Smoking
only in designated areas.
On Site Attractions/Nearby Points of Interest: The Presentation Center is situated on 264 acres of the rolling Santa Cruz mountains. Nature trails and hiking
around a beautiful lake surrounded by towering redwoods. Swimming pool, tennis,
and volleyball courts. Location is 30 minutes from Pacific beaches at Santa Cruz, or
an hour and a half from San Francisco.
Additional Information: The Center is a retreat house and welcomes individuals
and groups dedicated to the mission of a quiet, contemplative environment. No children. With a variety of accommodations, individuals or groups up to 100 people can
be provided for.

5. **Serra Retreat, Box 127, Malibu, CA 90265**
(213) 456-6631 ✤ **Contact:** Serra Retreat
✓Single Rooms   ✓Twin Rooms   ✓Other: Queen rooms
Guest Rate: $50.00 double occupancy; $65 single   **✓Includes 3 Meals Daily**
✓Reservations Required   ✓Advance Deposit: $20.00
Guest Rules: No smoking in buildings. Respect other retreatants' desire for quiet.
Minimum stay of 5 days.
On Site Attractions/Nearby Points of Interest: The Serra Retreat Center itself is
uniquely beautiful — an ideal setting on the Southern California coastline; Malibu
Lagoon and Museum, the J.P. Getty Art Museum, the historic Adamson House,
Santa Monica Mountains recreational area; nearby, Hollywood, Universal Studios
and Los Angeles attractions.

Additional Information: Non-profit or religious groups welcomed. Special rates, 96 people maximum with double occupancy. Children may be accommodated on special occasions.

6. **St. Paul Monastery, 44-660 San Pablo Ave., Palm Desert, CA 92260**
   (619) 568-2200 ✤ Contact: Paulist Center, Fr. Barnabas
✓**Single Rooms** ✓**Twin Rooms**
Individual Guest Rate: $40.00 ✓**Includes 3 Meals Daily**
✓**Reservations Required** ✓**Advance Deposit:** $10.00
On Site Attractions/Nearby Points of Interest: 15 miles east of Palm Springs. Heated pool and spa on the premises. Located on 1.5 acres amidst tall cedar trees, cacti and palms. Living Desert Reserve, Palm Springs Aerial Tramway, hot air balloon shows, desert golf and tennis tournaments, date festivals, gateway to Mt. San Jacinto State Park.
Additional Information: Groups can reserve 10 rooms for the weekend total of $900, maximum of 12 persons. Children OK.

7. **Shenoa Retreat Center, Box 43, Philo, CA 95466**
   (707) 895-3156 ✤ Contact: Reservation Office
✓**Single Rooms** ✓**Twin Rooms** ✓**Other:** Family and private cabins
Individual Guest Rate: $53.00 ✓**Includes 3 Meals Daily**
✓**Reservations Required** ✓**Advance Deposit:** 50%
Guest Rules: No smoking in buildings. Quiet time 10 p.m.-8 a.m.
On Site Attractions/Nearby Points of Interest: The Center is located 2½ hours NW of San Francisco, 35 miles NW of Cloverdale on Highway 138. Shenoa offers miles of walking paths through redwood forests, broad meadows, and along the Navarro River are opportunities to see abundant wildlife. Also, tennis courts, pool and river swimming, badminton, and volleyball are offered. Rave reviews for gourmet vegetarian cuisine from the organic gardens. Soothing massages and relaxation therapy sessions can be scheduled.
Additional Information: Children OK, prices negotiable. Campers welcome at $28 per person, includes meals. Groups of 20 or more welcome at discount rates.

8. **Santa Sabina Center, 1520 Grand Ave., San Rafael, CA 94901**
   (415) 457-7727 ✤ Contact: Harriet Hope
✓**Single Rooms** ✓**Twin Rooms** ✓**Other:** Individual Guest Rate: $25.00
✓**Reservations Required** ✓**Advance Deposit:** First day's rate
Guest Rules: No smoking; observe the quietude of the house; guests requested to use the time and space for retreat purposes — not as a stopover.
On Site Attractions/Nearby Points of Interest: The Center is located adjacent to the wooded area of Dominican College; swimming pool available, beautiful walking and hiking areas; nearby, Muir Woods, San Francisco beaches, Napa Valley—all the attractions of San Francisco and the Sausalito bayfront.
Additional Information: No children. Maximum stay is one week. Groups welcome; meals provided, rate varies.

9. **St. Andrew's Priory, Valyermo Retreat Center**
   31001 N. Valyermo Rd., Valyermo, CA 93563
   (805) 944-2178 ✤ Contact: Guestmaster
✓**Single Rooms** ✓**Twin Rooms**
Individual Guest Rate: $40.00 single, $35.00 double occupancy
✓**Includes 3 Meals Daily**
✓**Reservations Required** ✓**Advance Deposit:** $20.00

Guest Rules: Punctuality at meals. No pets. Overall quiet atmosphere requested. Guest house geared to persons who are self-directed and appreciate quiet time. Breakfast and dinner are usually eaten in silence.
On Site Attractions/Nearby Points of Interest: Valyermo is in the Mojave Desert in the northern foothills of the San Gabriel Mountains, 1 hour north of Los Angeles. The priory is known worldwide for its ceramics, which are on display and for sale at the gift shop. Close by is Devil's Punchbowl County Park and Wrightwood and Arrowhead ski areas and summer recreation sites.
Additional Information: Group retreats welcomed. No children.

10. Heartwood Institute, Ltd., 220 Harmony Lane, Garberville, CA 95542
  (707) 923-2021 ❖ **Contact:** Retreat Director
✓**Single Rooms** ✓**Twin Rooms** ✓**Other:** Camping accommodations available
Individual Guest Rate: $60.00 ✓**Includes 3 Meals Daily**
✓**Reservations Required** ✓**Advance Deposit:** $50.00
Guest Rules: Smoking in designated areas only.
On Site Attractions/Nearby Points of Interest: Garberville is about 185 miles north of San Francisco, 50 miles south of Eureka. The profoundly beautiful setting of Heartwood is on 200 acres of rolling mountains, meadows, forests of Douglas fir, live oak and madrone. The Institute trains professionals in the healing arts, massage therapies, and nutrition. The pool, sauna, and hot tub are important facilities in pursuit of the retreat's wellness goals. North of Garberville are 51,222 acres of redwoods (some of the tallest trees on the planet), Humboldt Redwoods State Park and the Avenue of the Giants.
Additional Information: No children. Mission to provide resources for physical, psychological, and spiritual well-being.

11. Mount Madonna Center, 445 Summit Rd., Watsonville, CA 95076
  (408) 847-0406 ❖ **Contact:** Program Office
✓**Single Rooms** ✓**Twin Rooms**
✓**Other:** Dormitory rooms for 4-7. Campgrounds and tent sites in redwood groves.
Individual Guest Rate: $28.00-$71.00 ✓**Includes 3 Meals Daily**
✓**Reservations Required** ✓**Advance Deposit:** None
Guest Rules: All prepared food is strictly vegetarian.
On Site Attractions/Nearby Points of Interest: Watsonville is about 110 miles south of San Francisco, near the Pacific coast, midway between Santa Cruz and Pebble Beach. The Center, a few miles east of Watsonville, rests atop Mt. Madonna with a spectacular view of all Monterey Bay. The 355 acres of open meadows and redwood forests include hiking trails, volleyball and tennis courts, a swimming lake, hot tub, gymnasium and herbal steam bath facilities. Of course, Monterey and Carmel are unrivaled regions of beauty, not to be missed.
Additional Information: Variety of meeting places for groups. Children OK. Yoga classes, scriptural study, health and spiritual growth, personal retreat space provided.

12. Angela Center, 535 Angela Dr., Santa Rosa, CA 95403
  (707) 528-8578 ❖ **Contact:** Tricia Schexnaydre
✓**Single Rooms** ✓**Twin Rooms** ✓**Other:** all rooms with twin beds — use as single or double
Individual Guest Rate: $20.00 ✓**Self-Catering Kitchenette**
Meals can be provided at an additional charge.
✓**Reservations Required** ✓**Advance Deposit:** None

Guest Rules: Respect for concern of others. The Center is not available to profit-making, sales promotion, or sport groups.

On Site Attractions/Nearby Points of Interest: Angela Center is in a lovely natural hillside setting near Santa Rosa, 60 miles north of San Francisco. From Santa Rosa, the Valley of the Moon scenic drive leads through the wine country to the Jack London Historical Park and Museum. The quaint villages of Kenwood and Glen Ellen, each with its own winery, are adjacent to the shops at Jack London Village. A half hour drive from the Center are the gourmet shops of the Sonoma Plaza and the Calistoga Hot Springs and geyser.

Additional Information: No children. Good food, clean comfortable surroundings for conference groups. Staff fosters a caring, non-intrusive environment. Inquiries welcomed.

13. Immaculate Heart Hermitage, Big Sur, CA 93920
   (408) 667-2456 ❖ Contact: Bookstore
✓Single Rooms ✓Other: 2 trailers for extended stay (1-4 weeks)
Individual Guest Rate: $30.00 (weekly rate $150.00) **✓Includes 3 Meals Daily**
✓Reservations Required ✓Advance Deposit: Call in ($50.00 for trailers)
Guest Rules: Atmosphere of quiet and recollection — no radios, musical instruments — meals are vegetarian.

On Site Attractions/Nearby Points of Interest: The Hermitage is located in the Santa Lucia Mountains on the rugged Big Sur coast, 85 miles north of San Luis Obispo and 25 miles south of Monterey. The precipitous cliffs scaling down to the waves of the Pacific provide one of the most spectacular stretches of scenery in California. A short drive south is the "Hearst Castle" which sits in solitary splendor among 123 acres of buildings, pools, and gardens.

Additional Information: No children. The Hermitage offers non-directive silent retreats and is operated by the Camaldolese Benedictine Monks. Because of the beauty and isolation of the Center, the Hermitage is running a six month reservation calendar for the nine private room retreat houses.

Immaculate Heart Hermitage, Big Sur, California

14. Mount Calvary Retreat House, P.O. Box 1296, Santa Barbara, CA 93102
   (805) 962-9855 ❖ **Contact:** Br. Larry Pearce
✓**Single Rooms** ✓**Twin Rooms**
Individual Guest Rate: $50.00 ($45.00 subsequent nights)
✓**Includes 3 Meals Daily** ✓**Reservations Required**
✓**Advance Deposit:** None for individuals; $30.00 for groups
Guest Rules: Reasonable quiet to be observed. No smoking inside buildings.
On Site Attractions/Nearby Points of Interest: The Retreat House, a Spanish colonial mansion, is dramatically situated on a ridge 1250 feet above Santa Barbara with a commanding view of the seacoast and Pacific Ocean. Santa Barbara, with its coastal setting, colonial architecture and mild climate, produces an idyllic Mediterranean ambiance. Within walking distance: the Santa Barbara Art Museum, the famed Mission, Rattlesnake Canyon, vista lookout hiking trails. Nearby: the yacht harbor, zoo, bird refuge, and botanical gardens.
Additional Information: No children. Weekdays usually open for individuals, weekends usually reserved one year in advance by groups. Mount Calvary, Episcopal, is a monastic community within the Anglican Communion.

15. Luther Glen Conference Center
   24876 N. Apple St. #F, Santa Clarita, CA 91321
   1-800-464-2417 or (805) 254-9866 ❖ **Contact:** Reservation Office
✓**Single Rooms** ✓**Twin Rooms** ✓**Other:** Option of triple or quad occupancy
Individual Guest Rate: $35.00-$50.00 ✓**Includes 3 Meals Daily**
✓**Reservations Required**
Guest Rules: No smoking in buildings.
On Site Attractions/Nearby Points of Interest: Luther Glen is 90 minutes east of Los Angeles, 90 minutes from Orange County, near Yucaipa off the I-10 freeway. The Center is nestled in a scenic glen at a 5000′ elevation bordered by the majestic San Gorgonio Mountains. A caring staff and relaxed atmosphere prevail at the Glen for uplifting one's faith: all-year hot tub open, swimming in the summer, ping pong on the patio; families love the petting zoo and Riley's Farm where guests can pick apples, press cider, and shuck corn. Homemade dining menu and numerous shops for browsing.
Additional Information: Children OK. Groups up to 50 welcomed. Six minute video on request: 1-800-464-2417. Excellent conference facilities.

16. Sacred Heart Retreat House, 920 E. Alhambra Rd., Alhambra, CA 91801
   (818) 289-1353, ext. 225 ❖ **Contact:** Sister M. James
✓**Single Rooms** ✓**Twin Rooms** ✓**Other:** Triples and suites
Individual Guest Rate: $45.00 ✓**Includes 3 Meals Daily**
✓**Reservations Required** ✓**Advance Deposit:** 30%
Guest Rules: Gates close at 8:15 p.m. No food in rooms.
On Site Attractions/Nearby Points of Interest: Alhambra is a 20 minute drive northeast of Los Angeles. The Retreat House has 42 single or double rooms along with six deluxe suites. A host of attractions are nearby: the Huntington Library and Museum, Disneyland, Knott's Berry Farm, picturesque Mexican Olvera Street, the Music Center's productions, Griffith Park's 4000 acres of mountains, gardens, picnic grounds, golf and tennis.
Additional Information: No children. Groups welcomed — schedule flexible. Teen groups OK if supervised.

17. Immaculate Heart Center for Spiritual Renewal
   888 San Ysidro Lane, Santa Barbara, CA 93108

(805) 969-2474 ❖ **Contact:** Retreat Office
✓**Single Rooms** ✓**Twin Rooms**
Individual Guest Rate: $45.00 **Guest Rate for Couples:** $55.00
✓**Includes 3 Meals Daily**
✓**Reservations Required** **No Advance Deposit**
Guest Rules: No smoking, alcohol, or pets.
On Site Attractions/Nearby Points of Interest: Santa Barbara is one of Southern California's most beautiful coastal cities, at the foothills of the Santa Ynez Mountains, one hour northwest of Los Angeles. The Center is situated among 18 acres of eucalyptus groves, with winding trails, a swimming pool and tennis court. Nearby are the estates and mansions of Montecito, and the "Queen of the Missions" in Santa Barbara marks the founding of the city by the Spanish in 1786. In Santa Barbara are the viewpoints from Stearns Wharf, the historic adobes of the El Paseo restoration, Keck Park Memorial Gardens with its 76 species of trees, the zoological gardens with its playground and miniature train, and the Sea Center Museum.
Additional Information: No children. Breakfast and lunch may be taken to picnic tables or room. Minimum stay, 2 days; maximum, 4 days.

18. La Casa de Maria Retreat Center
   800 El Bosque Rd., Santa Barbara, CA 93108
   (805) 969-5031 ❖ **Contact:** Conference Coordinator, Kathleen Jenks
The Center has a varied and extensive series of Friday to Sunday seminars and workshops. It is located on the grounds of the Immaculate Heart Center described above. Groups should contact the office well in advance because of the demand for such a beautiful facility. Send a self-addressed stamped envelope for a list of programs, prices, and reservation policy.
   The Center is a non-profit multi-denominational institute whose goal is to provide a place of peace where persons of all faiths can search for truth, engage in dialogue, experience personal growth and participate more effectively in the creation of a just and peaceful world.

19. Prince of Peace Abbey, 650 Benet Hill Road, Oceanside, CA 92054
   (619) 430-1305/430-1306 ❖ **Contact:** Fr. Sharbel Euen
✓**Single Rooms** ✓**Twin Rooms**
Individual Guest Rate: $30.00
✓**Includes 3 Meals Daily** ✓**Reservations Required** **Advance Deposit:** None
(Groups $10 pp)
Guest Rules: No smoking or alcohol.
On Site Attractions/Nearby Points of Interest: The Abbey is located on a majestic prominence which overlooks both the Pacific Ocean and the scenic San Luis Rey Valley. Nearby Oceanside, with its miles of white bathing beaches, has a protected harbor and marina that is a mecca for sportfishing, boating and cruises. Jutting out into the Pacific is Southern California's longest overwater pier (1,942 feet) featuring bait and gift shops, a restaurant and surf museum. In addition to the city's tennis, golf and riding facilities, visitors can enjoy the bird sanctuary, whale watching cruises, and self-guided tour to Camp Pendleton, the world's largest U.S. Marine Corps amphibious base. Less than an hour's drive to the south is Mexico.
Additional Information: No children. Groups welcomed (maximum of 20 persons). Refrigerator available for those on special diets or who wish to bring their own food.

20. Mission San Luis Rey Retreat Center
   4050 Mission Avenue, P.O. Box 409, San Luis Rey, CA 92068
   (619) 757-3659 ❖ **Contact:** Darlene Parker

✓**Single Rooms**   ✓**Twin Rooms**
Individual Guest Rate: $37.00   ✓**Includes 3 Meals Daily**
✓**Reservations Required**   **Advance Deposit:** Varies
Guest Rules: No alcohol or smoking in buildings.
On Site Attractions/Nearby Points of Interest: The Center is located on the expansive garden grounds of the Mission San Luis Rey, the largest of the historic Spanish missions of old California. A swimming pool and spa are available to guests. The inner courtyards, colonnaded archways, date palms and cactus gardens create in this setting of the golden San Luis Rey Valley a visible replica of old Spain. San Luis Rey is a short drive to the Pacific beaches of Oceanside, Del Mar and La Jolla. Within a 35 minute radius of the Center are the Scripps Aquarium, the Del Mar racetrack, the Wild Animal Park, the Bernardo Winery, and the Antique Gas and Steam Engine Museum. San Diego's Balboa Park and theater, Zoo (world's largest) and Sea World rank among the nation's premier visitor attractions. To the south are the bullfights and shopping bazaars of Tijuana, Mexico.
Additional Information: No children. Each room has 2 single beds. The Center has recently been remodeled, with new furnishings and private dorm bath facilities. Conference rooms available. Guests at the Center must be there explicitly for retreat experience.

COLORADO

---

1. Abbey of St. Walburga, 6717 So. Boulder Rd., Boulder, CO 80303
    (303) 494-5733 ✤ **Contact:** Sr. Emmanuel Luckman, OSB
✓**Single Rooms**   ✓**Twin Rooms**   **Individual Guest Rate:** $35.00
✓**Includes 3 Meals Daily**   ✓**Self-Catering Kitchenette**
✓**Reservations Required**   ✓**Advance Deposit:** $10.00 per person
Guest Rules: No smoking in buildings. Silence in main monastery requested.

On Site Attractions/Nearby Points of Interest: Beautiful 150 acre farm setting. 30 minute drive to Rocky Mountain resort sites. Boulder's Mall with its jugglers, magicians, musicians. Cultural events at the University of Colorado. Colorado Tourism Board promises 300 days of sunshine and crisp, clean air. Boulder is the Gateway to Estes Park and Grand Lake.

Additional Information: Groups welcomed on weekends. Children OK with adult supervision. Guests may wish to help with light farm chores.

2. Franciscan Center
   7665 Assisi Heights
   Colorado Springs, CO 80919
   (719) 598-5486
      Contact: Sister Christine Hayes
✓**Single Rooms**   ✓**Twin Rooms**
✓**Other:** Triple rooms

Mesa Verde National Park, Colorado

Individual Guest Rate: $23.00
✓**Reservations Required** ✓**Advance Deposit:** $10.00
Guest Rules: No smoking in buildings. Respect those who wish quiet. Required minimum length of stay is 2 weeks.
On Site Attractions/Nearby Points of Interest: Nestled at the foot of the Rampart Range Rocky Mountains. Scenic hiking areas and deer on the grounds. 10 minutes from Garden of the Gods, natural unique boulder and rock formations. The U.S. Air Force Academy adjoins the Center. Picturesque viewpoints in all directions. Nearby are Cave of the Winds and the Manitou Cliff Dwellings Museum.
Additional Information: 3 home-made meals provided at an additional $13.00 per person per day. No children. Groups welcomed. 5 meeting rooms available; dining room for 125.

3. Benet Pines, 15780 Route 83, Colorado Springs, CO 80921
  (719) 495-2574 ✤ **Contact:** Benedictine Sister
✓**Single Rooms** ✓**Twin Rooms**
Individual Guest Rate: $30.00 ✓**Includes 3 Meals Daily**
✓**Reservations Required** ✓**Advance Deposit:** $10.00 per person
Guest Rules: Quiet, meditative environment requested.
On Site Attractions/Nearby Points of Interest: Located on 30 acres of pine forest at an altitude of 7,000 feet with a spectacular view of Pikes Peak. Nearby: Garden of the Gods natural rock formations, local festivals, craft exhibits, and the Olympic Training Center. Close by is the Edward J. Peterson Space Command Museum and the U.S. Air Force Academy.
Additional Information: Children OK with family supervision. Families may set up tents. Groups welcomed.

4. Spiritual Life Institute, Nada Hermitage, Crestone, CO 81131
  (719) 256-4778 ✤ **Contact:** Sr. Susan Ryan
✓**Single Rooms** **Individual Guest Rate:** $45 first day; $35 additional days
✓**Includes 3 Meals Daily*** ✓**Self-Catering Kitchenette**
✓**Reservations Required** ✓**Advance Deposit:** $50.00
Guest Rules: Solitude is observed 2 days of the week. Couples may share a hermitage cabin at $55 the first day; $45 each additional day. Minimum stay 1 week.
On Site Attractions/Nearby Points of Interest: Located 150 miles south of Denver at an altitude of 7,600 feet in the majestic Sangre de Cristo Mountains. Beautiful pine forests, wildlife, streams nearby. Great Sand Dunes National Monument, a short drive south of Crestone, is the residue of thousands of years of wind-blown accumulation.
Additional Information: *Each kitchenette stocked with food. Individual hermitage cabins for one occupant at a time. Guests are invited to participate in the life of the Institute if they so desire. No children. No groups.

5. Spes in Deo Franciscan Family Retreat Center, Inc.
  21661 Hwy. 550, Montrose, CO 81401
  (303) 249-3526 ✤ **Contact:** Joyce Martin
✓**Rooms:** 4 rooms — 3 pers./room
Individual Guest Rate: $35.00 *(suggested)* ✓**Self-Catering Kitchenette**
✓**Reservations Required** ✓**Advance Deposit:** None
Guest Rules: No tobacco or alcohol. Contemplative community where quiet is respected — but a balance of work, play, and spiritual growth is offered.
On Site Attractions/Nearby Points of Interest: Located about an hour south of Grand Junction in the San Juan Mountains area. Nearby are Ridgway Reservoir

Recreation Area and Black Canyon National Monument. Center is in an orchard-farm setting. To the east of Montrose is Cureganti National Recreation Area. **Additional Information:** No children. Groups welcomed (no more than 12 persons).

6. **Bethlehem Center, 12550 Zuni, Northglen, CO 80234-2206**
   (303) 451-1371 ❖ Contact: Noel Dunne
✓**Single Rooms** ✓**Twin Rooms** ✓**Other:** Family accommodations
Individual Guest Rate: $30.00 ✓**Includes 3 Meals Daily**
✓**Reservations Required** ✓**Advance Deposit:** 10% of total cost
Guest Rules: No smoking in cafeteria. No food in the sleeping quarters.
On Site Attractions/Nearby Points of Interest: Restful locale in a rural setting, 20 minutes from Boulder and Denver. Situated in a natural wildlife sanctuary: eagles, hawks, cranes, Canadian geese, rabbits, prairie dogs, pheasants. Beautiful view of the Rocky Mountains. In Denver, the Art Museum, Museum of Natural History, Red Rocks Park, and 19th-century Larimer Square.
Additional Information: Families with children welcomed, as well as retreat groups.

7. **St. Benedict's Monastery, 1012 Monastery Rd., Snowmass, CO 81654**
   (303) 927-3311 ❖ Contact: Guestmaster
✓**Single Rooms** ✓**Twin Rooms**
Individual Guest Rate: Free-will donation ✓**Self-Catering Kitchenette**
✓**Reservations Required** ✓**Advance Deposit:** None
On Site Attractions/Nearby Points of Interest: Located 3½ hours west of Denver, just south of Glenwood Springs. The monastery property includes a ranch, stream, hills, aspen forests, and meadowlands. Ranch life and greenhouse. Nearby Aspen Ski Resort and cultural center. Tennis courts in Snowmass and the Aspen Music Festival runs from June to August.
Additional Information: No children. Small linen charge. Group retreats welcomed.

8. **St. Malo Center**
   10758 Highway 7
   Allenspark, CO 80510
   (Denver Office:
   200 Josephine
   Denver, CO 80206
   (303) 388-4411, Ext. 146
   Contact: Blake Fischer
✓**Single Rooms**
✓**Twin Rooms** *(all rooms with private bath)*
Individual Guest Rate:
$55 single, $44 double; more than 2 nights $47 single, $36 double
✓**Includes 3 Meals Daily**
✓**Reservations Required**
✓**Advance Deposit:**
$10.00 per night
Guest Rules: Retreat house atmosphere. Doors close at 10:00 p.m. No radios or televisions in guest rooms.

St. Malo Center, Allenspark, Colorado

On Site Attractions/Nearby Points of Interest: Nestled at the foot of Mt. Meeker in the heart of the Rockies, the 160-acre St. Malo Center is caressed by mountain streams and encircled by a forest of tall pines. (Allenspark is a little over an hour's drive NW of Denver, 25 miles north of Boulder.) The unique 3-story lodge, next to "Chapel on the Rock," has 49 beautifully decorated guest rooms with private verandas. Rocky Mountain National Park, with its alpine scenery and glacier-carved peaks, borders on the grounds of the Center. Popular Estes Park, nearby, offers golf, tennis, sightseeing tours, shopping.

Additional Information: Children OK with supervision. Best to have a minimum of 10 for group attendance — religious, educational, or non-profit. Many group facilities available.

CONNECTICUT

---

1. Our Lady of Calvary Retreat House
31 Colton St., Farmington, CT 06032
(203) 677-8519 ✤ **Contact:** Retreat Office
✓**Single Rooms** ✓**Twin Rooms**
Individual Guest Rate: $50.00 ✓**Includes 3 Meals Daily**
✓**Reservations Required** ✓**Advance Deposit:** None
Guest Rules: Smoking only in coffee room. No food in bedrooms. Atmosphere of quiet around chapel and sleeping areas.
On Site Attractions/Nearby Points of Interest: Located in the beautiful colonial town of Farmington, 12 miles west of Hartford, on 18 acres of lovely grounds. Library and gift shop on the premises. Nearby are the Mark Twain and Harriet Beecher Stowe houses (*Huckleberry Finn* and *Uncle Tom's Cabin* written here), and one of the best handcrafted merry-go-rounds in Bushnell Park.
Additional Information: Guests requested to furnish towels. Closed in August. Aim of the retreat house is to provide for others a sharing of life and growth. No children.

2. Wisdom House Retreat and Conference Center
229 E. Litchfield Rd., Litchfield, CT 06759
(203) 567-3163 ✤ **Contact:** Darlene Roy
✓**Single Rooms** ✓**Twin Rooms** ✓**Other:** Dormitories available
Individual Guest Rate: $50.00
✓**Includes 3 Meals Daily** ✓**Self-Catering Kitchenette**
✓**Reservations Required** ✓**Advance Deposit:** $30.00
Guest Rules: Printed and available in each room. No smoking in the buildings.
On Site Attractions/Nearby Points of Interest: Located on 58 acres of woods and meadows providing opportunities for hiking, nature walks, skiing. Outdoor swimming pool. Historic Litchfield situated among rolling hills on the Naguatuck River. Less than 9 miles away is Topsmead, a Connecticut State Forest.
Additional Information: Children 12 years and older OK. Can accommodate various kinds of private and group requests. Welcome all persons seeking peace and reflection.

3. Vikingsborg Guest House / Convent of St. Birgitta
Tokeneke Trail, Darien, CT 06820
(203) 655-1068
Contact: Director
✓**Single Rooms** ✓**Twin Rooms** ✓**Other:** Guest cottage for 4

Individual Guest Rate: $40.00
✓**Includes 3 Meals Daily**
✓**Half Board Available**
✓**Reservations Required**
✓**Advance Deposit:** Call in
On Site Attractions/Nearby Points of Interest: Park-like Darien is within a 2 hour drive NE of New York City. Nestled within hidden inlets of Long Island Sound, Vikingsborg offers a lush ambience of woodland walks and gardens, and a private dock for boating and swimming. Breathtaking views of the Sound can be had from the Abbey grounds, providing a unique setting for people of all faiths to enjoy the serenity of the surroundings. Library, recreation room, television, and grand piano available to retreatants.
Additional Information: No children. Groups welcomed.

Vikingsborg Guest House,
Darien, Connecticut

4. **Villa Maria Retreat House**
   159 Sky Meadow Dr.
   Stamford, CT 06903
   (203) 322-0107
   Contact: Sister M. Concetta Labenz
✓**Single Rooms** ✓**Twin Rooms** **Individual Guest Rate:** $35.00
✓**Includes 3 Meals Daily** *(buffet style)* ✓**Self-Catering Kitchenette**
✓**Reservations Required** ✓**Advance Deposit:** $10.00
On Site Attractions/Nearby Points of Interest: Stamford is 15 miles north of the New York border on Long Island Sound, a short distance NE of Greenwich. The affluent north end of town boasts the 118 acre Stamford Museum and Nature Center with a large display of early American artifacts, an observatory and planetarium. Attracting visitors worldwide is the Whitney Museum of American Art Champion— 20th-century American paintings and photography.
Additional Information: No children. Groups welcomed. The House has recently accommodated an increasing number of Christian groups as well as Jewish retreatants.

DELAWARE

---

1. **St. Francis Renewal Center, 1901 Prior Rd., Wilmington, DE 19809**
   (302) 798-1454 ❖ **Contact:** Fr. Vincent Fortunato
✓**Single Rooms** **Individual Guest Rate:** $20.00
✓**Includes 3 Meals Daily** ✓**Self-Catering Kitchenette**
✓**Reservations Required** ✓**Advance Deposit:** $20.00
On Site Attractions/Nearby Points of Interest: Famous Longwood Gardens. 30 minutes by rail to Philadelphia. Nearby is the Winterthur Museum, a collection of decorative arts from 1640-1840, and the Hagley Museum of American Industrial Growth.
Additional Information: No children. Groups welcomed.

1. **Marywood, 1714/5 State Rte. 13, Jacksonville, FL 32259**
   (904) 287-2525 ❖ **Contact:** Main office
   ✓**Single Rooms** ✓**Twin Rooms**
   Individual Guest Rate: $20.00 - 40.00
   ✓**Includes 3 Meals Daily** ✓**Self-Catering Kitchenette**
   ✓**Reservations Required** ✓**Advance Deposit:** 25% for groups
   On Site Attractions/Nearby Points of Interest: On the downtown riverfront is the new Jacksonville Landing Mall and the Riverwalk stretches along the opposite bank. The Cummer Gallery has an excellent art gallery and gorgeous gardens. Marywood is located on 100 acres of beautifully wooded terrain. Nearby, the first Spanish settlement in the U.S., St. Augustine, and now featuring a Marineland.
   Additional Information: Please inquire for group attendance.

2. **Our Lady of Florida Spiritual Center**
   1300 U.S. Highway 1, North Palm Beach, FL 33408
   (407) 626-1300 ❖ **Contact:** Retreat Director
   ✓**Single Rooms** ✓**Twin Rooms**
   Individual Guest Rate: $60.00 ✓**Includes 3 Meals Daily**
   ✓**Reservations Required** ✓**Advance Deposit:** 50%
   On Site Attractions/Nearby Points of Interest: North Palm Beach is on the Atlantic coast, about 80 miles north of Miami. Situated on 26 acres of waterfront, the Center overlooks Lake Worth and the Intracoastal Waterway. From the beautiful landscaped gardens, guests can observe pelicans diving for fish, dolphins bobbing by in the lake, golden sunrises, and palms gently swaying. Modern air-conditioned buildings, a gift shop, bookstore, two chapels, and outdoor shrines comprise the elegant setting.
   Additional Information: No children. Groups welcomed. Meals served by waitresses or buffet style. Special diets available.

Our Lady of Florida Spiritual Center, North Palm Beach, Florida

3. **San Pedro Center, 2400 Dike Rd., Winter Park, FL 32792**
   (407) 671-6322, ext. 227 ❖ **Contact:** Mary Mericle
   ✓**Single Rooms** ✓**Twin Rooms** ✓**Other:** Pavilion, cabins and dorms
   Individual Guest Rate: $35.00 single, $45.00 double
   (3 delicious home-style meals can be provided at $17 per person per day)
   On Site Attractions/Nearby Points of Interest: Winter Park, part of Orlando's
   Metro area, is a unique independent community. The 500 acre Center is away from
   the sounds of traffic, set among the peaceful paths and woods at the shore of Lake
   Howell. The campus allows for hiking, birdwatching, and jogging. Nearby are pub-
   lic-fee golf and tennis clubs. The many tourist attractions include Disney World,
   Universal Studios, Sea World, the Kennedy Space Center, all within a 40 minute
   drive.
   Additional Information: No children, groups welcomed.

GEORGIA

1. **Ignatius House, 6700 Riverside Dr. N.W., Atlanta, GA 30328**
   (404) 255-0503 ❖ **Contact:** Martha Rais
   ✓**Single Rooms**
   Individual Guest Rate: $57.00 w/3 meals; $35.00 w/kitchenette
   ✓**Self-Catering Kitchenette**
   ✓**Reservations Required** ✓**Advance Deposit:** $25.00
   On Site Attractions/Nearby Points of Interest: Located on a high bluff overlooking
   the Chattahoochee River and surrounded by 20 acres of beautiful trees, hills, streams.
   Atlanta is 15 miles south; Piedmont Art Festival; Dogwood Festival, featuring a
   nine-day celebration of parades, music and dance; and the Independent Film and
   Video Festival. Over 120 shops are in the redeveloped Atlanta Underground; CNN
   studio tours demonstrate 24-hour newscasting.
   Additional Information: No children. For groups, snacks are prepared, large conference rooms, meals served.

2. **Convent of St. Helena, 3042 Eagle Dr./PO Box 5645, Augusta, GA 30916**
   (706) 798-5201 ❖ **Contact:** Guest Mistress
   ✓**Single Rooms** ✓**Twin Rooms**
   Individual Guest Rate: Free-will donation ✓**Includes 3 Meals Daily**
   ✓**Reservations Required** ✓**Advance Deposit:** None
   Guest Rules: Silence requested after 10 p.m. and in certain outside areas during the
   day. Sound equipment must be used with earphones.
   On Site Attractions/Nearby Points of Interest: Augusta, the Classic South, with
   hundreds of antebellum mansions, the Cotton Exchange Building and the Old Slave
   Market Column. Convent located in wooded area with walking trails, views of the
   city skyline and of South Carolina across the Savannah River.
   Additional Information: Older children with adult supervision OK, but not advisable. Aim of the convent is to provide your stay with time for spiritual renewal
   and refreshment. Groups welcomed and a published calendar is provided which lists
   special programs.

IDAHO

1. **Nazareth Retreat Center, 4450 N. Five Mile Rd., Boise, ID 83704**
   (208) 375-2932 ❖ **Contact:** Ms. Frances Ourada

✓Single Rooms   ✓Twin Rooms   ✓Other: Double beds with private baths
Individual Guest Rate: Call for current rates   **✓Includes 3 Meals Daily**
✓Reservations Required   ✓Advance Deposit: Call in
On Site Attractions/Nearby Points of Interest: The Center has a panoramic view of the Salmon River Mountains, and its well-groomed lawns and paths surround the main lodge, conference room, library, and chapel. Boise is an environmentalist's delight: World Center for Birds of Prey (work with endangered species); M-K Nature Center for aquatic and riparian ecology; tigers, moose, petting farm at the Zoo; gateway to the 2,646,341 acre Boise National Forest; multitude of rivers and lakes in the region; recreation at Julia Davis Park.
Additional Information: Children OK, groups welcomed. After first night, discount on room charge.

ILLINOIS

---

1. Cenacle Retreat House, 513 Fullerton Pkwy., Chicago, IL 60614
   (312) 528-6300 *(9-5 Central)* ❖ **Contact:** Ministry Office
✓Single Rooms   ✓Twin Rooms
Individual Guest Rate: $45.00 - 60.00   **✓Includes 3 Meals Daily**
✓Reservations Required   ✓Advance Deposit: $25.00
Guest Rules: Atmosphere of the House is quiet, meals are in silence, except for workshops. The door is open to those who wish restful reflection.
On Site Attractions/Nearby Points of Interest: The Cenacle is a major complex located in the North (Lincoln Park) area of Chicago. Convenient to public transportation, and a 10-15 minute walk to Lake Michigan, Lincoln Park Zoo and the Conservatory. It is a quiet, peaceful retreat in the midst of a bustling city. Highlights of Chicago include theater, concerts, comedy revues, and seasonal events.
Additional Information: No children. Groups must be non-profit and church-related.

2. Cabrini Retreat Center, 9430 Golf Rd., Des Plaines, IL 60016
   (708) 297-6530 ❖ **Contact:** Phyllis Becherer
✓Single Rooms   ✓Other: Small apartment
Individual Guest Rate: Negotiable   **✓Includes 3 Meals Daily**
✓Reservations Required   ✓Advance Deposit: 10%
Guest Rules: Restricted smoking areas, eating in dining room only.
On Site Attractions/Nearby Points of Interest: On site year-round swimming pool, gymnasium, tennis courts. Flower gardens, wooded acreage, grotto, serene environment. Fisherman's dude ranch, 2 lakes, excellent food.
Additional Information: Children over 16 years OK. Groups welcomed and guideline memo furnished to assist guests.

3. St. Joseph Retreat Center, 353 N. River Rd., Des Plaines, IL 60016
   (708) 298-4070 ❖ **Contact:** Sister M. Dolores, CSFN
✓Single Rooms   ✓Twin Rooms
Individual Guest Rate: $45.00   **✓Includes 3 Meals Daily**
✓Reservations Required   ✓Advance Deposit: 25%
Guest Rules: No smoking.
On Site Attractions/Nearby Points of Interest: Only 15 minutes from O'Hare airport, close to all expressways. The Center provides expansive grounds for hiking trails and enjoying nature. Nearby to all of the attractions of Chicago: 110-story Sears Tower, Museum of Science and Industry, the Peace Museum.

Additional Information: Children 18 yrs. and over OK. Groups welcomed.

4. King's Retreat House, Box 165, Henry, IL 61537
   (309) 364-3084 ✤ **Contact:** King's House of Retreats
✓**Single Rooms** ✓**Twin Rooms**
Individual Guest Rate: $45.00 ✓**Includes 3 Meals Daily**
✓**Reservations Required** ✓**Advance Deposit:** $5.00
On Site Attractions/Nearby Points of Interest: Location is in a quiet, wooded area above the Illinois River, about 175 mi. SW of Chicago, and north of Peoria. Quiet farm country in the heart of the U.S. grain belt.
Additional Information: Rooms are air-conditioned. No children. Groups welcomed; meals are served family-style.

5. Bishop Lane Retreat House, Rte. 2, Box 214A, Rockford, IL 61102
   (815) 965-5011 ✤ **Contact:** Don Gamer
✓**Single Rooms** ✓**Twin Rooms**
Individual Guest Rate: $38.00 ✓**Includes 3 Meals Daily**
✓**Reservations Required** ✓**Advance Deposit:** Varies
On Site Attractions/Nearby Points of Interest: Located on 300 wooded acres with trails, pond, wildlife, gardens. Chicago is a 2-hour drive to the south.
Additional Information: All rooms are air-conditioned. Groups welcomed with rates negotiable. Children OK.

6. Dominican Conference Center, 7200 W. Division St., River Forest, IL 60305-1294
   (708) 771-3030 ✤ **Contact:** Jeffrey Olsen
✓**Single Rooms** ✓**Other:** Shared bath
Individual Guest Rate: $32.00 ✓**Includes 3 Meals Daily**
✓**Reservations Required** ✓**Advance Deposit:** 20%
Guest Rules: Goal of the Order: enrichment of individuals and society through communal searching for truth, the offering of warm hospitality to all guests.
On Site Attractions/Nearby Points of Interest: The Center, 30 minutes from Chicago's O'Hare airport, about 15 miles from downtown Chicago, is situated on 38 acres of attractive grounds with outdoor patios. Nearby Oak Park has the Studio of Frank Lloyd Wright, with the School of Architecture walking tour. Chicago's world class symphonies, theater, architecture and museums provide an inexhaustible menu to satisfy anyone's taste.
Additional Information: No children. Religious, business, educational and civic groups welcomed. Conference rooms with latest AV equipment.

INDIANA

---

1. John XXIII Center, 407 W. McDonald St., Hartford City, IN 47348
   (317) 348-4008 ✤ **Contact:** Sr. Maureen / Jan O'Neill
✓**Single Rooms** ✓**Twin Rooms** **Individual Guest Rate:** $15.00
✓**Self-Catering Kitchenette** *(use of main kitchen)*
✓**Reservations Required** ✓**Advance Deposit:** None
Guest Rules: No smoking in the house. Individuals provide and prepare own food. Small linen charge.
On Site Attractions/Nearby Points of Interest: Located half an hour from Muncie and Ball State University. The Center is a large mansion-style home, cozy and comfortable in a setting of peace and tranquility. Taylor University is situated in nearby

Upland.
Additional Information: Children OK. Groups welcomed at special rates. Meals available for groups. Weekdays usually available for individuals. Weekends scheduled by groups. Closed in July and August.

2. Solitude of St. Joseph, Box 983, Notre Dame, IN 46556
   (219) 239-5655 ✤ **Contact:** Director Brother John H. Kuhn, C.S.C.
✓**Single Rooms   Individual Guest Rate:** $25.00
✓**Includes 3 Meals Daily   ✓Self-Catering Kitchenette**
✓**Reservations Required   ✓Advance Deposit:** $35 for stays of 3 nights or more
Guest Rules: No smoking in House and silence observed. Guests prepare own meals from food provided. $5 charge for laundry and bed makeup.
On Site Attractions/Nearby Points of Interest: Located on the west edge of the University of Notre Dame between St. Mary's and St. Joseph's Lakes, and near the Notre Dame woods. University of Notre Dame student library, Smite Museum of Art, sports facilities nearby.
Additional Information: No children. Groups welcomed up to a maximum of 7 persons.

3. Mary's Solitude Prayer Center, St. Mary's, Notre Dame, IN 46556
   (219) 284-5599 ✤ **Contact:** Receptionist, Mary's Solitude
✓**Single Rooms   Individual Guest Rate:** $30.00   ✓**Includes 3 Meals Daily**
✓**Reservations Required   ✓Advance Deposit:** 15% (for more than 3 days)
Guest Rules: No smoking indoors. Quiet atmosphere.
On Site Attractions/Nearby Points of Interest: Located in South Bend with its two beautiful parks, Frank Lloyd Wright houses, the Notre Dame and Indiana University campuses, the celebrated auto museum. St. Joseph's and St. Mary's Lakes on the Notre Dame University grounds. St. Mary's College library.
Additional Information: No children. Groups limited to 16 persons.

4. Fatima Retreat House, 5353 E. 56th St., Indianapolis, IN 46226
   (317) 545-7681 ✤ **Contact:** Joe Madden
✓**Single Rooms   ✓Twin Rooms**
Individual Guest Rate: $46.00   ✓**Includes 3 Meals Daily**
✓**Reservations Required   ✓Advance Deposit:** 10%
On Site Attractions/Nearby Points of Interest: The House is set in a secluded and peaceful wooded area in the heart of Indianapolis. Flower gardens, nature walks. Various seasonal festivals in the city, the State Fair, African and Egyptian decor graces the Walker Theatre, native American art in the Eiteljorg Museum, and the "please touch" motto of the Children's Museum.
Additional Information: Children OK with adult supervision. Mission is to provide educational and spiritual enrichment.

5. Geneva Center, Box 646, Rochester, IN 46975
   (219) 223-6915 ✤ **Contact:** Teresa Michaelis
✓**Single Rooms   ✓Twin Rooms   ✓Other:** 5 cedar cabins (8 persons per cabin)
Individual Guest Rate: $32.50 double occupancy; $25.00 cabins
✓**Includes 3 Meals Daily   ✓Reservations Required**
Guest Rules: Talk sessions, recreation, music, games, etc., to be conducted in program areas after 10:30 p.m. No food to be brought into the Center. Use of alcoholic beverages allowed with discretion. No smoking in bedrooms or meeting rooms.
On Site Attractions/Nearby Points of Interest: Outdoor swimming pool, nature trails, water sport activities on Lake Manitou and the Tippecanoe River. Rochester

Fatima Retreat House, Indianapolis, IN

is located about 1¾ hours south of South Bend.
Additional Information: Children OK; 9 yrs. and younger half-price. Coffee and hot tea served at no additional cost. Mission aim is for person-centered educational purposes. 10% discount for Presbyterian groups. Center is operated by the Presbytery of Wabash Valley.

6. St. Meinard Archabbey Guest House, St. Meinard, IN 47577
    (812) 357-6585 ❖ **Contact:** Reverend Shappard
✓**Single Rooms** ✓**Twin Rooms**   **Individual Guest Rate:** $22.00
✓**Reservations Required** ✓**Advance Deposit:** None
On Site Attractions/Nearby Points of Interest: Located 50 miles NE of Evansville and 60 miles west of Louisville, KY. The abbey is situated on an impressive bluff overlooking the banks of the Anderson River. There is a college and seminary on the abbey grounds.
Additional Information: Children OK. Groups welcomed.

7. Norwich Lodge & Conference Center, 920 Earlham St., Richmond, IN 47374
    (317) 983-1575 ❖ **Contact:** Melissa Bickford
✓**Twin Rooms**   **Individual Guest Rate:** $25.00-$45.00 *(includes breakfast)*
✓**Reservations Required** ✓**Advance Deposit:** None
Guest Rules: No smoking or pets.
On Site Attractions/Nearby Points of Interest: Richmond is on the Whitewater River, 67 miles east of Indianapolis, close to the Ohio border and 34 miles west of Dayton, Ohio. The Center, hidden in a secluded wooded setting, has tennis courts, jogging trails, and playing fields. The city of 44,000 is home to Earlham College, Hayes Regional Arboretum that offers 3½ mile tours of the bird sanctuary, Glen Miller Park's shows at the outdoor amphitheater, water sports at Middlefield Reservoir, and antique cars and carriages at the County Historical Museum.
Additional Information: Children OK, groups welcomed. All rooms have recently been remodeled.

1. **Mississippi Abbey, 8400 Abbey Hill, Dubuque, IA 52003**
   (319) 582-2595 ❖ Contact: Sr. Carol Dvorak, OCSO
✓**Single Rooms** ✓**Twin Rooms**
Individual Guest Rate: Free-will donation ✓**Self-Catering Kitchenette**
✓**Reservations Required** ✓**Advance Deposit:** None
Guest Rules: Quiet to be observed in respect to others. Food is provided by guests to prepare their own meals. Maximum stay is two weeks.
On Site Attractions/Nearby Points of Interest: The Abbey is a 20-minute drive from Dubuque, picturesquely located on 580 acres of bluffs, woods, and creeks. The farm produces its own food; the main industry is producing and marketing Trappestine Creamy Caramels.
Additional Information: Small groups of 7 or 8 are welcome, including children.

2. **Emanuel Solitude Center, RR 2 Box 83, Iowa City, IA 52240**
   (319) 351-5839 ❖ Contact: Betsy Coester
✓**Single Rooms** ✓**Twin Rooms** ✓**Other:** Solitude Center
Individual Guest Rate: $15.00 or free-will donation
✓**Includes 3 Meals Daily** ✓**Self-Catering Kitchenette**
✓**Reservations Required** ✓**Advance Deposit:** None
Guest Rules: No pets or smoking.
On Site Attractions/Nearby Points of Interest: Beautiful woods, fields, trails for hiking, riding stable, within walking distance, boating and lake swimming. Nearby, famed Amana colonies experiment in communal utopianism; festivals and concerts in adjacent cities. Home of the University of Iowa; the gold dome of the old Capitol building serves as a centerpiece of both the university and town.
Additional Information: Children OK. Small groups welcomed — any number for campouts.

KANSAS

1. **Ursuline Retreat Center, E. Miami St., Paola, KS 66071**
   (913) 294-2349 ❖ Contact: Sister Frances Walker
✓**Single Rooms** ✓**Twin Rooms**
Individual Guest Rate: $27.00 ✓**Includes 3 Meals Daily**
✓**Reservations Required** ✓**Advance Deposit:** None
Guest Rules: No smoking.
On Site Attractions/Nearby Points of Interest: Located 40 miles SW of Kansas City, KS. About 1½ hours from Lawrence, home of the University of Kansas. In Lawrence are the Museum of Natural History, F. Spencer Museum of Art, Civil War relics in the E. Watkins Community Museum. Wide tree-lined avenues and gracious Victorian homes. Beautiful private gardens for strolling.
Additional Information: No children. Groups welcomed.

2. **Spiritual Life Center, 7100 E. 45th St. N., Wichita, KS 67226**
   (316) 744-0167 ❖ Contact: Front Desk
✓**Single Rooms** ✓**Twin Rooms** ✓**Other:** Dorm facilities
Individual Guest Rate: $35.00
✓**Includes 3 Meals Daily** ✓**Self-Catering Kitchenette**
✓**Reservations Required** ✓**Advance Deposit:** $10.00

Guest Rules: Silence in designated areas. No alcohol, TV, radios.
On Site Attractions/Nearby Points of Interest: New, state-of-the-art facility with private rooms and bath. Gorgeous walking paths around the lake. In the city is the Old Cowtown Historic Village Museum and the Mid-American Indian Center. Wichita State University campus displays an outdoor sculpture collection of 51 works by Moore, Rodin, Hepworth, and a huge glass mosaic mural by Miro.
Additional Information: No children. Groups welcomed; call well in advance for weekend dates.

3. **Manna Retreat Center, 325 E. 5th St., Box 675, Concordia, KS 66901**
   (913) 243-4428 ❖ **Contact: Secretary**
✓**Single Rooms** ✓**Twin Rooms** **Individual Guest Rate:** $28.00
✓**Includes 3 Meals Daily** ✓**Self-Catering Kitchenette**
✓**Reservations Required** ✓**Advance Deposit:** None
Guest Rules: No smoking in buildings.
On Site Attractions/Nearby Points of Interest: The Manna Center is on the border of and within walking distance of the small rural midwestern town of Concordia. On the Center's pleasant grounds are a library, bookstore, exercise room, chapel and swimming pool access. Concordia is on the Republican River about a 2 hour drive NW of Manhattan and Junction City. Within an hour's drive are the Eisenhower Center depicting Ike's career, "Old Abilene Cattle Town," and the Wild Bill Hickok Rodeo.
Additional Information: No children, groups welcomed. Interesting seminars presented throughout the year.

4. **Tall Oaks Conference Center, 12797 189th St., Linwood, KS 66052**
   (913) 723-3307 or 723-3213 ❖ **Contact:** Lori Davidson
Rooms: Dorm-style accommodations — cabin divided into 4 quadrants, with separate bath/shower campsites available for tents
Individual Guest Rate: $36.50 ✓**Includes 3 Meals Daily**
✓**Reservations Required** ✓**Advance Deposit:** Varies with stay
Guest Rules: No pets. Recycling center provided.
On Site Attractions/Nearby Points of Interest: Linwood is a 30 minute drive west from the greater Kansas City metropolitan area, 9 miles west of Bonner Springs. The 360 acres of the Center's native woods and meadows are ideal for hiking, wildlife and nature studies. Special features include an Olympic-size swimming pool, horseback riding, canoeing, fishing, and picnic areas. The open-air Matthews Chapel, surrounded by trees and meadows, is a highlight of the Center's environment.
Additional Information: Children OK, groups welcomed. Respect for other people and God's spirit of creation is at the heart of the Tall Oaks Community.

KENTUCKY

---

1. **Bethany Spring, 115 Dee Head Rd., New Haven, KY 40051**
   (502) 549-8277 ❖ **Contact:** Bethany Spring
✓**Single Rooms** ✓**Twin Rooms**
Individual Guest Rate: $30.00 ✓**Includes 3 Meals Daily**
✓**Reservations Required** ✓**Advance Deposit:** $10.00
On Site Attractions/Nearby Points of Interest: 55 miles south of Louisville in the north central part of the state. Close to the National Historic Site of Abraham Lincoln's birthplace, Stephen Foster's "Old Kentucky Home," Churchill Downs and famous horse farms. One mile from the Trappist farm where cheese production flourishes.

Half an hour away are hundreds of caves that wind through Mammoth Cave National Park. **Additional Information:** No children. Small retreat groups welcomed.

2. **Gethsemani Abbey**
   Trappist, KY 40051
   (502) 549-3117
   Contact: Guestmaster
   ✓Single Rooms
   Individual Guest Rate: Free-will donation
   ✓Includes 3 Meals Daily   ✓Reservations
   Required   ✓Advance Deposit: None
   Guest Rules: Smoking restricted and silence observed in specific areas. First week of each month for women only; remainder of month for men only.

*Matthews Chapel,
Tall Oaks Conference Center,
Linwood, Kansas*

On Site Attractions/Nearby Points of Interest: Located 50 miles south of Louisville on 1,200 acres of woods and countryside. The abbey was the home of author Thomas Merton. Farm setting where cheese and fruitcakes are produced. Idyllic setting for walks and hikes in forested surroundings.
Additional Information: No children. Minimum length of stay is two nights. Brochures available by writing to the Guestmaster. Groups of 10-15 persons welcomed.

LOUISIANA

---

1. **Ave Maria Retreat House, RR 1, Box 0368 AB, Marrero, LA 70072**
   (504) 689-3837 ✣ Contact: Lynn Milton
   ✓Single Rooms   Individual Guest Rate: $40.00   **✓Includes 3 Meals Daily**
   ✓Reservations Required   ✓Advance Deposit: Required for groups
   On Site Attractions/Nearby Points of Interest: Situated on the banks of the Bayou Barataria in the south part of greater New Orleans. Willow trees festooned with Spanish moss abound on the 20 acres of grounds. New Orleans Latin Quarter, the Mardi Gras, jazz concerts, plantations, Jean Lafitte Historical Park and Cajun country swamp tours are just part of the scene.
   Additional Information: Children OK and groups accommodated for their special requirements.

2. **Maryhill Renewal Center, 600 Maryhill Rd., Pineville, LA 71360**
   (318) 640-1378 ✣ Contact: Sr. Ann Lacour, MSC or Lisha Williams
   ✓Single Rooms   ✓Twin Rooms   ✓Other: 2 fully-equipped apartments
   Individual Guest Rate: $30.00
   ✓Reservations Required   ✓Advance Deposit: Call in
   Guest Rules: Provide own food or inquire about arrangements.
   On Site Attractions/Nearby Points of Interest: Located 135 miles NW of Baton Rouge on scenic and peaceful 184-acre woodland. Space, time and environment for spiritual refreshment and life-long learning.
   Additional Information: Groups welcomed. Children OK; ideal for families.

3. **Lumen Christi Retreat Center**
   100 Lumen Christi Lane, Schriever, LA 70395
   (504) 868-1523 ✣ Contact: Aimee Hebert

Lumen Christi Retreat Center, Schriever, Louisiana

✓**Single Rooms** ✓**Twin Rooms**
Individual Guest Rate: $40.00 ✓**Includes 3 Meals Daily**
✓**Reservations Required** ✓**Advance Deposit:** none
On Site Attractions/Nearby Points of Interest: Schriever is 60 miles southwest of New Orleans, about 6 miles south of Thibodaux. The Center complex is situated on 50 acres, next to a forested spring-fed lake, with beautiful natural lighting (hence "Lumen Christi"). Nearby are the shrimp and oyster fisheries of Houma and the castle-like Queen Anne mansion known as the Southern Plantation. Guided tours of Swamp Gardens and Heritage Park exhibit the fishing pirogues and life in the bayou.
Additional Information: No children. Groups welcomed (20 person minimum).

MAINE

---

1. **Hersey Retreat, P.O. Box 1183, Stockton Springs, ME 04981**
   Winter Address: P.O. Box 810, Brooks, ME 04921
   (207) 722-3405 ❖ **Contact:** David Greeley
✓**Single Rooms** ✓**Twin Rooms** **Individual Guest Rate:** $30.00
✓**Includes 3 Meals Daily** ✓**Self-Catering Kitchenette**
✓**Reservations Required** ✓**Advance Deposit:** $20.00
Guest Rules: No pets. No smoking in buildings. Individuals welcomed as part of a non-profit group: wedding parties, family reunions, youth camps, conference gathering, etc.
On Site Attractions/Nearby Points of Interest: Mid-coast Maine at its best, the lodge sits on a bluff overlooking the meeting of the Penobscot River and Bay. At the tip of Sandy Point are acres of meadows and woods and a long beach for strolling or swimming. One hour from Acadia National Park. Nearby are seaports at Belfast, Camden and Searsport.
Additional Information: Unitarian-Universalist operation. Open May through October. Children OK. Groups encouraged.

2. **St. Joseph-by-the-Sea, 235 Pleasant Ave., Peaks Island, ME 04108**
   (207) 766-2284 ❖ Contact: Sr. Ann Murphy SND
   ✓**Single Rooms   Individual Guest Rate:** $30.00
   ✓**Includes 3 Meals Daily   ✓Reservations Required**
   ✓**Advance Deposit:** $50.00
   Guest Rules: Women only. Minimum stay 2 days. No smoking. Silence one of the most important aspects here.
   On Site Attractions/Nearby Points of Interest: Rooms are on high land sloping to the bay and beach. Peaks Island is one of the best located of the 300 islands of Casco Bay. Close to Portland shops and seafood festivals/restaurants. Beautiful rocks, coves, spruce and pine woods and visits to nearby islands. Breathtaking scenery; fishing docks.
   Additional Information: No children. Groups up to 10 persons.

3. **Bay View Villa Guest/Retreat House**
   Rte. 9/187 Bay View Rd., Saco, ME 04072
   (207) 283-3636 ❖ Contact: Sister Anita Therrien
   ✓**Single Rooms   ✓Twin Rooms**
   Individual Guest Rate: $25.00-34.00 *(includes breakfast)*
   ✓**Reservations Required   ✓Advance Deposit:** First night's rental
   Guest Rules: No smoking in House. Quiet is a courtesy to other guests. Minimum stay 2 days off season, 7 days during the summer.
   On Site Attractions/Nearby Points of Interest: A few minutes south of Portland, Saco overlooks beautiful Saco Bay. Old Orchard Beach offers an uninterrupted seven-mile walk around the bay. Rare and used bookstores line the way to nearby Kennebunkport. A one-mile walk in Wells reveals the haunts of numerous rare birds, home of the Rachel Carson National Wildlife Refuge.
   Additional Information: Groups accommodated. Children 5 years and older OK.

4. **Goose Cove Lodge, Deer Isle, Sunset, ME 04683**
   (207) 348-2508 ❖ Contact: Jane Kretchman
   ✓**Single Rooms   ✓Twin Rooms   ✓Other:** Cottages — sleep 4-6
   Individual Guest Rate: $100.00, includes 2 meals, July-August
   ✓**Reservations Required   ✓Advance Deposit:** Inquire
   Guest Rules: Open from mid-May to mid-October. Minimum stay in July and August is 7 days. Other months $50 per person, breakfast only.
   On Site Attractions/Nearby Points of Interest: 75 acres of nature trails overlooking Penobscot Bay. Miles of beach, canoeing, swimming. Barred Island Nature Preserve accessible by sand bar. Raw natural beauty of Maine seacoast with views of other islands. Beautiful haven described as "End of Beyond." Maine State Ferry Service runs boats to various islands in Penobscot Bay.
   Additional Information: Excellent meals served in main dining room. Cabins have fireplaces and private baths, verandas. Children OK. Retreat groups welcomed in months other than July and August, and 3 meals per day can be arranged.

5. **Ferry Beach Park Association, 5 Morris Ave., Saco, ME 04072**
   (207) 282-4489 or (207) 284-8612 *(summer)* ❖ **Contact:** Receptionist
   Rooms: Housing in dormitory-style buildings or campgrounds. Tent and trailer sites with hookups. Special $ rates.
   Individual Guest Rate: $20.00 (3 meals can be provided at $24 per person)
   ✓**Reservations Required   ✓Advance Deposit:** $20.00
   Guest Rules: No smoking in buildings. Swimming when lifeguard on duty.
   On Site Attractions/Nearby Points of Interest: The Ferry Beach campus is lo-

cated 20 miles south of Portland, on beautiful Saco Bay in southern Maine. Historic Quillen House, center of the 35 acre campus, houses a store and a dining room with wrap-around porches that overlook the sea. Nearby Kennebunkport and Cape Arundel provide an auto museum, aquarium, boat rentals, whale watching and the Ogunquit Museum of Art.

Additional Information: The seaside camp and conference center is rooted in Universalist principles of inherent human worth and dignity, free spiritual exploration, ethical responsibility and social justice. Open mid-June to Labor Day. Groups and children welcomed. Small linen charge.

6. China Lake Conference Center, P.O. Box 149, China, ME 04926
   (207) 968-2101 ✤ **Contact:** Beverly Stanhope
✓**Single Rooms** ✓**Twin Rooms**
✓**Other:** Semi-private rooms and dormitory facilities
Individual Guest Rate: $25-$40 ✓**Includes 3 Meals Daily**
✓**Reservations Required** ✓**Advance Deposit:** On request
Guest Rules: No pets, radios or television.
On Site Attractions/Nearby Points of Interest: The Center is 20 miles NW of Augusta, 10 miles SE of Waterville. Set in a pastoral open hillside of 300 acres of fields and woodland, the Center has a commanding view of China Lake. The property owns 200 feet of shoreline with athletic fields and tent and trailer camping areas.
Additional Information: No children, groups welcomed. Owned and operated by the American Baptist Churches, the Center is accessible year-round.

7. St. Paul's Retreat House and Cursillo Center
   136 State St., Augusta, ME 04330
   (207) 622-6235 ✤ **Contact:** Fr. Michael Lauze
✓**Single Rooms** ✓**Twin Rooms**
Individual Guest Rate: $38.00 ✓**Includes 3 Meals Daily**
✓**Reservations Required** ✓**Advance Deposit:** None
Guest Rules: No smoking or alcohol. Subdued conversation time and space for slowing down and silent reflection.
On Site Attractions/Nearby Points of Interest: The state capital of Maine, Augusta is 54 miles north of Portland, 39 miles in from the sea. St. Paul's House enjoys the elegant trappings of the former governor's mansion and is centrally located downtown. The State House towers above Capitol Park, the Kennebel River, Maine State Museum and restored Old Fort Western. The region is in the center of the Belgrade and China Lake Resort area, and a half hour from the campuses of Bates and Colby colleges.
Additional Information: Children OK (ages 4 and above) with supervision. Large complex; groups welcome for Friday night to Sunday afternoon attendance.

MARYLAND

---

1. Christian Brothers Spiritual Center, Box 29, Adamstown, MD 21710
   (301) 874-5180 ✤ **Contact:** Patricia Burriss
✓**Single Rooms** ✓**Twin Rooms**
Individual Guest Rate: $33.00 ✓**Includes 3 Meals Daily**
✓**Reservations Required** ✓**Advance Deposit:** None
On Site Attractions/Nearby Points of Interest: Located in the far western part of the state, near the Civil War battlefields of Gettysburg, Antietam, Harpers Ferry.

Historic city of Frederick a 30-minute drive away. Ski lodge on the Center's grounds. **Additional Information:** Youth groups accommodated, but cannot offer hospitality to groups or families with small children. Adult groups OK.

2. Manresa-on-Severn Retreat House, Box 9, Annapolis, MD 21404
(410) 974-0332 ✤ **Contact:** Lucille Oliver
✓**Single Rooms** ✓**Twin Rooms**
✓**Other:** Rooms with double bed
Individual Guest Rate: $42.00 ✓**Includes 3 Meals Daily**
✓**Reservations Required** ✓**Advance Deposit:** $25.00
Guest Rules: Quiet, peaceful atmosphere for meditation and reflection.
On Site Attractions/Nearby Points of Interest: Home of the U.S. Naval Academy — one square mile of downtown designated by U.S. Department of the Interior as a historical district — many landmarks of the 18th and 19th century still stand. City dock area with restored City Market, shops, and seafood restaurants. Manresa is on the Severn River overlooking Annapolis and Chesapeake Bay.
Additional Information: Children 8 years and older OK. Groups welcomed.

3. Silent Retreat Center at Dayspring
11301 Neelsville Church Rd., Germantown, MD 20874
(301) 428-9348 ✤ **Contact:** Carol Wilkinson
✓**Single Rooms** **Individual Guest Rate:** $25.00
✓**Self-Catering Kitchenette**
✓**Reservations Required** ✓**Advance Deposit:** None
Guest Rules: Only silent retreats.
On Site Attractions/Nearby Points of Interest: A 200-acre working farm with rolling hills, woods, meadows, 30 minutes NW of Baltimore. In Baltimore, the B&O Railroad Museum, USS Constellation, the National Aquarium, Fort McHenry ("Star Spangled Banner") National Monument.
Additional Information: Groups welcome for silent retreats. No children.

Manresa-on-Severn Retreat House, Annapolis, Maryland

4. Bon Secours Spiritual Center
   1525 Marriottsville Rd., Marriottsville, MD 21104
   (410) 442-1320 ❖ **Contact:** Office
✓**Single Rooms** ✓**Twin Rooms** **Individual Guest Rate:** $60.00
✓**Includes 3 Meals Daily** ✓**Self-Catering Kitchenette**
✓**Reservations Required** ✓**Advance Deposit:** Groups only
Guest Rules: Facilities and staff offer services to individuals seeking solitude and spiritual reflection.
On Site Attractions/Nearby Points of Interest: Nestled in 300 acres of rolling hills in the Maryland countryside, the center is ideal for nature walks in the nearby woods. There are ponds, gardens, and a swimming pool. Near to Baltimore city attractions and Washington, DC.
Additional Information: Groups welcomed, children accommodated depending on sponsorship.

5. Loyola-on-Potomac, Faulkner, MD 20632
   (301) 870-3515 ❖ **Contact:** Mrs. Clare Foster
✓**Single Rooms** ✓**Twin Rooms**
Individual Guest Rate: $45.00 ✓**Includes 3 Meals Daily**
✓**Reservations Required** ✓**Advance Deposit:** $15.00
Guest Rules: No smoking in public areas. Respect for those on silent retreat.
On Site Attractions/Nearby Points of Interest: Located on the shores of the Potomac River, with a view of all types of sailing and motor craft coming out of Chesapeake Bay and the upper Potomac. Nearby is the Clement Island recreational area and St. Mary's City, located some 70 miles SE of Washington, D.C. Interesting architecture of the south Maryland peninsula is found at St. Ignatius Church and the St. Thomas Manor.
Additional Information: No children. Groups up to 75 welcome.

6. St. Gabriel's Retreat House, P.O. Box 3106, Catonsville, MD 21228-0106
   (410) 747-6767 ❖ **Contact:** Retreat Reservations
✓**Single Rooms** ✓**Twin Rooms**
Individual Guest Rate: $70-80 per weekend ✓**Includes 3 Meals Daily**
✓**Reservations Required**
Guest Rules: Rules vary with groups. We encourage stays on the premises during retreats—not to be used as a tourist stopover.
On Site Attractions/Nearby Points of Interest: The Retreat House is on the property of All Saints Convent (see #8). It is surrounded by 88 acres of wooded and landscaped lands, and beyond that the Patapsco State Park. Part of the Episcopalian Community.
Additional Information: Children OK with supervision, groups welcomed.
NOTE: The Annunciation Monastery (P.O. Box 21238, Catonsville, MD 21228, ph. 410-747-6140), on the grounds of St. Gabriel's, has accommodations for men only. Contact Fr. Edwards.

7. Drayton Retreat Center, 12651 Cooper's Lane, Worton, MD 21678
   (410) 778-2869 ❖ **Contact:** Carol Shaw
✓**Single Rooms** ✓**Twin Rooms** ✓**Other:** Cluster rooms, 3-9 occupants
Individual Guest Rate: $45.00-$67.00 ✓**Includes 3 Meals Daily**
✓**Reservations Required** ✓**Advance Deposit:** 25% of total bill
Guest Rules: No smoking in manor house, no alcohol or pets.
On Site Attractions/Nearby Points of Interest: The Center lies on a small penin-

sula, half a mile east of Chesapeake Bay. Worton is directly east of Baltimore, across the bay. The Center's primary building is an impressive Georgian Manor House with 23 rooms, teak floors, Waterford chandeliers, hand-carved woodwork, gold draperies, and a drawing room overlooking a sloping hill to Still Pond Creek. An outdoor swimming pool, tennis court, formal gardens and nature trails grace the 36 acre estate. Nearby: scenic rivers and bays, Remington Farms Nature Conservancy, small tucked-away fishing villages.
Additional Information: Setting for diversity and inspiration sponsored by Peninsula-Delaware Conference of the United Methodist Church. Groups welcomed. Children OK with prior approval.

8. All Saints Convent, Box 3127, Catonsville, MD 21228
   (410) 747-4104 ✣ Contact: Sr. Julia Mary
✓**Single Rooms   ✓Twin Rooms**
Individual Guest Rate: Freewill offering or $30-40
✓**Includes 3 Meals Daily   ✓Reservations Required**
Guest Rules: Silence requested 8:00 p.m. - 9:30 a.m. Women only. Prefer that retreatants remain on grounds during their stay. Spiritual objectives emphasized.
On Site Attractions/Nearby Points of Interest: Catonsville is about 9 miles east of Baltimore city center off of Highway I-95. The beautiful stone Gothic Revival Convent is set on 88 acres of natural woodlands on the crest of a hill, all of which is surrounded by woods. The Convent abuts Patapsco State Park where there are numerous trails for walks and hikes.
Additional Information: No children under 14. Groups welcomed (inquire about rates). An Episcopalian community.

MASSACHUSETTS

1. Eastern Point Retreat House, Gonzaga, Gloucester, MA 01930
   (508) 283-0013 ✣ Contact: Retreat Secretary
✓**Single Rooms   Individual Guest Rate:** $40.00   ✓**Includes 3 Meals Daily**
✓**Reservations Required   ✓Advance Deposit:** 25%
Guest Rules: Respectful of the silence. Guests enabled to develop inner strength through reading, meditation, and resolving problems.
On Site Attractions/Nearby Points of Interest: Beautiful mansion overlooking Brace's Cove on the back shore of Gloucester, some 45 miles NE of Boston. Each room has a dramatic view of the sea. Walks along the oceanfront and country lanes add to the serenity of the retreat experience. Tea, coffee and snacks are available all day. Historic wharves of Gloucester village blanket the waterfront; one of the world's foremost fishing ports.
Additional Information: No children. Groups welcome.

2. Glastonbury Abbey, 16 Hull St., Hingham, MA 02043
   (617) 749-2155 ✣ Contact: Retreat Office
✓**Single Rooms   ✓Twin Rooms**
Individual Guest Rate: $40.00 first night; $35.00 each additional night
✓**Includes 3 Meals Daily**
✓**Reservations Required   ✓Advance Deposit:** $35.00
On Site Attractions/Nearby Points of Interest: The Abbey is on 60 acres of woods bordered by stone fences; part of an old estate. Hingham, just 16 miles south of Boston, was founded in 1635. The Old Ship Church in Hingham is the last standing Puritan church in America. The Abbey itself is less than 2 miles from the Atlantic

Ocean.

Additional Information: Groups welcomed. No children. Guest houses are large comfortable homes and non-institutional in nature.

3. St. Joseph's Abbey Retreat House, Spencer, MA 01562*
   (508) 885-3010 ✠ **Contact:** Guestmaster
✓Single Rooms
Individual Guest Rate: Free-will donation (average $30-40 per night)
✓Includes 3 Meals Daily
✓Reservations Required   ✓Advance Deposit: None
Guest Rules: Men only. Respect the quiet of the guests. Minimum stay: weekend or 2 nights.
On Site Attractions/Nearby Points of Interest: Property consists of 1,800 acres, approximately 800 of which are rented to nearby farmers, and 1,000 are wooded. Income is from the famous Trappist jams and jellies sold throughout the country. Located a few miles west of Worcester.
Additional Information: Reservations accepted in advance for only two people at a time, preferable by telephone rather than in writing. No children or groups.

4. St. Benedict Priory, 250 Still River Rd., Box 67, Still River, MA 01467
   (508) 456-3221 ✠ **Contact:** Fr. Xavier Connelly, OSB
✓Single Rooms   ✓Twin Rooms
Individual Guest Rate: $30.00   **✓Includes 3 Meals Daily**
✓Reservations Required   ✓Advance Deposit: None
On Site Attractions/Nearby Points of Interest: The Priory comprises several old colonial homes replete with sacred art. The 68-acre farm is professionally managed. The buildings are situated on a knoll looking across a wide valley to low mountains. Twenty minutes away is historic Lexington and Concord; Boston is a 1-hour drive. Fruitlands Museum within walking distance.
Additional Information: Groups welcomed, children OK. St. Schalastica Priory, a sister monastery, is 45 minutes away in Petersham, MA. Guest facilities available by calling (508) 724-3213.

5. Emery House, Emery Lane, West Newbury, MA 01985
   (508) 462-7940 ✠ **Contact:** Guestmaster
✓Single Rooms   ✓Twin Rooms   Individual Guest Rate: $45.00
✓Includes 3 Meals Daily   ✓Self-Catering Kitchenette
✓Reservations Required   ✓Advance Deposit: $45.00
Guest Rules: Guests join Society members in services and meals. Quiet is observed.
On Site Attractions/Nearby Points of Interest: Located an hour north of Boston, on 120 acres of fields and woods, adjacent to the 400-acre Mandsley State Park. The House is bordered by the Merrimack and Artichoke Rivers. Old Town Newbury and the historic fishing and shipping center of Newburyport are close by.
Additional Information: No children. Groups should reserve far in advance.

6. Mount St. Mary's Abbey, 300 Arnold Rd., Wrentham, MA 02093
   (508) 528-1282 ✠ **Contact:** Sr. M. Denise

---

*Mary House, ¼ mile away, is where men and women (married or single) may stay in a gracious and relaxed atmosphere of contemplation. Meals are self-prepared in a fully equipped kitchen. Donation of $17 per person per night or more according to one's means. Mary House, PO Box 20, Spencer, MA 01562; (508) 885-5450. Also, inquire about Brunelle House for informal stays: (508) 885-3010.

✓**Single Rooms**   ✓**Twin Rooms**
Individual Guest Rate: $12.00 to $15.00   ✓**Self-Catering Kitchenette**
✓**Reservations Required**   ✓**Advance Deposit:** None
Guest Rules: Guests are to respect the atmosphere of rest and solitude of their fellow guests. A reasonable supply of food (excluding meat) is provided in the kitchen where guests prepare their own meals. Smoking kept to a minimum.
On Site Attractions/Nearby Points of Interest: A working farm with gardens, orchards, and woods on 600 acres, the Abbey is located 40 miles west of Boston. There are 50 cows on the grounds and Trappistine Quality Candy is produced on the premises. Fresh bread is sold twice a week, and a gift shop sells convent-made candy and greeting cards. Historic Boston just one hour away.
Additional Information: Children OK with adult supervision. Groups welcome. Reservations to be made not later than 4 or 5 days in advance.

7. Calvary Retreat Center, 59 South St., Shrewsbury, MA 01545
   (508) 842-8821 ❖ **Contact:** Retreat Office
✓**Single Rooms**   ✓**Twin Rooms**   ✓**Other:** Large colonial house w/twin rooms
Individual Guest Rate: $25.00 ($85.00 weekend)   ✓**Includes 3 Meals Daily**
✓**Reservations Required**   ✓**Advance Deposit:** $25.00 for weekend
On Site Attractions/Nearby Points of Interest: Shrewsbury is just a stone's throw to the north of Worcester. The Center is close to the city's hub and its grounds offer a serene and restful ambiance. The region is dotted with lakes, and nearby is a verdant park for walking, jogging, or picnicking.
Additional Information: No children. Groups welcomed and technical support equipment is provided.

8. Sirius Community, Baker Rd., Shutesbury, MA 01072
   (413) 259-1836 ❖ **Contact:** Guest Office
✓**Single Rooms**   ✓**Twin Rooms**

Gathering at Sirius Community, Shutesbury, Massachusetts

Individual Guest Rate: $40-$55 ✓Includes 3 Meals Daily
✓**Reservations Required** ✓**Advance Deposit:** $25.00
Guest Rules: No pets or alcohol. Bring towel, flashlight, outdoor wear.
On Site Attractions/Nearby Points of Interest: Shutesbury is a 15 minute drive NE of Amherst and about 25 minutes NE of Northampton. Situated between the Quabbin Reservoir and the Connecticut River, the 80 acre Community, with its pond and community gardens, is nestled in the eastern hills of the Pioneer Valley. In Amherst: University of Massachusetts, Amherst; Hampshire College; and the Emily Dickinson homestead. Courses given at Sirius: holistic health, organic gardening, group meditation, spiritual growth, massage.
Additional Information: Initial visit requirement to attend Community Living Experience Weekend ($120, Fri.-Sun., meals included). CLE offered each month on 3rd weekend. After participation, all other visits accepted. Groups accepted, max. 20. Children OK; 3-15 yrs., $5 per day.

9. Adelynrood Conference and Retreat Center
   Society of the Companions of the Holy Cross, Byfield, MA 01922
   (508) 462-6721 ✥ **Contact:** Retreat Director
✓**Single Rooms** ✓**Twin Rooms**
Individual Guest Rate: $45.00 ✓**Includes 3 Meals Daily**
✓**Reservations Required** ✓**Advance Deposit:** Call in
On Site Attractions/Nearby Points of Interest: Adelynrood is 30 miles north of Boston and 10 miles south of the New Hampshire state line. The Center, owned and operated by an international sisterhood of 700 Episcopalian women, is open from late May to late September. The Center has large open areas for lawn games, picnics, meeting rooms, library, chapels and dining areas. Nearby: historic Newburyport bay and beaches, Plum Island National Bird Sanctuary, Parker River National Wildlife Refuge — 4,662 acres of marine and bird life, marshes, dunes, berry patches.
Additional Information: No children, groups welcomed. One of the oldest retreat centers in continuous operation in the U.S.

Adelynrood Conference and Retreat Center, Byfield, Massachusetts

10. Sacred Heart Retreat House, Route 1A, Box 567, Ipswich, MA 01938
   (508) 356-3838 ❖ **Contact:** Receptionist
✓**Single Rooms** ✓**Twin Rooms**
Individual Guest Rate: $35.00   ✓**Includes 3 Meals Daily**
✓**Reservations Required** ✓**Advance Deposit:** Call in
On Site Attractions/Nearby Points of Interest: Sacred Heart is located 28 miles north of Boston on Route 1A. Central to this 75 acre estate is a majestic brick mansion housing a floor-to-ceiling library and scores of comfortable bedrooms. Surrounding the broad lawns and fields are two baseball diamonds, a soccer field, two tennis courts, an outdoor swimming pool and a basketball court. Nearby: the Salem Witch Museum, Newburyport's Waterfront Park and Promenade, and the Parker River National Wildlife Refuge for surf fishing and cranberry picking.
Additional Information: Children OK and groups up to 40 are welcomed.

11. Rowe Conference Center, Kings Highway Rd., Rowe, MA 01367
   (413) 339-4954 ❖ **Contact:** Retreat Office
✓**Single Rooms** ✓**Twin Rooms**
✓**Other:** Dorm housing—6 to 8 beds per room in farmhouse and cabins
Individual Guest Rate: $20-40
✓**Includes 3 Meals Daily** ✓**Self-Catering Kitchenette**
NOTE: Meals can be provided on weekends for an additional charge.
✓**Reservations Required** ✓**Advance Deposit:** 50% of total
Guest Rules: No pets and no smoking inside buildings.
On Site Attractions/Nearby Points of Interest: The Rowe Center lies at the foothills of the Northern Berkshires, 20 miles NE of Pittsfield in the northwestern corner of the state. Skirting the Center is the 67-mile Mohawk Trail, which winds its way to Shelbourne Falls, a picture-book replica of small-town Americana. The colorful Bridge of Flowers spans the Deerfield River here; further downriver is tiny Deerfield Village, half of which is a museum site of 18th century houses.
Additional Information: Children OK and groups welcomed. Summer camp programs. Workshops offered.

12. Campion Renewal Center, 319 Concord Rd., Weston, MA 02193
   (617) 894-3199 ❖ **Contact:** Renewal Office
✓**Single Rooms** ✓**Twin Rooms**
Individual Guest Rate: $51.00   ✓**Includes 3 Meals Daily**
✓**Reservations Required** ✓**Advance Deposit:** $25.00
On Site Attractions/Nearby Points of Interest: The many attractive buildings of the Renewal Center are found on the outskirts of Boston, about 30 minutes from city center. Close by are the historical landmarks of Lexington and Concord: the Museum of Our National Heritage; the Munroe Tavern, built in 1635 and now open to the public; the Hancock-Clarke House, where Paul Revere shouted the wake-up call; the old North Bridge and Walden Pond. Many tours available in the Boston area.
Additional Information: No children. The Center has six "function areas" that accommodate 15-200 people.

13. St. Stephen Priory Spiritual Life Center
   20 Glen St., Box 370, Dover, MA 02030
   (508) 785-0124 ❖ **Contact:** Retreat Secretary
✓**Single Rooms** ✓**Twin Rooms**
Individual Guest Rate: $50.00   ✓**Includes 3 Meals Daily**
✓**Reservations Required** ✓**Advance Deposit:** $25.00
Guest Rules: No smoking.

On Site Attractions/Nearby Points of Interest: The Priory is about a 30 minute drive southwest of Boston, 10 miles east of Wellesley. The Priory, on 76 acres of property bordering the Charles River, is the former mansion of the Cheney family. On the property are forest trails, cross-country skiing, basketball, handball, baseball fields, swimming pool and a canoe wharf. Buffet-style meals served in a cozy dining room. Workshops stress individual renewal.
Additional Information: No children, groups welcomed.

14. Kripalu Center for Yoga and Health, P.O. Box 793, Lenox, MA 02140
    1-800-967-3577 ✤ **Contact:** Reservation Office
✓**Single Rooms** ✓**Twin Rooms** ✓**Other:** Dorm-style also available
Individual Guest Rate: $56.00 and up ✓**Includes 3 Meals Daily**
✓**Reservations Required** ✓**Advance Deposit:** 25%
Guest Rules: No smoking or alcohol. Food is vegetarian, silent dining, conservative dress.
On Site Attractions/Nearby Points of Interest: Lenox is in the far west of Massachusetts, about 10 miles south of Pittsfield. The Center is expansive — 4 acres of carpeting were purchased to cover the floors. It is adjacent to the Tanglewood Music Festival grounds, and is a non-profit spiritual and holistic health center offering programs in yoga, bodywork, spiritual attainment and self-discovery. Set in the beautiful Berkshire Mountains, the facility overlooks a lake with a public beach. Over 13,000 guests per year are served and there is always a lively spirit of mutual help and respect.
Additional Information: Children OK during specific times. No groups. For those on limited budgets, opportunities for work exchange provided. Phone (413) 448-3123.

MICHIGAN

1. St. Francis Retreat House, 703 E. Main St., DeWitt, MI 48223
    (517) 669-8321 ✤ **Contact:** Marie Bower or Janie Bollman
✓**Single Rooms** ✓**Twin Rooms**
Individual Guest Rate: $7.00-10.00 ✓**Self-Catering Kitchenette**
✓**Reservations Required** ✓**Advance Deposit:** Varies — call ahead
Guest Rules: Peaceful and quiet environment.
On Site Attractions/Nearby Points of Interest: Located on 95 acres of pine forest, fruit tree orchards, rolling hills. A 15-minute drive to the campus of Michigan State University, the state Capitol building in Lansing, and the Michigan Outdoor TV Studio and Museum.
Additional Information: Children 14 years and older OK. A very hospitable staff to meet individual and group requests.

2. St. Augustine House, P.O. Box 125, Oxford, MI 48371
    (313) 628-5155 ✤ **Contact:** Fr. Richard Herbel
✓**Single Rooms**
Individual Guest Rate: $15.00-20.00 ✓**Includes 3 Meals Daily**
✓**Reservations Required** ✓**Advance Deposit:** None
Guest Rules: No smoking indoors.
On Site Attractions/Nearby Points of Interest: Located between Flint and Pontiac, about 45 miles north of Detroit. The retreat house stands on a hillside, a rural setting, with views for many miles. The only Lutheran monastery in the USA.
Additional Information: No children. Groups of 8-10 persons welcomed.

St. Claire Capuchin Retreat, St. Clair, Michigan

3. St. Claire Capuchin Retreat, 1975 North River Rd., St. Clair, MI 48079
   (313) 329-9011 ❖ **Contact:** Jan Markel
✓**Single Rooms** ✓**Other:** Large bedrooms, 4-5 beds per room
Individual Guest Rate: $20.00
✓**Reservations Required** ✓**Advance Deposit:** $20.00
Guest Rules: No smoking or alcoholic beverages.
On Site Attractions/Nearby Points of Interest: The Retreat House is a Tudor mansion on 50 acres of land located directly on the St. Clair River. Near to Detroit and the Philip A. Hart Plaza, a 10-acre "citizen center" that holds free concerts, ethnic festivals, and ice skating in the winter.
Additional Information: Children of high school age OK. Youth and youth groups are given priority preference. 25 person minimum — $50 per person, includes 5 meals.

4. St. Lazare Retreat House, 18600 W. Spring Lake Rd., Spring Lake, MI 49456
   (616) 842-3370 ❖ **Contact:** St. Lazare Retreat House
✓**Single Rooms** **Individual Guest Rate:** Free-will donation
✓**Reservations Required** ✓**Advance Deposit:** None
Guest Rules: Retreats with silent reflection. Meals by arrangement.
On Site Attractions/Nearby Points of Interest: St. Lazare is 10 miles west of Grand Rapids and a short distance to Grand Haven on the shore of Lake Michigan. Water sport activities at Spring Lake.
Additional Information: Weekends for individuals; weekdays reserved for groups. No children.

5. St. Joseph Home Retreat Center, 1000 E. Porter, Jackson, MI 49202
   (517) 787-3320 ❖ **Contact:** Sr. Concepta, Administrator
✓**Single Rooms** ✓**Twin Rooms**
Individual Guest Rate: $35.00 ✓**Includes 3 Meals Daily**

✓**Reservations Required**   ✓**Advance Deposit:** $25.00
On Site Attractions/Nearby Points of Interest: The Center is an hour's drive west from Detroit, 35 miles due west of Ann Arbor. The Center's large complex is in a semi-residential wooded area with peaceful surroundings. The Michigan Space Center displays the Gemini trainer, Apollo 9 Command Module, orbiters, moon rocks, rocket engines, etc. Cascade Falls Park has picnicking, paddle-boating, tennis courts, miniature golf and more. Balloon festivities in the summer and 5 miles of nature trails are at the Dahlem Environmental Education Center.
Additional Information: No children. Conference rooms for groups.

6. **Full Circle House of Prayer, 2532 South Blvd., Port Huron, MI 48060**
   (810) 364-3326 ❖ **Contact:** Office
✓**Single Rooms   Individual Guest Rate:** $25.00
✓**Includes 3 Meals Daily**   ✓**Self-Catering Kitchenette:** for breakfast and lunch
✓**Reservations Required**   ✓**Advance Deposit:** None
Guest Rules: Respect privacy of guests.
On Site Attractions/Nearby Points of Interest: This small, charming turn-of-the-century House is one hour north of Detroit, southern tip of Lake Huron, at the junction of the Black and St. Clair Rivers. Lakeport State Park is a 565-acre recreation site on the shores of Lake Huron, and at the Museum of Arts and History are Thomas Edison's boyhood exhibits, lighthouses, Indian lore. From the city, the famous Blue Water Bridge crosses over to Sarnia, Canada.
Additional Information: No children, no groups. Opportunity to pitch in and cultivate the organic vegetable garden.

7. **Queen of Angels Retreat**
   3400 S. Washington St., Box 2026, Saginaw, MI 48605-2026
   (517) 755-2149 ❖ **Contact:** Carolyn Hartman
✓**Single Rooms   Individual Guest Rate:** $35.00
✓**Includes 3 Meals Daily**
✓**Reservations Required**   ✓**Advance Deposit:** Call in
On Site Attractions/Nearby Points of Interest: Saginaw is about 115 miles NW of Detroit, 35 miles north of Flint. The Retreat, on 17 parklike acres of woods and old oak trees, has 59 single rooms, chapels, conference rooms, large dining area, library and lounge. Saginaw attractions include: Japanese Cultural Garden, Rose Garden with 60 varieties and 1000 bushes, and the French Chateau Castle Museum. Nearby Frankenmuth has boat tours on the Cuss River and Bronners is the world's largest Christmas store, 50,000 trims and gifts.
Additional Information: No children (under 18). Groups welcomed.

MINNESOTA

1. **Benedictine Center of St. Paul's Priory**
   2675 E. Larpenteur Ave., St. Paul, MN 55109
   (612) 777-7251 ❖ **Contact:** Karen Luxem, Secretary
✓**Single Rooms**   ✓**Twin Rooms**
Individual Guest Rate: $40.00 ($30.00 for religious community members)
✓**Includes 3 Meals Daily**   ✓**Self-Catering Kitchenette** *(for snacks only)*
✓**Reservations Required**   ✓**Advance Deposit:** None
Guest Rules: No smoking in buildings. Dining times are set.
On Site Attractions/Nearby Points of Interest: The Benedictine Center of St. Paul's Priory is located within ½ hour from the State Capitol, Guthrie and Ordway Theatres,

St. Paul's Priory, St. Paul, Minnesota

the Metrodome, Target Center and Civic Center for sports and cultural events. It is within an hour's drive to many of the lake resorts of Minnesota and northern Wisconsin and within 20 minutes' drive to the beautiful Afton State Park on the scenic St. Croix River. Spacious grounds for walking; 90 acres of woodland and meadow for outdoor activities.

Additional Information: No children. A unique and quiet setting for reading, writing, thought, and spiritual regeneration. Groups welcomed.

2. Good Counsel Education Centre, PO Box 8968, Mankato, MN 56002
   (507) 389-4287 ✤ Contact: Hospitality Director
✓Single Rooms   ✓Twin Rooms   ✓Other: Quad rooms with shared bath
Individual Guest Rate: $20.00
✓Reservations Required   ✓Advance Deposit: None
Guest Rules: No smoking or alcohol. Peaceful atmosphere.
On Site Attractions/Nearby Points of Interest: Mankato, at the confluence of the Minnesota and Blue Earth Rivers, is 1½ hours SW of the twin cities of St. Paul and Minneapolis. The Center is adjacent to the tree-shaded campus of Mankato State College. Sibley, Minneopa, and Tourtelotte Parks are open to camping, pools, fishing, picnicking, boating, scenic river views. Cross-country skiing at nearby Flandrau State Park — you will meet deer, peacocks and geese in their natural habitat at Deer Park.
Additional Information: No children. Multi-purpose facility, meals, available to groups.

3. Mount St. Benedict Center, E. Summit Ave., Crookston, MN 56716
   (218) 281-3441 ✤ Contact: MSB Center Director
✓Single Rooms   ✓Twin Rooms   ✓Other: 30 dorm beds in bays of 5 each
Individual Guest Rate: $23.00 (double room)   **✓Includes 3 Meals Daily**
✓Reservations Required   ✓Advance Deposit: $10.00

Mount St. Benedict Center, Crookston, Minnesota

Guest Rules: No tobacco or alcohol. Respect for a peaceful lifestyle.
On Site Attractions/Nearby Points of Interest: Located on a ridge overlooking the Red Lake River in the sugar belt country of Red River Valley. The Center spreads its meadows eastward away from town. Ideal for snowy-night walks and cross-country skiing. On campus are monastic crafts, rug looming, candlemaking, and bread baking. Site of University of Minnesota/Crookston. Elderhostel classes. Crookston is in the far northwest corner of Minnesota, close to the North Dakota border.
Additional Information: Children OK if "beyond the cradle stage". Groups welcome — advance registration.

4. St. Francis Center, 116 SE Eighth Ave., Little Falls, MN 56345
   (612) 632-2981 ❖ Contact: Sister Lydia Langer
✓Single Rooms   ✓Twin Rooms   ✓Other: 2 winterized hermitages
Individual Guest Rate: $13.00-18.00   ✓Self-Catering Kitchenette
✓Reservations Required   ✓Advance Deposit: $50.00 for groups
Guest Rules: Atmosphere for growth and reflection.
On Site Attractions/Nearby Points of Interest: Little Falls is on the Mississippi River about 2½ hours NW of St. Paul. The center has an indoor swimming pool, hot tub, sauna, exercise room, and tennis court. Sports medicine therapy and massage are available. Two state parks are nearby, with pine forests, a nature trail and streams. Little Falls features the historic Charles Lindbergh home.
Additional Information: Children OK, but must be well supervised. Some group retreats offered.

5. Center for Spiritual Development
   211 10th St., Box 538, Bird Island, MN 55310
   (612) 365-3644 ❖ Contact: Reservation Office
✓Single Rooms   ✓Other: Limited number of rooms for couples
Individual Guest Rate: $25.00   ✓Includes 3 Meals Daily
✓Reservations Required   ✓Advance Deposit: None

Guest Rules: No smoking.
On Site Attractions/Nearby Points of Interest: Bird Island is about 100 miles west of Minneapolis near Buffalo Lake, and minutes away from some of Minnesota's 10,000 other lakes.
Additional Information: Groups welcomed — non-refundable deposit required. No children.

6. **Benedictine Resource Center**
   St. Benedict's Convent, St. Joseph, MN 56374
   (612) 363-7112 or 363-7114 ❖ **Contact:** Julie Schleper, OSB
   ✓**Single Rooms** ✓**Twin Rooms**
   Individual Guest Rate: Varies with food arrangement
   ✓**Includes 3 Meals Daily** ✓**Self-Catering Kitchenette**
   ✓**Reservations Required** ✓**Advance Deposit:** None
   Guest Rules: Respect other's wishes and quiet time.
   On Site Attractions/Nearby Points of Interest: NW of Minneapolis near St. Cloud, St. Joseph is a small town in a rural setting. Home of the College of St. Benedict, founded in 1913, and of the Liturgical Press of St. John's University. Areas for walking through the woods and meadows, and close to lakefront water sports.
   Additional Information: Welcomes groups. Children OK with parent or guardian.

7. **Christian Brothers Retreat Center**
   15525 St. Croix Trail N., Marine-on-St. Croix, MN 55047
   (612) 433-2486 ❖ **Contact:** Guestmaster
   ✓**Single Rooms** ✓**Twin Rooms**
   Individual Guest Rate: $40.00 ✓**Includes 3 Meals Daily**
   ✓**Reservations Required** ✓**Advance Deposit:** None
   Guest Rules: Respectful of others.
   On Site Attractions/Nearby Points of Interest: Just 40 minutes north of St. Paul, one of the most beautiful canal trips in the country is down the St. Croix River. At the Center there is tennis, swimming, boating, and cross-country skiing. Beautiful walking viewpoints along the riverfront and in the Croix Valley.
   Additional Information: Groups welcomed. Inquire for children.

8. **Franciscan Retreat Center**
   16385 St. Francis Lane, Prior Lake, MN 55372
   (612) 447-2182 ❖ **Contact:** Br. Ambrose, Director; or the secretary
   ✓**Single Rooms** **Individual Guest Rate:** By special arrangement
   ✓**Reservations Required** ✓**Advance Deposit:** None
   Guest Rules: Common courtesy to guests.
   On Site Attractions/Nearby Points of Interest: In the Minneapolis area. Lake of Isles, ringed by stately mansions, and bikers, skaters and joggers near Lake Calhoun on the west end. The Walker Art Center, and world-famous Minneapolis Institute of Arts and Sculpture Garden are highlights of the city. Theater, concerts, musicals, zoo — other attractions to be found in the Twin Cities.
   Additional Information: Groups welcomed. No children.

MISSISSIPPI

---

1. **Diocesan Renewal Center, 2225 Boling St., Jackson, MS 39213**
   (601) 982-5020 ❖ **Contact:** Mary Davenport
   ✓**Single Rooms** ✓**Twin Rooms** ✓**Other:** Triple rooms

Individual Guest Rate: $12.00
✓Reservations Required ✓Advance Deposit: None ($100 for groups)
Guest Rules: No smoking. No food in bedrooms.
On Site Attractions/Nearby Points of Interest: The city, named for Andrew Jackson, has much to recommend, starting with the Zoological Park, a natural 100 acre habitat for 500 animals; the antique-filled Governor's Mansion; the Davis Planetarium (largest in the southeast); the Dizzy Dean Museum; the Eudora Welty Library (southern writer's exhibits); and noontime concerts in Smith Park.
Additional Information: No children. Groups welcomed.

MISSOURI

1. St. John's Diocesan Center, 2015 E. 72nd St., Kansas City, MO 64132
   (816) 363-3585 ✤ **Contact:** Ann Freeman
✓Single Rooms   ✓Twin Rooms   ✓Other: Dormitories
Individual Guest Rate: $33.00   **✓Self-Catering Kitchenette**
✓Reservations Required   ✓Advance Deposit: Dependent on total fee
On Site Attractions/Nearby Points of Interest: The Crown Center Plaza in Kansas City has a multitude of restaurants and shops, all fronted by a hotel and 5-story waterfall. The Coterie Children's Theatre and Ice Terrace always pleases the kids. An elevator takes one to the top of the Liberty Memorial for a view of Arrowhead and Royals Stadium.
Additional Information: Children OK and groups welcomed.

2. Rickman Center, Box 104298, Jefferson City, MO 65110
   (314) 635-0848 ✤ **Contact:** LaDonna Hopkins or Paula McCurren
✓Single Rooms   ✓Twin Rooms   ✓Other: Cabins; can accommodate 10
Individual Guest Rate: $26.00-40.00   **✓Includes 3 Meals Daily**
✓Reservations Required   ✓Advance Deposit: 20%
On Site Attractions/Nearby Points of Interest: 2½-3 hours west of St. Louis, the Center is situated on 220 acres of beautiful wooded forest. Hiking trails and sport fields circle around the property and lead to the swimming pool. The city is near the confluence of the Missouri and Osage Rivers, and is a gateway to the famed Ozark Mountains and Osage Beach.
Additional Information: Group retreats and children welcomed.

3. Seton Center, 7800 Natural Bridge Rd., St. Louis, MO 63121
   (314) 382-6866 or 382-2800, x288 ✤ **Contact:** Sr. Jacqueline Muster, CSJ
✓Single Rooms   ✓Twin Rooms
Individual Guest Rate: Depends on length of stay
✓Includes 3 Meals Daily   ✓Self-Catering Kitchenette
✓Reservations Required   ✓Advance Deposit: 10% of total
On Site Attractions/Nearby Points of Interest: In St. Louis is Forest Park, the largest urban park in America. At the Riverfront and Laclede's Landing tugs and sternwheelers slug along the powerful Mississippi. The tallest monument in the U.S., Gateway Arch, is accessible by elevated train rides. Gateway Riverboat Cruises leave on the hour from the base of the Arch. In addition, St. Louis offers cathedrals, museums, gardens, the Magic House, and much more.
Additional Information: No children. Call for group retreat accommodations.

4. Caroline Hall, 320 E. Ripa St., St. Louis, MO 63125
   (314) 544-0455 ✤ **Contact:** Sr. Marie Kevin

✓**Single Rooms** ✓**Other:** Dorm room with 24 spaces
Individual Guest Rate: $42.00 (group rate) — call for individual rate
✓**Includes 3 Meals Daily**
✓**Reservations Required** ✓**Advance Deposit:** 25%
Guest Rules: Make up one's own bed.
On Site Attractions/Nearby Points of Interest: The Hall is a modern facility in south St. Louis County overlooking the Mississippi River, north of historic Jefferson Barracks Park. The Hall borders acres of landscaped hills, has an indoor swimming pool and gymnasium. St. Louis presents the Municipal Opera productions, the Opera Theatre, and the St. Louis Symphony Orchestra.
Additional Information: Prices different for individuals, since the minimum number of persons required for opening the kitchen is 15. Closed most of September. Children 5 years and older OK. Groups OK.

5. Queen of Haven Solitude, Route 1, Marionville, MO 65705
 (417) 744-2011 ✤ **Contact:** Queen of Heaven Solitude
✓**Single Rooms** ✓**Other:** Individual cabins
Individual Guest Rate: Goodwill offering ✓**Includes 3 Meals Daily**
✓**Reservations Required** ✓**Advance Deposit:** None
Guest Rules: Maintaining silence in order to enjoy the benefits of solitude. Each cabin self-contained with all the amenities, including heat and air-conditioning. Meals taken privately.
On Site Attractions/Nearby Points of Interest: Rugged, spacious grounds, with forest trails and mountain views. Located a few miles SW of Springfield, near to the James River.
Additional Information: No children. Cannot accept groups.

6. Christina House, P.O. Box 69, Abbey Lane, Pevely, MO 63070
 (314) 479-3697 ✤ **Contact:** Christina House
✓**Single Rooms** ✓**Other:** 8 underground hermitages
Individual Guest Rate: $12.50 ✓**Self-Catering Kitchenette**
✓**Reservations Required** ✓**Advance Deposit:** None
Guest Rules: Maximum privacy in the earth homes — each is equipped with appliances for light cooking and has its own bath.
On Site Attractions/Nearby Points of Interest: Pevely is 30 minutes south of St. Louis on the Mississippi River.
Additional Information: No children. Cannot accept groups.

7. Maria Fonte Solitude, Box 322, High Ridge, MO 63049
 (314) 677-3235 ✤ **Contact:** Sister Mary Catherine
✓**Rooms:** 6 individual cabins, each with shower
Individual Guest Rate: Free-will donation ✓**Includes 3 Meals Daily**
✓**Reservations Required** ✓**Advance Deposit:** None
Guest Rules: Silence to be observed within the community except for the director.
On Site Attractions/Nearby Points of Interest: Grounds are rugged, but spacious. Located about 20 miles SW of St. Louis. Hermitages self-contained and well-equipped.

8. Kenrick Pastoral Center, 7800 Kenrick Road, St. Louis, MO 63119
 (314) 961-4320, Ext. 114 ✤ **Contact:** Deacon Robert Snyder
✓**Single Rooms** ✓**Twin Rooms** ✓**Other:** 16 rooms with bath between
Individual Guest Rate: $28.00
✓**Reservations Required** ✓**Advance Deposit:** $10.00

Main seminary building,
Kenrick Pastoral Center,
St. Louis, Missouri

Guest Rules: No smoking or alcohol. Quiet atmosphere.

On Site Attractions/Nearby Points of Interest: The Center is operated in conjunction with the Kenrick Theological Seminary, which is located in the suburbs of St. Louis in a quiet setting with park-like grounds. Highlights of St. Louis: capsule transportation to 630-foot Gateway Arch, Museum of Westward Expansion, Zoological Park with 3,400 animals in natural settings, sternwheeler Riverboat Cruises on the Mississippi, renovated pre-Civil War buildings with shops and restaurants at Laciede's Landing.

Additional Information: Children OK age 10 and over. Groups welcomed — no charge for conference rooms, 25 overnight maximum.

9. **Thompson Retreat**
   and Conference Center
   12145 Ladue Road
   St. Louis, MO 63141
   (314) 434-3633
   Contact: Facilities coordinator

✓**Single Rooms** ✓**Twin Rooms** Individual Guest Rate: $22.00-$35.00
✓**Reservations Required** ✓**Advance Deposit:** $25.00

On Site Attractions/Nearby Points of Interest: The Center, with the elegance and graciousness of a country estate, is at the end of a winding driveway bordered by

Thompson Retreat and Conference Center, St. Louis, Missouri

landscaped and wooded areas that roll gently on 32 acres. Drive carefully! — deer may be strolling by from the salt lick. The Center has all the necessities for study and rest — no telephones or television. However, when it's time for a break, use the Center's tennis courts, outdoor track, basketball and volleyball courts, or golf at the nearby 9-hole course.
Additional Information: No children. Meals for groups can be prepared by the Center's caterer.

MONTANA

---

1. Christhaven Retreat House, Box 948, Anaconda, MT 59711
   (406) 563-7803 ❖ **Contact:** Christhaven
✓**Single Rooms** ✓**Twin Rooms**
Individual Guest Rate: $30.00 to $40.00 ✓**Includes 3 Meals Daily**
✓**Reservations Required** ✓**Advance Deposit:** For groups — please inquire.
Guest Rules: Make bed upon leaving.
On Site Attractions/Nearby Points of Interest: A short drive NW of Butte. Nearby are Lost Creek State Park, with waterfalls, Fairmont Hot Springs (therapy pools), ski areas, Mt. Haggin (10,665 ft.), all surrounded by rivers, lakes, and rugged mountain ranges. Seven North American Indian tribes still reside in Montana.
Additional Information: Children in their teens OK if adequately supervised. Groups welcomed.

2. Ursuline Center, 2300 Center Ave., Great Falls, MT 59401
   (406) 452-8585 ❖ **Contact:** Harry Tholen
✓**Single Rooms** ✓**Twin Rooms** ✓**Other:** Dorm accommodations
Individual Guest Rate: $14.00 ✓**Self-Catering Kitchenette**
✓**Reservations Required** ✓**Advance Deposit:** $10.00
Guest Rules: Meals can be served by arrangement.
On Site Attractions/Nearby Points of Interest: The Center is listed on the National Register of Historic Places. Tucked in between the 9,000-foot mountains of the Continental Divide, the Center's grounds provide spectacular vistas. Great Falls is on the upper reaches of the Missouri River, the home of the Charles Russell Museum, and a gateway to Glacier National Park. Fishing, boating, outdoor recreation area in summer and winter.
Additional Information: Children OK and groups welcomed.

3. Sacred Heart Renewal Center, 26 Wyoming Ave., Billings, MT 59101
   (406) 252-0322 ❖ **Contact:** Office
✓**Single Rooms** ✓**Twin Rooms** **Individual Guest Rate:** $20.00
3 meals can be provided for $13.50. ✓**Self-Catering Kitchenette**
✓**Reservations Required** ✓**Advance Deposit:** None
On Site Attractions/Nearby Points of Interest: Billings, in south central Montana on the west bank of the Yellowstone River, is about a 2 hour drive to the north entrance of Yellowstone National Park. Sacred Heart provides a comfortable environment in the heart of Billings. A final resting place for gunmen who died with their boots on is at Boot Hill Cemetery. One has breathtaking views of Yellowstone Valley and the Custer National Forest. Pictographs 4,500 years old are in nearby caves — and in the present day, Riverfloat festivals send inner tubes, canoes, rafts and launches swirling downstream.
Additional Information: Children OK with families, groups welcomed.

4. Boulder Hot Springs, P.O. Box 930, Boulder, MT 59632
   (406) 225-4339 ❖ **Contact:** Barb Reiter
✓**Single Rooms** ✓**Twin Rooms** ✓**Other:** Tents, campers welcome (no hookups)
Individual Guest Rate: $30.00 (meals can be provided for an extra charge)
✓**Reservations Required** ✓**Advance Deposit:** 10% of total
Guest Rules: No alcohol, smoking, pets, candles, fire of any kind.
On Site Attractions/Nearby Points of Interest: Nestled in the heart of Montana's Peace Valley, Boulder Hot Springs is at an altitude of 5,068 feet on 274 acres of fertile land at the edge of Deerlodge National Forest. Centuries ago, native Americans selected this spot as a holy sanctuary. Boulder lies midway between the state capital of Helena and Butte. Highlights of the Center are the 104° geothermal therapeutic baths, and in summer, outdoor swimming in the cool spring-fed pools. Moose, deer, fox and antelope roam in the area. Nearby is Elkhorn Ghost Town and Radon Mines, famed for healing properties.
Additional Information: Children OK, groups welcomed and rates negotiable. Separate geothermal bathing facilities for men and women available. Host to all groups, especially those interested in recovery, spirituality and healing.

NEBRASKA

---

1. Niobrara Valley House of Renewal, Box 117, Lynch, NE 68746
   (402) 569-3433 ❖ **Contact:** Kathryn Purviance
✓**Single Rooms** ✓**Twin Rooms**
Individual Guest Rate: Free-will donation; $15.00 suggested
✓**Self-Catering Kitchenette**
✓**Reservations Required** ✓**Advance Deposit:** None
Guest Rules: No alcohol.
On Site Attractions/Nearby Points of Interest: Lynch is located in the NE corner of Nebraska near the Ponca and Santee Indian Reservations, and across from the South Dakota border. Nearby: Ashfall, prehistoric fossil beds; boating and fishing on the Niobrara and Missouri Rivers; Fort Randall, an early American Western fort and church; Native American arts and crafts stores; western antiques.
Additional Information: Children OK; groups welcomed. Individual, marriage, engaged, encounter retreats; seminars, workshops, support groups.

2. Notre Dame Center, 3501 State St., Omaha, NE 68112
   (402) 455-4083 ❖ **Contact:** Kris Krajicek
✓**Twin Rooms** ✓**Other:** Dormitory facilities
Individual Guest Rate: $12.50 ✓**Self-Catering Kitchenette**
✓**Reservations Required** ✓**Advance Deposit:** $10.00
On Site Attractions/Nearby Points of Interest: Situated in a peaceful wooded area. Gymnasium available. Several museums in Omaha, including the architectural displays in the Western Heritage Museum. The Omaha Children's Museum features science exhibits, and the Henry Doorly Zoo has the largest enclosed aviary in North America. The Omaha Magic Theater presents innovative American musicals.
Additional Information: Children OK; groups welcomed. Provide own linens.

3. Columban Retreat Center, St. Columbans, NE 68056
   (402) 291-1920 ❖ **Contact:** Fr. Denis Bartley
✓**Single Rooms** ✓**Twin Rooms**
Individual Guest Rate: Call for rates; very reasonable.

✓Reservations Required   ✓Advance Deposit: $12.00
On Site Attractions/Nearby Points of Interest: Located 20 minutes from Omaha on 40 acres of partially wooded terrain. Very private and tranquil. Boys Town nearby.
Additional Information: Caters to weekend retreats only. No children.

4. Crosier Renewal Center, 223 E. 14th St., PO Box 789, Hastings, NE 68902
  (402) 463-3188 ❖ Contact: Mary Ann Warner
✓**Single Rooms** ✓**Twin Rooms**
Individual Guest Rate: $30.00   ✓**Includes 3 Meals Daily**
✓**Reservations Required** ✓**Advance Deposit:** $15.00
Guest Rules: No smoking except in coffee room.
On Site Attractions/Nearby Points of Interest: Gymnasium, tennis court, game room. Within 30 minutes: Pioneer Village and the city of Grand Island. Indian and Native American art displayed in the Hastings Museum.
Additional Information: Children OK; groups welcomed.

5. Christ the King Priory, PO Box 528, Schuyler, NE 68661
  (402) 352-2177, Ext. 320 ❖ Contact: Fr. Volker Futter
✓**Single Rooms** ✓**Twin Rooms**
Individual Guest Rate: $20.00   ✓**Includes 3 Meals Daily**
✓**Reservations Required** ✓**Advance Deposit:** None
On Site Attractions/Nearby Points of Interest: Schuyler is 65 miles west of Omaha, 15 miles east of Columbus. The priory is unique — it is literally encased into the natural landscape of the area, its roof and outer walls covered by a verdant carpet of grass. Fremont, to the east, has a recreation area with 25 lakes and its Vally Railroad offers train rides on vintage rail cars. Columbus, to the west, has horse racing at Agricultural Park and boating, fishing, swimming, etc. at Loup and Pawnee Park.
Additional Information: No children, no groups.

NEW HAMPSHIRE

---

1. The Common, #182 Old Street Rd., Peterborough, NH 03458-1699
  (603) 924-6060 ❖ Contact: Retreat House Director
✓**Single Rooms** ✓**Twin Rooms** ✓**Other:** Rooms have 2-4 beds.
Individual Guest Rate: $52.00   ✓**Includes 3 Meals Daily**
✓**Reservations Required** ✓**Advance Deposit:** $40-50
Guest Rules: No televisions or radios.
On Site Attractions/Nearby Points of Interest: Two hours northwest of Boston and surrounding the hilltop mansion of the Common are 173 acres of meadows and

The Common, Peterborough, New Hampshire

woodlands in the Monadnock Mountain region of southern New Hampshire. The Common has its own museum, outdoor swimming pool, and cross-country skiing trails. Peterborough features the MacDowell Artist Colony, a puppet theatre, and a repertory group. A 15 minute drive away is Monadnock State Park.
Additional Information: Children OK and the Common can sleep groups up to 34 persons. Deposit required.

2. Epiphany Monastery
   P.O. Box 60, Scobie Rd., New Boston, NH 03070-0060
   (603) 487-3020 ❖ **Contact:** Guestmaster
✓**Single Rooms** **Individual Guest Rate:** $30.00
✓**Includes 3 Meals Daily** ✓**Self-Catering Kitchenette**
✓**Reservations Required** ✓**Advance Deposit:** None
Guest Rules: Observe atmosphere of quiet.
On Site Attractions/Nearby Points of Interest: The monastery is a 1½ hour drive NW of Boston, 30 miles west of Manchester. The Center's charming guest rooms, dining hall and sitting rooms occupy the main building situated on a rural hundred acres of woods and wetlands. Swimming at Scobie Pond, a beautiful clean 160 acres of transparent water. Nearby recreational activities at Sheiling Forest, Greenfield State Park and Mt. Monadnock State Park. Nearby Hancock town preserved as an historical district.
Additional Information: No children. Meeting rooms for conferences.

NEW JERSEY

---

1. Cenacle Retreat House, 411 River Rd., Highland Park, NJ 08904
   (908) 249-8100) ❖ **Contact:** Retreat Office
✓**Single Rooms** ✓**Twin Rooms**
Individual Guest Rate: Depends on length of stay & needs
✓**Includes 3 Meals Daily**
✓**Reservations Required** ✓**Advance Deposit:** Varies
On Site Attractions/Nearby Points of Interest: On 12 wooded acres within the metropolitan New York commuting area, overlooking the Raritan River; adjacent to Rutgers University in New Brunswick.
Additional Information: No children. Request guests to attend for purpose of reflection and spiritual growth. Closed July to August 10.

2. Emmaus Retreat House, 101 Center St., Perth Amboy, NJ 08861
   (908) 442-7688 ❖ **Contact:** Emmaus House
✓**Single Rooms** ✓**Twin Rooms** ✓**Other:** 2 suites
Individual Guest Rate: $35.00 ✓**Includes 3 Meals Daily**
✓**Reservations Required** ✓**Advance Deposit:** $25.00
On Site Attractions/Nearby Points of Interest: Perth Amboy is a short distance from New York City. There is a waterfront marina near the Retreat House and 3 minutes away is the local YMCA for exercise and swimming (small fee).
Additional Information: No children; groups welcomed (maximum of 15 persons).

3. Xavier Center, P.O. Box 211, Convent Station, NJ 07961
   (201) 292-6488 ❖ **Contact:** Mary Sheehan
✓**Single Rooms** ✓**Twin Rooms**
Individual Guest Rate: $50.00 ($30.00/no meals) ✓**Includes 3 Meals Daily**
✓**Reservations Required** ✓**Advance Deposit:** For groups (varies)

Guest Rules: Smoking restricted. Quiet on bedroom floors.

On Site Attractions/Nearby Points of Interest: The Center is located about one hour west of New York City near the historic city of Morristown and Morristown National Park. A few miles west are the various antique shops of Chester, and an hour to the east is the Jersey coast and Gateway National Recreation Area.

Additional Information: Children's groups OK by day (no overnights). Groups welcomed.

4. Francis House of Prayer, Box 392, Rancocas, NJ 08073
 (609) 877-0509 ✠ **Contact:** Fr. Joseph Tedesco or Sr. Marcy Springer
✓**Single Rooms** ✓**Twin Rooms**
Individual Guest Rate: $25.00 *(meals by arrangement)*
✓**Reservations Required** ✓**Advance Deposit:** $25.00

On Site Attractions/Nearby Points of Interest: Rancocas is just half an hour away from historic Philadelphia, in the farmland of New Jersey. Easily accessible from the New Jersey turnpike.

Additional Information: No children. Small groups for overnight; 25 persons for day retreats.

5. Loyola House of Retreats, 161 James St., Morristown, NJ 07960
 (201) 539-0740 ✠ **Contact:** Sr. Irene Garvey
✓**Single Rooms** **Individual Guest Rate:** $35.00 ✓**Includes 3 Meals Daily**
✓**Reservations Required** ✓**Advance Deposit:** call in

Guest Rules: No smoking. Quiet observed. Guests welcomed for quiet reflection and meditation.

On Site Attractions/Nearby Points of Interest: Loyola is located in a peaceful section of Morristown (about 25 miles east of Newark) surrounded by 30 acres of lawns, gardens, swimming pool, paths, and woods. There are 85 comfortable private rooms, a well-stocked library, and a kitchen that prepares tasty, nutritional meals. The principal structure is a Georgian revival mansion, and has the proportions and appearance of Buckingham Palace.

Additional Information: No children. Groups welcomed, cost dependent on services required, and accommodated Tuesday to Thursday.

Loyola House of Retreats, Morristown, New Jersey

6. St. Marguerite's Retreat House, Convent of St. John Baptist
   P.O. Box 240, Mendham, NJ 07945
   (201) 543-4641 ❖ **Contact:** Retreat Center Sister
✓**Single Rooms   Individual Guest Rate:** $50.00   ✓**Includes 3 Meals Daily**
✓**Reservations Required   ✓Advance Deposit:** Inquire for groups
Guest Rules: No smoking in buildings. No alcohol.
On Site Attractions/Nearby Points of Interest: Mendham is 10 miles west of Morristown, one hour from New York City, 50 minutes from Newark Airport. Ninety-three acres of woodland surround the Episcopalian convent, with its spacious bedrooms and burnished wood paneled meeting rooms which reflect an old world charm and elegance. Home-cooked buffet meals are served up by a professional cook. Morristown landmarks: restorations of 18th and 19th century homes — political cartoonist Thomas Nast, Stephen Vail, Alexander Hamilton House, the Ford Mansion (where George Washington plotted military maneuvers).
Additional Information: No children. Groups welcomed.

7. St. Joseph by the Sea, 400 Route 35 North, South Mantoloking, NJ 08738
   (908) 892-8494 ❖ **Contact:** Secretary
✓**Single Rooms   Individual Guest Rate:** Varies
✓**Reservations Required   ✓Advance Deposit:** Call for rates
Guest Rules: Atmosphere of quiet and solitude.
On Site Attractions/Nearby Points of Interest: South Mantoloking is a shoreline village at the north end of Island Beach, minutes east of Breton Woods, and about 20 miles south of Asbury Park. The Center's conference room has a commanding view of the ocean, the loft overlooks Barnegat Bay to the west; there is direct access to both bay and ocean from the Center's all-weather solarium. Two natural recreational areas offer swimming, seasonal fishing, nature tours, whale watching, picnicking.
Additional Information: No children. Groups welcomed — 16 minimum for day, 18 for weekends.

8. St. Joseph's Villa - Guest and Retreat House, Peapack, NJ 07977
   (908) 234-0334 ❖ **Contact:** Sister Roberta
✓**Single Rooms   ✓Twin Rooms**
Individual Guest Rate: $50.00   ✓**Includes 3 Meals Daily**
✓**Reservations Required   ✓Advance Deposit:** Call in
Guest Rules: No smoking, no shorts. Women only as guests.
On Site Attractions/Nearby Points of Interest: Peapack, half an hour southwest of Morristown, half an hour north of Somerville — all in all, less than 50 miles from New York City. The Villa: a three story mansion built in 1902-1904 for 2 million dollars. A 425 acre estate, mountain top view, with hedged fields that lead to Ravine Lake. Mirrored lagoon entranceway, reminiscent of the Taj Mahal, bordered with busts of Roman emperors. Two terraces run the length of the baronial chateau, accented by several waterfall fountains. Crystal chandeliers, walnut-paneled library, two elevators. Opulent, but serene and lovely — and a place to share.
Additional Information: No children. Groups welcomed: day, 25-50 persons; weekend, 20 persons.

9. St. Mary's Abbey - Delbarton, 270 Mendham Rd., Morristown, NJ 07960
   (201) 538-0550/538-3231 ❖ **Contact:** Rev. Justin Caputo
✓**Single Rooms   ✓Twin Rooms**
Individual Guest Rate: $40.00   ✓**Includes 3 Meals Daily**
✓**Reservations Required   ✓Advance Deposit:** None
Guest Rules: No smoking in main buildings.

St. Joseph's Villa - Guest and Retreat House, Peapack, New Jersey

On Site Attractions/Nearby Points of Interest: The Center is located 3 miles west of Morristown, about 25 miles west of Newark. It is situated on over 400 acres of open fields and wooded grounds, and borders two 1,000 acre parks: Lewis Morris County Park and Jockey Hollow State Park. The main mansion and separate buildings are air-conditioned, with a pool and tennis available to guests. Morristown, once the headquarters of General Washington, has never lost its aura of affluence, and its magnificent pre-Revolutionary mansions are reminders of titled British gentry.
Additional Information: Children 8 years and older OK. Groups welcomed. Tradition of hospitality.

NEW MEXICO

---

1. Monastery of Christ in the Desert, Abiquiu, NM 87510
   (505) 843-3049 ✤ **Contact:** Guestmaster
✓**Single Rooms** ✓**Twin Rooms**
Individual Guest Rate: $25.00 suggested donation   ✓**Includes 3 Meals Daily**
✓**Reservations Required** ✓**Advance Deposit:** None
Guest Rules: No pets. No red meat served at meals. Guests encouraged to share in some of the work. Quiet atmosphere maintained.
On Site Attractions/Nearby Points of Interest: Located in a picturesque canyon, 6,500 feet above sea level, in northwestern New Mexico. The breath-taking landscape is surrounded by miles of federal wilderness lands. Nearby: the Navajo Indian Reservation, Rio Chama River, the Ranches of Taos, and Los Alamos. Long hikes possible in the National Wilderness Area south of the monastery.
Additional Information: No children, no groups. Weather is quite cold in winter and warm on summer days. Accessible only by car.

2. Our Lady of Guadalupe Abbey
   Pecos Benedictine Community, Pecos, NM 87552
   (505) 757-6415/6600 ✤ Contact: Any staff member
✓Single Rooms ✓Twin Rooms
Individual Guest Rate: $35.00 (5 days: $150.00) ✓Includes 3 Meals Daily
✓Reservations Required ✓Advance Deposit: $30.00
Guest Rules: No smoking or alcohol. No pets.
On Site Attractions/Nearby Points of Interest: A former dude ranch on 1,000 acres of property, the Abbey at Pecos is just 25 miles from the popular tourist city of Santa Fe. At the heart of the Pecos National Monument are the well-preserved Indian pueblos. The skiing center of Taos is nearby, including the Millicent Rogers Ceramic Museum and the natural hot springs.
Additional Information: No children; groups welcomed. Holistic lifestyle combined with renewal and self-healing.

NEW YORK

---

1. Graymoor Christian Unity Center, Garrison, NY 10524
   (914) 424-3671 ✤ Contact: Retreat Office
✓Single Rooms ✓Twin Rooms
Individual Guest Rate: $70.00 single; $60.00 double ✓Includes 3 Meals Daily
✓Reservations Required ✓Advance Deposit: $30.00 per person
On Site Attractions/Nearby Points of Interest: Garrison is 4 miles north of Peekskill in the beautiful Lower Hudson River Valley, about an hour and 15 minutes from New York City. Close by is the Appalachian Trail, West Point Military Academy, the rolling hills along the Hudson with the restored mansions.
Additional Information: No children. Groups welcomed.

2. House of the Redeemer, 7 E. 95th St., New York, NY 10128
   (212) 289-0399 ✤ Contact: Alicia Benoist
✓Single Rooms ✓Twin Rooms Individual Guest Rate: $35.00-50.00
✓Reservations Required ✓Advance Deposit: Inquire
Guest Rules: Minimum stay 1 week. Guests must be retreatants who seek quiet time for reflection, not as a stopover. No structured schedule.
On Site Attractions/Nearby Points of Interest: An elegant 5-story East Side townhouse a few steps from 5th Avenue, close to New York's Museum Mile. A few steps away are the Metropolitan Museum of Art, the Central Park Zoo, the Wollman Skating Rink, and the famed art auction gallery of Sotheby's. Tours of what will one day be the world's largest Gothic cathedral — St. John the Divine — are conducted daily. Other New York attractions too numerous to list.
Additional Information: Groups welcomed. Children over 12 OK with supervision.

3. Our Lady of the Resurrection Monastery
   Barmore Rd., La Grangeville, NY 12540
   Contact: Guestmaster
✓Single Rooms ✓Twin Rooms Individual Guest Rate: $35.00
✓Includes 3 Meals Daily ✓Self-Catering Kitchenette *(for breakfast)*
✓Reservations Required ✓Advance Deposit: None
Guest Rules: No smoking. Quiet respected. Simplicity and serenity of life. Maximum stay one week.
On Site Attractions/Nearby Points of Interest: In the tucked-away area of Dutchess County north of New York City, the monastery sits peacefully on 22 acres of hilltop

land. Herb and flower gardens web the farm in an area where sheep graze. Historic sites are in many nearby towns — West Point Military Academy on the Hudson River.
Additional Information: No children. Groups welcomed.

4. **Abode of the Message, Box 1030D Shaker Rd., New Lebanon, NY 12125**
   (518) 794-8090/9720 ✤ Contact: Maria Cristina Fernandez
   ✓**Single Rooms** ✓**Twin Rooms** ✓**Other:** Retreat huts for solitude
   Individual Guest Rate: $40.00 ✓**Includes 3 Meals Daily**
   ✓**Reservations Required** ✓**Advance Deposit:** $40.00
   Guest Rules: Minimum stay of 3 days suggested. Mission: a break fom the routine of life in order to gain greater self-understanding and a sense of meaningfulness. A rejuvenation of body, mind and spirit.
   On Site Attractions/Nearby Points of Interest: Situated 39 miles east of Albany, the Abode is couched in 430 acres of the beautiful Berkshire Mountains. Nearby, the famed Tanglewood music festivals, Berkshire Ballet, skiing at Brodie Mountain and Jiminie Peak. Plenty of lakes, parks, museums in the vicinity.
   Additional Information: Children 3 years and older OK. Groups welcomed.

5. **Jesuit Retreat House, Martyr's Shrine, Auriesville, NY 12016**
   (518) 853-4496 ✤ Contact: Director
   ✓**Single Rooms** ✓**Twin Rooms**
   Individual Guest Rate: $40.00 ✓**Includes 3 Meals Daily**
   ✓**Reservations Required** ✓**Advance Deposit:** None
   Guest Rules: Respect the quiet required of guests.
   On Site Attractions/Nearby Points of Interest: Located a short distance NW of Schenectady, the House perches on a hilltop with extended views far to the north and east. Miles of trails extend around the 600 acres of beautifully landscaped grounds that is a haven for scores of different birds. The Erie Canal and mysterious Howe Caverns are close by.
   Additional Information: Transportation provided from nearby bus and train stations. Children OK; groups welcomed.

6. **Bethany Retreat House, County Route 105, Highland Mills, NY 10930**
   (914) 928-2213 ✤ Contact: Secretary
   ✓**Single Rooms** ✓**Twin Rooms**
   Individual Guest Rate: $30.00 ✓**Includes 3 Meals Daily**
   ✓**Reservations Required** ✓**Advance Deposit:** $25.00 for longer stays
   On Site Attractions/Nearby Points of Interest: Lovely lake on the spacious grounds of the House. Located just ½ hour from the West Point Military Academy, north of New York City; near Woodbury Common with its scores of outlet stores. Walking trails in all directions.
   Additional Information: No children. Retreat groups welcomed.

7. **St. Joseph Spiritual Life Center, RD #5 Box 113, Valatie, NY 12184**
   (518) 784-9481 ✤ Contact: Brother Aubert Harrigan
   ✓**Single Rooms** ✓**Twin Rooms**
   Individual Guest Rate: $35.00 M-Th; $40.00 Fr.-Sat.
   ✓**Includes 3 Meals Daily**
   ✓**Reservations Required** ✓**Advance Deposit:** 10% of total cost
   Guest Rules: No smoking. Quiet on bedroom floors.
   On Site Attractions/Nearby Points of Interest: Located half an hour south of Albany in a verdant rural setting of 400 acres. The grounds include meadows, a pond,

tennis courts, a horseshoe set, a basketball backboard, and hiking trails. The Hudson Valley is rich in 17th and 18th century historical sites. Albany, at the end of the Hudson River, showcases the Rockefeller Empire State Plaza, with its museum and performing arts center. Worth seeing is the Schuyler Mansion, where Benjamin Franklin and George Washington dined.
Additional Information: Children and groups welcomed.

8. Mount St. Francis Hermitage, Box 276, Maine, NY 13802
    (607) 754-9813 ❖ **Contact:** Brother Daniel Gallucci
✓**Single Rooms** ✓**Twin Rooms** ✓**Other:** 12 cabins, retreat house
Individual Guest Rate: $10.00 cabins; $15.00 retreat house
✓**Self-Catering Kitchenette**
✓**Reservations Required** ✓**Advance Deposit:** None
Guest Rules: Provide own food and bedding for cabins and retreat house. Aim is to assist in self-discovery through trust and devotion.
On Site Attractions/Nearby Points of Interest: On 200 acres of wooded land, with ponds and viewpoint trails. Located a few miles NW of Binghamton, not too far from the Finger Lakes to the north. For those so inclined, participation in work projects — tending the gardens, cleaning paths, etc. — is always appreciated.
Additional Information: No children. Groups welcomed.

9. Transfiguration Monastery, R.D. 2, Box 2612, Windsor, NY 13865
    (607) 655-2366 ❖ **Contact:** Sr. Jeanne Marie
✓**Single Rooms** ✓**Twin Rooms**
Individual Guest Rate: Donation ($25.00 suggested)
✓**Includes 3 Meals Daily**
✓**Self-Catering Kitchenette** *(breakfast or snacks)*
✓**Reservations Required** ✓**Advance Deposit:** None
Guest Rules: Quiet in rooms. Early morning silence in kitchen. Tapes and radios with headphones. Time for sacred music and reflection.
On Site Attractions/Nearby Points of Interest: Located near Binghamton on 100 acres of fields and wooded land in the Susquehanna Valley at the base of Horeb Mountain. Great natural beauty, valley trails for walking. Next to an 18-acre golf course. Wine is produced from their own grapes and delicious food — French country cuisine — is superb.
Additional Information: Small groups (7 maximum) are welcomed. Children are OK with careful supervision.

10. St. Cuthbert's House and St. Aidan's House
    Melrose, R.D. 2, Federal Hill Rd., Brewster, NY 10509
    (914) 278-2610 ❖ **Contact:** Sr. Mary Winifred, C.H.S.
✓**Single Rooms** ✓**Twin Rooms**
Individual Guest Rate: $50.00 ✓**Includes 3 Meals Daily**
✓**Reservations Required** ✓**Advance Deposit:** For groups
Guest Rules: No smoking.
On Site Attractions/Nearby Points of Interest: Located on 127 acres of rolling hills and woodlands, the House is just 1½ hours north of New York City. Nearby are countless museums, antique shops, music centers (Music Mountain), the Charles Ives Center. Various workshops are presented throughout the year: Writers' Workshop, Setting Personal Boundaries, Discovering Intimacy, Book Reviews.
Additional Information: Children OK if accompanied by parents. Groups welcomed.

11. St. Andrew's House, 89 Saint Andrew's Rd., Walden, NY 12586
   (914) 778-3707 ✢ Contact: Father Andrea Ansbro, C.P.
✓Single Rooms   ✓Twin Rooms   ✓Other: Large cottage
Individual Guest Rate: $90.00/weekend; $150.00/married couple per weekend
✓Includes 3 Meals Daily
✓Reservations Required   ✓Advance Deposit: 50%
Guest Rules: No smoking in bedrooms. Prepare bed before departure. Respectful quiet.
On Site Attractions/Nearby Points of Interest: Fourteen acres of lawn and woods surround the House in Walden — about 2½ hours NW of New York City. Nearby are the Hudson River historical sights, West Point, and the mountains which encircle the Walden area.
Additional Information: Athletic facilities available. Individuals and groups welcomed. No children under 16 years. Aim is to provide a comforting household for those who want a relaxed atmosphere that will help clarity of vision in decision-making.

12. Convent of St. Helena, P.O. Box 426, Vails Gate, NY 12584
   (914) 562-0592 ✢ Contact: Guest Mistress
✓Single Rooms   ✓Twin Rooms
Individual Guest Rate: Varies according to needs; $25.00 suggested
✓Includes 3 Meals Daily
✓Reservations Required   ✓Advance Deposit: Negotiable
Guest Rules: No alcohol, radio, TV sets; sensitivity to others' request for quiet. An atmosphere conducive to the enhancement of the spirit.
On Site Attractions/Nearby Points of Interest: An hour and an half or so north of New York City through Central Valley. Nearby are Bear Mountain, Hudson River sights; the convent itself is placed in an attractive section of woods and fields.
Additional Information: Children OK so long as they are adaptable to the needs of other guests. Groups welcomed.

13. St. Mary's Convent, John St., Peekskill, NY 10566
   (914) 737-0113 ✢ Contact: Guest Mistress
✓Single Rooms   ✓Twin Rooms
Individual Guest Rate: $35.00 suggested donation   ✓Includes 3 Meals Daily
✓Reservations Required   ✓Advance Deposit: $10.00
Guest Rules: No smoking indoors. Silence requested at specific times and as a courtesy to others.
On Site Attractions/Nearby Points of Interest: Located near Peekskill, about an hour and a half from New York City. The convent was built from granite quarried on the property and rests on a beautifully landscaped bank of the Hudson River.
Additional Information: Groups welcomed as long as they participate in the convent's prayer and way of life in some way. No children.

14. Little Portion Friary, St. Joseph's Retreat House
   P.O. Box 399, Mt. Sinai, NY 11766
   (516) 473-0553 ✢ Contact: Guest Brother
✓Single Rooms   ✓Twin Rooms   ✓Other: Dormitory with 4 beds
Individual Guest Rate: $45.00   ✓Includes 3 Meals Daily
✓Reservations Required   ✓Advance Deposit: None
On Site Attractions/Nearby Points of Interest: Located almost centrally on the north shore of Long Island, the friary's 60 acres border a wildlife sanctuary and Mt.

Sinai Harbor. In nearby Nassau County is the Cradle of Aviation Museum, which houses scores of vintage airplanes; Sagamore Hill, crammed with Teddy Roosevelt memorabilia; the Vanderbilt Museum and the formal English gardens at Old Westbury.
Additional Information: Groups welcome, deposit required. Children OK.

15. Abbey of the Genesee, River Rd., Piffard, NY 14533
(716) 243-2220 ✤ **Contact:** Bethlehem Retreat House
✓**Single Rooms** ✓**Other:** Additional houses for groups
Individual Guest Rate: $30.00 suggested donation
✓**Includes 3 Meals Daily** ✓**Self-Catering Kitchenette**
✓**Reservations Required** ✓**Advance Deposit:** $50.00 for groups of 5 or more
Guest Rules: Silence observed at mealtime — a climate for quiet reflection. Minimum stay of 3 days. Buffet or self-prepared meals.
On Site Attractions/Nearby Points of Interest: Located 35 miles south of Rochester, the Abbey comprises almost 2,200 acres of a working farm that grows wheat, corn and soybeans. A successful bakery on the premises markets 25-30,000 loaves of Monk's Bread each week. Guests are invited to share in the work of the Abbey if they wish. Nearby is Letchwork Park on the Genesee River, and the educational center of the State University of NY at Geneseo.
Additional Information: No children. Groups welcomed.

16. St. Margaret's House, Jordan Rd., New Hartford, NY 13413
(315) 724-2324 ✤ **Contact:** Guest Sister
✓**Single Rooms** ✓**Other:** Facilities to house 2-8 persons
Individual Guest Rate: $30.00 ✓**Includes 3 Meals Daily**
✓**Self-Catering Kitchenette** *(for hot and cold drinks)*
✓**Reservations Required**
✓**Advance Deposit:** None
Guest Rules: No smoking. Silence observed from 9 p.m. until after breakfast.
On Site Attractions/Nearby Points of Interest: The House is just south of Utica on 10 acres of land with trees, landscaped lawns and gardens. This beautiful farm country is 2 hours from the Fingerlakes region and about an hour from Syracuse and Oneida Lake. A well-stocked lending library is on House grounds.
Additional Information: Usually no children. Groups welcomed.

17. Mount Savior Monastery
Pine City, NY 14871
(607) 734-1688
Contact: Guestmaster
✓**Single Rooms** ✓**Twin Rooms**
✓**Other:** 2 cottages & an apartment
Individual Guest Rate: $30.00
✓**Includes 3 Meals Daily**
✓**Self-Catering Kitchenette**
(in cottages and apt.)
✓**Reservations Required**

Mount Savior Monastery

✓Advance Deposit: None
Guest Rules: Guests are to arrange their own time and activities that meet their need for quiet self-contemplation. Option for work opportunities.
On Site Attractions / Nearby Points of Interest: Located just south of Elmira on over 250 acres of land. Market lambs and sheep are raised, yarn and pelt products sold. Nearby are the Fingerlakes of Seneca, Owasco, and Cayuga, which are steeped in Indian lore. Bridges spanning deep river gorges can lead you to Cornell University, high on the hills in Ithaca. Book and gift store on the premises.
Additional Information: Children OK. Groups welcomed at special rates.

18. Holy Cross Monastery, P.O. Box 99, West Park, NY 12493
    (914) 384-6660 ❖ **Contact:** Guesthouse
✓Single Rooms ✓Twin Rooms
Individual Guest Rate: $60.00 **✓Includes 3 Meals Daily**
✓Reservations Required ✓Advance Deposit: $35.00 per person
Guest Rules: No smoking or alcohol.
On Site Attractions/Nearby Points of Interest: Two hours north of New York City, Holy Cross sits on 26 acres of meadowland facing the Hudson River. Directly across the river is the Vanderbilt Museum as well as Hyde Park, the home of Franklin D. Roosevelt, now a museum and library. Nearby are the Catskills and West Point. Holy Cross has an ongoing artists-in-residence program and provides space and time for reading, writing, and reflection.
Additional Information: Children OK if 13 years and older. Groups welcomed — non-refundable and non transferable deposit required. Closed Mondays and the month of August.

19. Wainwright House, 260 Stuyvesant Ave., Rye, NY 10580
    (914) 967-6080, Ext. 109 ❖ **Contact:** Mrs. Terry Poly, Retreat Coordinator
✓Single Rooms ✓Twin Rooms ✓Other: Dorm rooms (2-6 persons per room)
Individual Guest Rate: $25 (meals can be provided for an additional charge)
✓Reservations Required ✓Advance Deposit: 25%
Guest Rules: No smoking in buildings. Guests must arrive before 10:00 p.m.
On Site Attractions/Nearby Points of Interest: Rye is 30 minutes NE of New York City. The House is actually a French chateau with 33 rooms and two outbuildings — a carriage house and a 5-bedroom home. The five acre estate of footpaths and gardens overlooks Long Island Sound. In addition to the myriad cultural attractions of NYC are the Rye Nature Center, the Bruce Museum in Greenwich (wildlife diorama, impressionist paintings) and the Bronx's Botanical Gardens.
Additional Information: No children. Courses and seminars offered year-round for individuals and groups. Institutes of Health and Healing, Global Issues, Spiritual Development.

20. Passionist Spiritual Center, 5801 Palisade Ave., Bronx, NY 10471
    (718) 549-6500 ❖ **Contact:** Retreat Secretary
✓Single Rooms ✓Twin Rooms
Individual Guest Rate: $75.00 **✓Includes 3 Meals Daily**
✓Reservations Required ✓Advance Deposit: $50.00
Guest Rules: Strictly a center for group or individual retreats, not be be construed as an overnight guest house for travelers.
On Site Attractions/Nearby Points of Interest: The Bronx is the northernmost borough of New York City, between the Harlem River and Long Island Sound. Tours of the city and Westchester County, boat trips on the Hudson can be a starting point for getting an overview of the grandeur of the region, before or after a retreat stay.

Additional Information: No children. Groups welcomed.

21. Mariandale Center, 299 N. Highland Ave., Ossining, NY 10562
(914) 941-4455 ❖ **Contact:** David Wixted, Director
✓**Single Rooms Individual Guest Rate:** $40.00 - $50.00
✓**Includes 3 Meals Daily**
✓**Reservations Required** ✓**Advance Deposit:** 20%
Guest Rules: No smoking in buildings.
On Site Attractions/Nearby Points of Interest: Located on the east bank of the Hudson River, Ossining is about an hour north of New York City. The Center is surrounded by 60 acres of sprawling lawns and woodlands with a 12 mile south view of the river. Playing fields, picnic areas, hiking trails, and an outdoor pool are available to guests. Personal and social wellness services available — including therapeutic massage. Nearby: West Point Academy, Sleepy Hollow Mansions, Croton Dam Gorge, Bear Mountain.
Additional Information: No children. Large and small conference rooms — air-conditioned.

22. Stella Maris Retreat Center, 130 E. Genesee St., Skaneateles, NY 13152
(315) 685-6836 ❖ **Contact:** Sister J. Olivia
✓**Single Rooms** ✓**Twin Rooms**
Individual Guest Rate: $38.00 ✓**Includes 3 Meals Daily**
✓**Reservations Required** ✓**Advance Deposit:** $10.00
Guest Rules: Quiet atmosphere, no pets.
On Site Attractions/Nearby Points of Interest: The Stella Maris Center is located in upstate New York, 35 miles SW of Syracuse, a short distance east of Auburn. The Center rests on the north shore of Lake Skaneateles, highest of the Finger Lakes. The 16-mile lake curves between gently rolling hills and rises to majestic heights at the headwaters. The main building is on a 10 acre estate that was once owned by heirs of the Smith/Corona typewriter company. Skaneateles is a town of wealth and elegance.
Additional Information: No children. Groups welcomed.

23. St. Francis Center, RD 1, Box 1365, Oyster Bay, NY 11771
(516) 922-3545 or (516) 922-3708 ❖ **Contact:** Br. Roman Morris
✓**Single Rooms** ✓**Twin Rooms**
Individual Guest Rate: Varies ✓**Includes 3 Meals Daily**
✓**Reservations Required** ✓**Advance Deposit:** Call in
On Site Attractions/Nearby Points of Interest: Oyster Bay is about a 45 minute drive from New York City, on the north shore of Long Island Sound. The Center's Italian style mansion is situated in a rural environment on a magnificent estate which was once the "Spring House" of Frederick Wheeler, president of American Can Co. French tile, Italian stonework, and European woodwork were used in the construction. Nearby: Planting Fields Arboretum (150 acre country estate), Sagamore Hill (Victorian mansion of President Theodore Roosevelt), a bird sanctuary and Coe Hall Tudor manor.
Additional Information: No children. Hermitage for private time. Workshops and special interest groups invited.

24. Marian Shrine and Don Bosco Retreat Center
PO Box 9000, West Haverstraw, NY 10993
(914) 947-2201 ❖ **Contact:** Rev. Gerard Pellegrino
✓**Single Rooms** ✓**Other:** Rooms with double bed

Individual Guest Rate: $36.00 *(weekend rates somewhat higher)*
✓**Includes 3 Meals Daily**
✓**Reservations Required**   ✓**Advance Deposit:** 25%
On Site Attractions/Nearby Points of Interest: West Haverstraw is on the west bank of the Hudson River, about 30 miles north of New York City. The Shrine, on 200 acres of pristine expanses of woods, views west and north to the widest angle of the River. Beyond the mile-long Rosary Way is a modern living structure with 50 double rooms. Here is the gateway to the Lower Catskill Mountains and 15 minutes from West Point, the U.S. Army training ground since 1802. Many Revolutionary War sites are in the region—Stony Point Battlefield, where George Washington held off superior British forces. Nearby Nyack is an antique and arts center.
Additional Information: Two different retreat facilities — one for youth (teens), one for adults.

25. Chapel House, Colgate University, Hamilton, NY 13346
   (315) 824-7675 ❖ **Contact:** Director
✓**Single Rooms**   ✓**Twin Rooms**
Individual Guest Rate: $36.00   ✓**Includes 3 Meals Daily**
✓**Reservations Required**   ✓**Advance Deposit:** None
Guest Rules: Respect the privacy of others. No smoking or alcohol. Minimum stay 2 days.
On Site Attractions/Nearby Points of Interest: Hamilton is 20 miles south of Utica in upstate New York. Chapel House itself, built on a hill amidst beautiful woods above Colgate University, has a library with 5,000 volumes, many works of religious art, a music room, serene chapel, and dining facilities. The House, administered by Colgate University, welcomes anyone of any religious persuasion (or none at all) to use its facilities to discover the insights in the books, art, music, and quiet. Since 1959, Chapel House has welcomed guests from all over the world, of every faith and vocation.
Additional Information: No children. Not a conference center. Rooms include a private bedroom/bath, desk, lamp, reading chair and overlook the surrounding woods.

NORTH CAROLINA

---

1. Aqueduct Conference Center
   P.O. Box 17299, Chapel Hill, NC 27516-7299
   (919) 933-5557 ❖ **Contact:** Tom Tyson, Executive Director
✓**Single Rooms**   ✓**Twin Rooms**
Individual Guest Rate: $80.00 Conference (call for non-conference rate)
✓**Includes 3 Meals Daily**
✓**Reservations Required**   ✓**Advance Deposit:** None
Guest Rules: "Make yourself at home." Each bedroom has a private bath and sleeps 2 people.
On Site Attractions/Nearby Points of Interest: In Chapel Hill are tennis courts, boating and fishing in Jordan Lake, and golf at Finley Golf Course. the Moorhead Planetarium contains the famous Zeiss Star Projector and shows are given daily. Sporting events and concerts at the University of North Carolina. A few minutes north is Durham, home of the scenic and prestigious Duke University. The tobacco giant Washington Duke has left his estate intact and it is still a working farm. Picnicking in the Sarah Duke Gardens.
Additional Information: Various speakers present a wide variety of topics. Children OK and groups welcomed. Well-equipped for conference use.

2. Avila Retreat House, 711 Mason Rd., Durham, NC 27712
    (919) 477-1285 ❖ Contact: Kathy Bigg or Sister Damian Marie, Director
✓**Single Rooms** ✓**Twin Rooms** ✓**Other:** 1 private room with bath available
Individual Guest Rate: $40.00   ✓**Includes 3 Meals Daily**
✓**Reservations Required** ✓**Advance Deposit:** $10.00 per person
Guest Rules: No smoking in bedrooms. No alcohol.
On Site Attractions/Nearby Points of Interest: Meditation trail through the fields,
forests, streams and hillside of the 51 acres comprising the Center. The Duke estate,
Sarah Duke Gardens, and Bennett Place are all open to the public. Durham, home of
Duke University, is also the Diet Capital of the World, since the erstwhile tobacco
capital has become devoted to medicine. Visitors shed thousands of pounds of ex-
cess weight at the various clinics.
Additional Information: No children. Meeting rooms, 2 dining rooms, and screened-
in gazebo for groups.

3. In The Oaks Episcopal Retreat Center
    P.O. Box 1117, Black Mountain, NC 28711
    (704) 669-2117 ❖ Contact: Conference Coordinator
✓**Twin Rooms** ✓**Other:** 8 rustic cabins (seasonal); youth center
Individual Guest Rate: $48.00   ✓**Includes 3 Meals Daily**
✓**Reservations Required** ✓**Advance Deposit:** 5%
On Site Attractions/Nearby Points of Interest: The charming community of Black
Mountain is 15 miles east of Asheville on Interstate 40. The focal point of the Oaks
is the majestic mansion built 70 years ago in the English country tradition, and
esconced in 65 wooded acres of the Blue Ridge Mountains. A library, meditation
rooms, a heated indoor swimming pool, and a large gymnasium are just a part of the
public areas. Sojourners of all faiths can find rest, inspiration and values renewal In
The Oaks.
Additional Information: Children OK, groups welcomed.

In The Oaks Episcopal Retreat Center, Black Mountain, North Carolina

NORTH DAKOTA

1. Queen of Peace Retreat Center, 1310 N. Broadway, P.O. Box 1750, Fargo, ND 58107
(701) 293-9286 ✤ **Contact:** George Lacher, Director
✓**Single Rooms** ✓**Twin Rooms**
Individual Guest Rate: $14.50 first night; $12.50 additional nights
✓**Self-Catering Kitchenette**
✓**Reservations Required** ✓**Advance Deposit:** None
Guest Rules: No smoking in buildings.
On Site Attractions/Nearby Points of Interest: Fargo is in the easternmost part of the state, adjacent to the Minnesota border. Named after William Fargo of the Wells Fargo Express Company, the city is proud of its North Dakota State University (herbarium and wildlife museum), the Fargo Theater and Wurlitzer organ concerts and Moorhead Community Theater. Bonanzaville USA is a reconstructed western town of 45 buildings — train depot, sod houses, log cabins, church, etc. — and on Pioneer days period costumes are worn.
Additional Information: Children OK, groups welcomed.

OHIO

1. Sacred Heart Retreat Center, 3128 Logan Ave., Youngstown, OH 44501
(216) 759-9539 ✤ **Contact:** Barbara Witt
✓**Single Rooms** ✓**Twin Rooms**
Individual Guest Rate: $35.00 ✓**Includes 3 Meals Daily**
✓**Reservations Required** ✓**Advance Deposit:** For groups (depending on size)
Guest Rules: No smoking.
On Site Attractions/Nearby Points of Interest: In a quiet residential area, the Center is set in 27 acres of woods, paths and a lake. Nearby is Mill Creek Park with walking paths, lakes, golf course and tennis courts. The Center is close to many excellent restaurants, the Butler Institute of American Art, and the local YMCA, which is open to the public.
Additional Information: No children. Can accommodate groups up to 60.

2. St. Francis Center, 10290 Mill Rd., Cincinnati, OH 45231
(513) 825-9300 ✤ **Contact:** Sharon Huber
✓**Single Rooms** ✓**Other:** Private rooms, dormitories
Individual Guest Rate: Varies — call ahead ✓**Includes 3 Meals Daily**
✓**Reservations Required** ✓**Advance Deposit:** Depends on length of stay
Guest Rules: No food or beverages in dormitory facility. Smoking in restricted areas. Quiet after 11 p.m.
On Site Attractions/Nearby Points of Interest: Situated on 125 acres of woods, gardens, and a lake. In Cincinnati are the Taft Museum, the Mount Airy Arboretum, the Zoo, King's Island, the Contemporary Arts Center, and many parks and theaters. The Riverwalk and Serpentine Wall offer promenade areas along the Ohio River, and free summer concerts are held at the Pavilion.
Additional Information: Children OK with supervision. Groups welcomed.

3. Friarhurst Retreat House, 8136 Wooster Pike, Cincinnati, OH 45227
(513) 561-2270 ✤ **Contact:** Mert Seibert or Linda Scott
✓**Single Rooms** ✓**Twin Rooms**
Individual Guest Rate: Varies — depends on length of stay

✓Includes 3 Meals Daily

✓Reservations Required   **✓Advance Deposit:** Depends on length of stay

Guest Rules: Courtesy to other guests and respect for property. The "golden rule" concept adds to the hospitality and good food that is offered to all of our guests.

On Site Attractions/Nearby Points of Interest: Located on beautiful grounds with a grotto for silent meditation. Interesting sights in Cincinnati are the Union Terminal, a superb example of art deco architecture and the world's highest unsupported dome; tours of the world's largest soap manufacturer, Ivorydale; sports at Riverfront Stadium and Riverfront Coliseum; and fireworks at Riverfest.

Additional Information: No children. Non-profit groups welcomed.

4. St. Joseph Renewal Center, 200 St. Francis Ave., Tiffin, OH 44883

(419) 447-0435 ✣ Contact: Sister Barbara Westrick

✓Single Rooms   Individual Guest Rate: $35.00   **✓Includes 3 Meals Daily**

✓Reservations Not Required   **✓Advance Deposit:** $20.00 at time of booking

Guest Rules: No smoking. Quiet, peaceful atmosphere.

On Site Attractions/Nearby Points of Interest: A beautiful campus with pool, a modern facility, wide open spaces — bicycles provided. Massage therapy and reflexology available. Bright, cheerful rooms with spacious lounge. Tiffin is an hour away from Ohio's scenic playground, the Lake Erie islands, offshore from Sandusky. Nearby Cedar Point Amusement Park is slightly SE of Marblehead Peninsula and Catawba Island. Ferry rides, boating, bicycling, and the Erie County Vineyard Days add to the enjoyment of the region.

Additional Information: Groups welcomed. No children.

5. Maria Stein Center, 2365 St. Johns Rd., Maria Stein, OH 45860

(419) 925-4538 ✣ Contact: Suzanne Budde

✓Single Rooms   **✓Twin Rooms**

Individual Guest Rate: $27.00 single; $37.00 double (for 2 persons) Meals provided at an extra charge.

✓Reservations Required   **✓Advance Deposit:** Call in

Guest Rules: No smoking.

On Site Attractions/Nearby Points of Interest: Maria Stein, in northwestern Ohio, is 40 miles south of Lima and 10 miles west of Minster on State Route 119. The Center, 200 acres of farm and wooded land, lends itself to walking, hiking, bicycling, jogging and general relaxation. A short drive north to Wapakoneta brings you to the Neil Armstrong Museum, displaying stratospheric balloons, spacecraft, plus an aerospace show. Close by is Grand Lake for water sports, and a summer community arts festival in Lima.

Additional Information: No children, groups welcomed. 60 rooms available, all with private bath.

OREGON

1. Our Lady of Peace Retreat, 3600 SW 170th Ave., Beaverton, OR 97006

(503) 649-7127 ✣ Contact: Sr. Anne Marie, OSF

✓Single Rooms   **✓Twin Rooms**

Individual Guest Rate: $30.00   **✓Includes 3 Meals Daily**

✓Reservations Required   **✓Advance Deposit:** $5.00

Guest Rules: No smoking inside building.

On Site Attractions/Nearby Points of Interest: In Oregon's clean, pure air, the retreat house is located just 12 miles south of the center of Portland on 20 acres in the breathtaking Tualatin Valley. The house is surrounded by expansive lawns, an orchard, and a grove of evergreens. The Pacific Ocean beaches are an hour away and Mt. Hood's hiking and skiing are 3/4 of an hour away. Four famous gardens lie within the city of Portland, along with the Washington Park Zoo and McCall Waterfront Park.

Additional Information: Groups and children welcomed.

2. Loyola Retreat House, 3220 SE 43rd Ave., Portland, OR 97206
(503) 777-2225 ✤ Contact: Mary Kay Murphy
✓**Single Rooms** ✓**Twin Rooms**
Individual Guest Rate: $35.00 ✓**Includes 3 Meals Daily**
✓**Reservations Required** ✓**Advance Deposit:** $25.00
Guest Rules: Quiet atmosphere. Doors close by 10:00 p.m. Purpose of visit is for quiet meditation and reflection, not for use as a hotel/motel.
On Site Attractions/Nearby Points of Interest: The Loyola House is located in a quiet neighborhood just 10 minutes from downtown Portland. The beautiful landscaped grounds have 5 acres of old growth evergreens and 800 varieties of rhododendrons. Facilities include private rooms, library, spacious dining rooms, music room, fireplace area, and chapel. In Portland: Rose City Riverboat Cruises, Performing Arts Center, the sky bridges of the World Trade Center, Washington Park Zoo, McCall Waterfront Park.
Additional Information: No children, groups welcomed.

3. St. Benedict Lodge Dominican Retreat Center
56630 North Bank Rd., McKenzie Bridge, OR 97413-9614
(503) 822-3572 ✤ Contact: Reservation Office
✓**Single Rooms** **Individual Guest Rate:** $12.75 ✓**Self-Catering Kitchen**
✓**Reservations Required** ✓**Advance Deposit:** Varies
Guest Rules: No smoking in buildings. No pets. Show consideration to others.
On Site Attractions/Nearby Points of Interest: McKenzie Bridge is 50 miles east of Eugene on Highway 126 in the heart of the McKenzie River Recreational Region. The Lodge has a wide river view frontage, a swimming pool, meadows, and outdoor game area. Hiking, river rafting, and fishing are found among the towering Douglas firs and glistening waterfalls in the Three Sisters National Wilderness Area.
Additional Information: Children OK. Groups welcomed, minimum 30 in winter, 40 in the summer. Minimum stay: weekend or two overnights. Linen service: $4.00.

PENNSYLVANIA

---

1. Mount St. Macrina Retreat Center
510 W. Main St., Box 878, Uniontown, PA 15401
(412) 438-7149 ✤ Contact: Sister Carol Petrasovich
✓**Twin Rooms** ✓**Other:** Large dorm-style rooms, can accommodate 1-4
Individual Guest Rate: $20.00
✓**Reservations Required** ✓**Advance Deposit:** None
Guest Rules: Meals by arrangement. No smoking. The center is a source of regeneration and serenity.
On Site Attractions/Nearby Points of Interest: The center is on 210 acres of rolling hills in the Laurel Mountains of southwestern Pennsylvania, about 2 hours south of Pittsburgh. The Laurel Highlands cradles many historical sites, landmarks, museums, and white frothy rivers. Nearby are Ohiopyle State Park, whose 18,000 acres supply hiking, fishing, winter sports, and river rafting; and historic Ft. Necessity,

with demonstrations of musket firing and infantry dressed as French and English soldiers.
Additional Information: Groups welcomed. Children 14 and older OK.

2. St. Francis Center for Renewal
   395 Bridle Path Rd., Bethlehem, PA 18017
   (215) 866-2597 ❖ **Contact:** Sister M. Anita, OSF
✓**Single Rooms** ✓**Twin Rooms Individual Guest Rate:** $25.00
✓**Self-Catering Kitchenette**
✓**Reservations Required** ✓**Advance Deposit:** $25.00
On Site Attractions/Nearby Points of Interest: During the holiday season, practically the entire city center is aglow with Christmas lights and decorations. The center is adjacent to Allentown, close to the Pocono Mountains, resort areas, and the Moravian settlements. Philadelphia is a little over 2 hours to the south.
Additional Information: No children. Groups welcomed.

3. Fatima Renewal Center, 1000 Seminary Rd., Dalton, PA 18414
   (717) 563-8500 ❖ **Contact:** Mrs. Mary Franceschelli
✓**Single Rooms** ✓**Twin Rooms**
Individual Guest Rate: $32.00 ✓**Includes 3 Meals Daily**
✓**Reservations Required** ✓**Advance Deposit:** $10.00 for weekend
Guest Rules: Brochure given with reservations. Price on weekends $46.50 for one night with 3 meals; 2 nights on weekend $70.00 with 5 meals.
On Site Attractions/Nearby Points of Interest: Located 30 minutes north of Scranton, the center has walking trails, a small lake and a gymnasium. A beautiful setting in the northern Pocono Mountains. In nearby Wilkes-Barre, the Cherry Blossom Festival is held every June.
Additional Information: Groups welcomed. Children OK with close adult supervision.

4. St. Margaret's House, 5419 Germantown Ave., Philadelphia, PA 19144
   (215) 844-9410 ❖ **Contact:** Guest Sister
✓**Single Rooms** ✓**Twin Rooms**
Individual Guest Rate: $30.00 ✓**Includes 3 Meals Daily**
✓**Reservations Required** ✓**Advance Deposit:** None
Guest Rules: No smoking or alcohol in the house. Silence from 9:00 p.m. until after breakfast (lounge excepted).
On Site Attractions/Nearby Points of Interest: The Fairmount Park Trolley Tour of Philadelphia will show you Independence Hall, the Liberty Bell, Ben Franklin's home at Franklin Court, Congress Hall and most other historical sites. Home of six college campuses, five art museums, and the largest fresh water port in the world at Penn's Landing. Philadelphia hosts outdoor summer concerts at the Mann Music Center — everything from ballet, jazz, rock to classical compositions. 16 miles away is the 2000-acre Valley Forge Park, the historic site of George Washington's headquarters.
Additional Information: No children. Overnight groups of 15-20 persons welcomed; during the day, 25-30. Fees arranged for each group. Programs and workshops offered for interested groups.

5. Emmaus, Daylesford Abbey, 200 So. Valley Rd., Paoli, PA 19301
   (215) 647-2530 ❖ **Contact:** Jean D'Ambrosio, Administrator
✓**Single Rooms Individual Guest Rate:** $35.00
✓**Includes 3 Meals Daily** ✓**Self-Catering Kitchenette**

✓**Reservations Required** ✓**Advance Deposit:** None
On Site Attractions/Nearby Points of Interest: Emmaus is a house separate from the abbey. Situated on 136 acres, the property is charming and serene, a sanctuary for both man and wildlife. Nearby are the reconstructed soldier huts, fortifications and parade grounds that were once the headquarters of George Washington at Valley Forge. In the park is a free museum with guided tours, a picnic area and a 5-mile bike trail. A 40-minute drive to the east takes you into the heart of Philadelphia. **Additional Information:** No children. Groups of up to 57 persons can be accommodated at the abbey. The abbey's Institute for Religion and Culture offers programs focused on cultural sensitivity.

6. St. Raphaela Mary Retreat House
   616 Coopertown Rd., Haverford, PA 19041
   (215) 642-5715
✓**Single Rooms** ✓**Twin Rooms** **Individual Guest Rate:** $35.00
✓**Includes 3 Meals Daily** ✓**Reservations Required** ✓**Advance Deposit:** $20.00
Guest Rules: Smoking and beverages allowed in the lounge or outside. Prepare bed before leaving. Relax and be comfortable in your home away from home.
On Site Attractions/Nearby Points of Interest: A three-story mansion on 8 acres of Philadelphia's Main Line suburbs. Beautifully kept grounds, pathways, a grotto, guest areas for relaxation. All of the historic sites, the recreation, and culture of Philadelphia are within a 20-minute drive. Near to Rosemont, Bryn Mawr, and Villanova colleges.
Additional Information: No children. Can accommodate groups and provide workshops. Air-conditioned, remodeled rooms. Aim to provide a quiet restful place to concentrate and learn in relaxed surroundings.

7. Orthodox Monastery of the Transfiguration
   RD 1, Box 184x, Ellwood City, PA 16117
   (412) 758-4002 ✤ **Contact:** Office
✓**Single Rooms** ✓**Twin Rooms** **Individual Guest Rate:** Free-will donation
✓**Includes 3 Meals Daily** ✓**Self-Catering Kitchenette**
✓**Reservations Required** ✓**Advance Deposit:** None
Guest Rules: No smoking. No shorts.
On Site Attractions/Nearby Points of Interest: Ellwood City is about 1½ hours NW of Pittsburgh, close to the Ohio border, and situated on the Beaver River. Pleasant surroundings on 100 acres of the rolling hills of western Pennsylvania. Abundance of trees and private walking trails.
Additional Information: A newer and larger monastery is nearing completion. Children OK, and groups up to 8 persons welcomed. Snacks available anytime in the guest area.

8. Pendle Hill, 338 Plush Mill Rd., Wallingford, PA 19086
   (215) 566-4507 ✤ **Contact:** Irene Ramsay, Registrar
✓**Single Rooms** ✓**Twin Rooms** ✓**Other:** Triple rooms
Individual Guest Rate: $38.00 *(includes breakfast)*
✓**Reservations Required** ✓**Advance Deposit:** None
Guest Rules: No smoking, alcohol or drugs. Quaker mission is to live in an educational environment, doing cooperative work, exploring spiritual worth, and to translate the values of harmonious interdependence to the community at large.
On Site Attractions/Nearby Points of Interest: Pendle Hill Center is located 12 miles southwest of Philadelphia, a quiet campus of 22 acres with more than 125 varieties of trees and shrubs on its grounds. All of the historic sights of Philadelphia

are within easy access via public transportation. Nearby are the colorful Longwood Gardens, the Brandywine Museum (Andrew Wyeth), and the distinct Anabaptist communities of the Amish, Mennonites, and Brethren of Lancaster County, where the residents use horse-drawn carriages and wear old-fashioned dress.

Additional Information: Children OK — 12 and under half price. Groups welcomed. Lunch and dinner (delicious buffet-style food) are $4.00 and $6.00. Many interesting workshops are offered, including pottery and weaving. No guests the last two weeks in August.

9. Cornelia Connelly Center
1341-1359 Montgomery Avenue, Rosemont, PA 19010
(215) 527-4813 *(9:00 a.m.-1:00 p.m. Eastern time)*
✓**Single Rooms Individual Guest Rate:** $25.00
✓**Includes 3 Meals Daily   ✓Self-Catering Kitchenette**
✓**Reservations Required** *(for 6 days or more)*   ✓**Advance Deposit:** $30.00

Guest Rules: No smoking inside buildings. Guests are requested to prepare beds prior to departure. Simple, functional lifestyle.

On Site Attractions/Nearby Points of Interest: The Center is on the grounds of a former main line estate west of the Philadelphia city center. Spread out under tree-shaded grounds are sculptured works, terraced lawns, garden fountains and a running stream. Half an hour away is the 2000-acre Valley Forge National Historic Park, with its Revolutionary War trappings and George Washington memorabilia. Of course, Philadelphia is rife with historical landmarks, an urban center with its shopping malls, cultural arts and entertainment.

Additional Information: No children. Groups welcomed. Laundry facilities, books and tapes available.

10. St. Paul of the Cross Retreat House
148 Monastery Ave., Pittsburgh, PA 19010
(412) 381-7676 ✤ **Contact:** R.H. office or Betty Borsh
✓**Single Rooms   ✓Twin Rooms**
Individual Guest Rate: $35.00 *(meals additional)*
✓**Reservations Required   ✓Advance Deposit:** First night, 20% for groups

St. Paul of the Cross Retreat House, Pittsburgh, Pennsylvania

Guest Rules: No alcohol. Request participation in some services. Programs and workshops emphasize spiritual renewal and personal growth. Individuals are encouraged to find their own level of interaction. Relaxed fellowship. If part of one's plans include seeing the sights, assistance can be given for booking excursions. **On Site Attractions/Nearby Points of Interest:** The House is situated on 14 acres of landscaped grounds and quiet gardens with a panoramic view of the Pittsburgh skyline. The private serenity of the hilltop location with its tree-shaded lanes contrasts with the busy urban life below. Pittsburgh's highlights include the 42-story Cathedral of Learning and the glass tower of PPG Place, the acres of flowers and Edwardian homes at Schenley Park, the 200-foot fountain at Point State Park, the Shakespeare and Three Rivers Art Festival, the zoo, and the city university. The Gateway Clipper Fleet offers sightseeing cruises on three rivers. **Additional Information:** Children OK with supervision. Non-profit, charitable and philanthropic groups welcomed. Well-balanced, home-cooked meals. Special coordinators to assist with arrangements. Small and large meeting rooms. Fenced parking lot.

11. **Laurelville Mennonite Church Center**
    Box 145, Route 5, Mt. Pleasant, PA 15666
    (412) 423-2056 ❖ **Contact:** Betty Miller or Mike Zehie
    ✓**Twin Rooms** ✓**Other:** Motel-type units, lodge, cabins and guesthouse
    Individual Guest Rate: $30.00 to $55.00 ✓**Includes 3 Meals Daily**
    ✓**Reservations Required** ✓**Advance Deposit:** 50%
    Guest Rules: No smoking in buildings. No alcohol. 11:00 p.m. noise curfew.
    On Site Attractions/Nearby Points of Interest: Laurelville Center is located 75 miles southeast of Pittsburgh on 180 acres of wooded land in the beautiful Laurel Mountains. Close by are whitewater rafting rides for summer enjoyment and the Seven Springs Ski Resort for winter sports. On the premises are a pool, tennis court, miniature golf course, and a volleyball court. Within a half-hour's drive one can visit Frank Lloyd Wright's architectural masterwork "Fallingwater," and see the restored Fort Ligonier, where various groups enact 18th-century battles and camp life on summer weekends.

Laurelville Guest House, Mt. Pleasant, Pennsylvania

Additional Information: Children OK. Groups welcomed. 7 meeting rooms for groups of 30 to 250. Large dining hall capacity serving home-style meals.

12. Trinity Spiritual Center, 3609 Simpson Ferry Rd., Camp Hill, PA 17011
    (717) 761-7355 ✤ **Contact:** Dr. Mary Ann Boyarski
✓**Single Rooms** ✓**Twin Rooms** **Individual Guest Rate:** $30.00 with breakfast
✓**Reservations Required** ✓**Advance Deposit:** 10%
Guest Rules: No smoking. No food or beverages in sleeping quarters.
On Site Attractions/Nearby Points of Interest: Camp Hill is 10 miles south of the state capital of Harrisburg. The compelling Harrisburg Riverfront is a 5-mile-long park along the shores of the Susquehanna River, with views of majestic bridges and the city skyline. In the middle of the river is City Island, a recreational center featuring the *Pride of Susquehanna*, a 65-foot paddle-wheeler that cruises the river during the summer. The Museum of Scientific Discovery is a "hands on" show of scientific apparatus. The Center itself has extensive gardens and paths for walking.
Additional Information: No children. Groups welcomed.

13. St. Gabriel's Retreat House
    631 Griffin Pond Rd., Clarks Summit, PA 18411
    (717) 586-4957 ✤ **Contact:** Alene Perry
✓**Single Rooms** ✓**Twin Rooms**
Individual Guest Rate: $25.00 ✓**Includes 3 Meals Daily**
(St. Gabriel's is famed for its home-baked bread)
Reservations Required ✓**Advance Deposit:** 25%
Guest Rules: No smoking or alcohol. Quiet atmosphere observed.
On Site Attractions/Nearby Points of Interest: Clarks Summit is located just 6 miles north of Scranton, a little over 2 hours west of New York City. The House, a large single floor modern building, affords beautiful mountain views on 50 acres of wooded countryside. In Scranton: Steamtown Historical Site, collection of steam locomotives and offers old-fashioned 58 mile train excursion; Montage and Elk Mountain ski areas (300 acres of mountainside trails); Nay Aug and McDade Park provide wide variety of recreational activities.
Additional Information: Children OK, groups welcomed. Large lounge meeting rooms with TV/VCR. St. Gabriel's is grateful to those who may contribute more than the asking fee.

St. Gabriel's Retreat House, Clarks Summit, Pennsylvania

14. Fatima House, 601 Rolling Hills Rd., Ottsville, PA 18942
   (215) 795-2947 ❖ Contact: Regina Cullen
✓Single Rooms   ✓Twin Rooms
Individual Guest Rate: $25.00   ✓Self-Catering Kitchenette
✓Reservations Required   ✓Advance Deposit: 25%
Guest Rules: No smoking.
On Site Attractions/Nearby Points of Interest: Ottsville is a few minutes north of Doylestown (about 22 miles north of Philadelphia) in the scenic beauty and rich historical milieu of Bucks County. The restored barn and guest rooms are in a lovely country setting not far from Nockumixon State Park. At the Moravian Pottery Works, tiles are handcrafted on the premises. Nearby New Hope is a gathering place for artists, literary, and theatrical personalities.
Additional Information: Children OK, groups of up to 75 accommodated for day meetings.

15. Spruce Lake Retreat, RR 1 Box 605, Canadensis, PA 18325-9749
   (717) 595-7505 ❖ Contact: Accommodations Manager
✓Single Rooms   ✓Twin Rooms
✓Other: 60 wooded campsites with bathhouse, bunkhouse
Individual Guest Rate: $28.00   ✓Self-Catering Kitchenette
(3 meals provided @ $17.50. Vegetable and fruit snacks: price varies.))
✓Reservations Required   ✓Advance Deposit: $25.00 per room; $12.50 per campsite
Guest Rules: No smoking in buildings, no alcohol or pets. Quiet hours between 11:00 p.m. and 7:00 a.m.
On Site Attractions/Nearby Points of Interest: Canadensis is north of Philadelphia, 55 miles east of Wilkes-Barre and 2 hours west of New York. The Retreat is located on 325 acres of woodlands, with streams, waterfalls, wildlife, 2 small lakes and hiking trails. Fifty-one motel-type rooms with private bath, 8 conference rooms, 60 wooded campsites — the Retreat can accommodate 20 to 200 people. Recreation facilities: 2 tennis courts, volleyball, swimming, miniature golf, skiing, ice skating, tobogganing, indoor pool, ping pong.
Additional Information: Children OK. Groups welcomed, special rates. Deposits non-refundable if reservation cancelled. Linens can be provided.

RHODE ISLAND

1. Mount St. Joseph Spiritual Life Center
   13 Monkey Wrench Lane, Bristol, RI 02809
   (401) 253-5434 ❖ Contact: Sister Irene Escobar, SSD
✓Single Rooms   ✓Twin Rooms   Individual Guest Rate: $35.00
✓Includes 3 Meals Daily   ✓Self-Catering Kitchenette
✓Reservations Required   ✓Advance Deposit: $30.00
Guest Rules: Special attention given to those who wish personal direction.
On Site Attractions/Nearby Points of Interest: Bristol is located midway between Providence and Newport; the center itself occupies 25 acres of woods and peaceful scenery overlooking Mount Hope Bay and the Bay Bridge. The historical town of Bristol is home to the Blitheweld Arboretum, the Heffenrater Museum, and Colt State Park, where many local and national bands play in the summer. In nearby Providence are Brown University, a famous repertory company, theatres and art shops. To the south, Newport jazz festivals, the Naval War College Museum, and grandiose mansions.

Additional Information: Groups and children accepted for day programs. Additional beds available at Columbia Fathers Seminary — inquire for further information. Bicycles are available to use on the 10-mile bicycle trail.

2. Providence Zen Center, 528 Pound Rd., Cumberland, RI 02864
(401) 658-1464 ❖ Contact: J.W. Harrington
✓**Rooms:** Dormitory-style accommodations
Individual Guest Rate: $30.00   ✓**Includes 3 Meals Daily**
✓**Self-Catering Kitchenette**
✓**Reservations Required**   ✓**Advance Deposit:** 50%
Guest Rules: Strictly vegetarian; no shoes, no smoking indoors. General environment is quiet and meditative. Discounted rates to those joining in the Zen Center's daily meditation practices.
On Site Attractions/Nearby Points of Interest: Situated on a quiet 50 acres with trees, pathways, and a pond just 15 miles north of Providence. One hour to the south is Newport, with its imitative neoclassical and baroque mansions of yesteryear. In Providence is the Rhode Island State Capitol's unsupported marble dome, second in size to St. Peter's in Rome, and the Waterfront Festival with its craft and art booths, harbor cruises, and speedboat races.
Additional Information: Children OK. Groups welcomed, vegetarian buffet meals, use of halls, guestmaster very willing to take care of any needs.

3. St. Paul's Priory Guest House, 61 Narragansett Ave., Newport, RI 02840
(401) 847-2423 ❖ Contact: Guest Mistress
✓**Single Rooms**   ✓**Twin Rooms**
Individual Guest Rate: Free-will donation   ✓**Self-Catering Kitchenette**
✓**Reservations Required**   ✓**Advance Deposit:** None
Guest Rules: No smoking. The guiding principle of the House is to help others in every aspect of life: spiritually, intellectually, emotionally. Minimum stay 2 days.
On Site Attractions/Nearby Points of Interest: Located on a 3-acre estate encircled by the famed mansions of Newport. Only two blocks from the ocean, the House is 10 minutes away from Cliff Walk, the pedestrian throughway where one can stroll for hours along the rugged shoreline. In Newport, the first synagogue ever built in the U.S.; the Bannister's Wharf Marina berths the ships from the America's Cup races, and visitors are invited to step aboard. Fort Adams State Park has picnic areas and 2 fishing piers.
Additional Information: Groups welcomed if they prepare their own meals and have their own Retreat Master. Individuals will find a well-stocked kitchen. Inquire about children.

4. Nazareth Center, 12 Cliff Terr., Newport, RI 02840
(401) 847-1654 ❖ Contact: Sr. Rachel Gonthier
✓**Single Rooms**   ✓**Twin Rooms**
Individual Guest Rate: $30.00   ✓**Includes 3 Meals Daily**
✓**Reservations Required**   ✓**Advance Deposit:** $25.00
Guest Rules: The Center provides the environment for quiet reflection. Not an overnight stopover.
On Site Attractions/Nearby Points of Interest: Adjacent to the famed Cliff Walk of Newport, each bedroom has a marvelous view of the sea. The Walk offers an extended tour of the lavish mansions and also affords a panoramic view of the ocean. A 10-mile bicycle loop provides breathtaking scenery and gives you a gander of Hammersmith Farm, childhood home of Jackie Onassis and the "summer White House" of JFK.

Additional Information: No children. Groups of 8 persons maximum welcomed. Swimming pool accessible. Closed July and August.

SOUTH CAROLINA

1. Emmanuel House, 1916 N. Pleasantburg Dr., Greenville, SC 29609
   (803) 244-4514/268-5065 *(evenings)* ✣ **Contact:** Sr. Helen Godfrey, OSC
✓**Single Rooms** ✓**Twin Rooms**
Individual Guest Rate: $20.00 or free will donation   ✓**Self-Catering Kitchen**
✓**Reservations Required** ✓**Advance Deposit:** None
Guest Rules: Women only. No smoking or pets. A fully equipped kitchen is available for guests to prepare snacks or full meals.
On Site Attractions/Nearby Points of Interest: Greenville, in the northwestern corner of the state, is 74 miles SW of Charlotte, NC, and 99 miles NW of Columbia, SC. The House is a quiet and comfortable center on the grounds of the Monastery of St. Clare. Guests are free to follow their own schedule in the spirit of solitude. Reedy River flows over the falls in the heart of Greenville and winds through tree-lined streets. Bob Jones University has a collection of rare bibles and sacred religious art. The Zoo area has lighted tennis courts, a park, and bicycle trails. Nearby are 11,000 acres of forest, parks, and lakes.
Additional Information: No children. Groups limited to 4 persons.

SOUTH DAKOTA

1. Harmony Hill Center, RR3, Box 254, Watertown, SD 57201
   (605) 886-6777 ✣ **Contact:** Sister Joan Sand
✓**Single Rooms** ✓**Twin Rooms**
Individual Guest Rate: $30.00   ✓**Includes 3 Meals Daily**
✓**Reservations Required** ✓**Advance Deposit:** $30.00
On Site Attractions/Nearby Points of Interest: Watertown is located near the South Dakota/Minnesota border. Nearby are Lake Kampeska and Lake Poinsett, which offer swimming, fishing, and other waterfront activities. There are numerous walking trails on the Center's premises, which is an accredited branch campus of Mt. Marty College. Both the historical Heritage House and Mellette House are in Watertown.
Additional Information: Groups welcomed, but must bring their own director. Inquire about children.

TENNESSEE

1. Stritch Conference Center, 2455 Avery Ave., Memphis, TN 38112
   (901) 722-0243 ✣ **Contact:** Director
✓**Single Rooms** ✓**Twin Rooms**
Individual Guest Rate: $30.00   ✓**Includes 3 Meals Daily**
✓**Reservations Required** ✓**Advance Deposit:** None
On Site Attractions/Nearby Points of Interest: The Center is located on the beautiful campus of the Christian Brothers University. The University swimming pool, tennis and handball courts, and exercise facility are available to guests of the Center. In Memphis is the Elvis Presley memorial, Graceland, and his car museum across the street. The Great American Pyramid holds the American Music Hall of Fame, the Memphis Music Experience, and a 20,000-seat arena. Many museums

and parks, the Zoo and Aquarium, and the Orpheum Theatre make Memphis a mecca for everyone's taste.
Additional Information: Children OK. Groups welcomed. Coordinator of 30 or more persons receives a free room.

2. **Dubose Conference Center, Box 339, Monteagle, TN 37356**
   (615) 924-2353 ✤ **Contact:** Randy Schulte or Kim Terry
   ✓**Single Rooms** ✓**Twin Rooms** ✓**Other:** 4 cabins, camp-style
   Individual Guest Rate: $40.00 to $60.00 ✓**Includes 3 Meals Daily**
   ✓**Reservations Required** ✓**Advance Deposit:** For groups of 50 or more
   Guest Rules: That guests respect the needs of other guests, treat the grounds and buildings as their own, and join in a spirit of community and fellowship.
   On Site Attractions/Nearby Points of Interest: Located on 65 acres of wooded countryside with swimming pool and hiking trails. The national historical landmark Claiborne Hall is on the premises. Nearby in Sewanee is the University of the South with golf and tennis available. Lake Woods and Tim's Ford Lake are part of the South Cumberland State Recreation Area, attracting swimmers, fishing, and boating enthusiasts. Monteagle is 95 miles SE of Nashville, just south of Tullahoma.
   Additional Information: Children OK. Groups welcomed with advance notice and coordinator provided. Dubose is steeped in tradition and is a place dear to the hearts of guests over the past 45 years.

3. **House of the Lord, 1306 Dellwood Rd., Memphis, TN 38127**
   (901) 357-7398 ✤ **Contact:** Sr. Mary Ann Coccaro or Sr. Terry Starr
   ✓**Single Rooms** ✓**Twin Rooms**
   Individual Guest Rate: Free-will donation ✓**Self-Catering Kitchenette**
   ✓**Reservations Required** ✓**Advance Deposit:** None
   Guest Rules: The welcome door is open to all. Some meals with resident community depending on length of stay.
   On Site Attractions/Nearby Points of Interest: The facility is an old monastery where guests share a simple, comfortable, relaxed environment. A seven-acre walking/running/exercise loop adjoins the House. Memphis, the city steeped in music from blues to jazz to rock'n'roll, now has it all in the 32-story Great American Pyramid, with its Music Hall of Fame, the Music Experience, music theater and a 20,000-seat sports arena. Beautiful sunset walks along the Mississippi, where the river runs clear, are memorable; and in Overton Park you can stroll through the Memphis Zoo and Aquarium.
   Additional Information: No children. Small groups welcomed.

4. **Penuel Ridge Retreat Center, 1440 Sams Creek Rd., Ashland City, TN 37015**
   (615) 792-3734 ✤ **Contact:** Retreat Coordinator
   ✓**Single Rooms** ✓**Twin Rooms**
   Individual Guest Rate: $18.00 ✓**Self-Catering Kitchenette**
   ✓**Reservations Required** ✓**Advance Deposit:** None
   Guest Rules: No pets.
   On Site Attractions/Nearby Points of Interest: Ashland is about 20 miles NW of Nashville off of I-40. The Center is located on 120 acres of beautiful countryside adjoining the Cheatham Wildlife Preserve, with nature trails that wind through wooded ridges and around a tranquil spring-fed lake. The ecumenical Center invites persons who seek time to be out-of-doors, write in a journal, browse through books, or simply reflect on life's goals. Nashville, the state capital, popularly known for its Coun-

try Music Hall of Fame and Opryland, USA, is also famous for its eight institutions of higher learning.
Additional Information: Younger children OK if part of family group. Groups welcomed.

TEXAS

1. Montserrat Retreat House, Box 398, Lake Dallas, TX 75065
   (817) 497-2221 ✤ **Contact:** Montserrat Office
✓**Single Rooms** ✓**Twin Rooms**
Individual Guest Rate: $50.00 or free-will donation ✓**Includes 3 Meals Daily**
✓**Reservations Required** ✓**Advance Deposit:** None
Guest Rules: To facilitate personal renewal, growth and reflection, an atmosphere of quiet is essential.
On Site Attractions/Nearby Points of Interest: Gracious lakeside setting with 33 acres of woodlands, trails, hills. Nearby is the Dallas-Ft. Worth metroplex. In Dallas, the arts district houses the Museum of Art; in Thanksgiving Square, a below-street-level enclosure has gardens and waterfalls, and in State Fair Park are a plethora of museums, including the Aquarium and the Age of Steam Museum.
Additional Information: No children. Groups welcomed Monday through Wednesday.

2. Camp Allen, Rte. 1 Box 426, Navasota, TX 77868
   (409) 825-7175 ✤ **Contact:** Jeremiah Ward
✓**Twin Rooms   Individual Guest Rate:** $50.00
✓**Includes 3 Meals Daily**
✓**Reservations Required**
✓**Advance Deposit:** 50%
On Site Attractions/Nearby Points of Interest: Navasota is about an hour's drive NW of Houston. The camp is situated by an 8-acre lake, with an Olympic size swimming pool, tennis courts, and a full court basketball and volleyball pavilion. In Houston the models of Gemini, Apollo and Skylab are displayed at the LBJ Space Center, which is also the home of Mission Control. The Houston Tunnel System connects all the major buildings in downtown, extending from the Civic Center to the Hyatt Regency, encompassing hundreds of shops and scores of restaurants.
Additional Information: Children OK and groups welcomed.

The Alamo, San Antonio, Texas

73

3. **Benedictine Retreat Center, HCR 2 Box 6300, Sandia, TX 78383**
   (512) 547-3257 ✤ Contact: Rev. Louis Hacker, O.S.B.
✓**Single Rooms** ✓**Twin Rooms**
Individual Guest Rate: $20; $50/weekend; $75 married couple/weekend
✓**Includes 3 Meals Daily**
✓**Reservations Required** ✓**Advance Deposit:** $50.00 for groups only
Guest Rules: No smoking in buildings. No shorts in church.
On Site Attractions/Nearby Points of Interest: Sandia, about 40 miles NW of
Corpus Christi, has two large park areas for camping and picnics. The Center is on
the shore of Lake Corpus Christi, with fishing, swimming and hiking at water's
edge. The Corpus Christi shoreline boardwalk beckons visitors to climb aboard the
restaurant showboats and sightseeing ferries. The Harbor Playhouse presents summertime melodramas as well as musicals.
Additional Information: Children OK. Groups welcomed to fully-equipped meeting rooms.

4. **Bishop Defalco Retreat Center**
   2100 N. Spring St., Amarillo, TX 79107
   (806) 383-1811 ✤ Contact: Patsy Kuehler
✓**Single Rooms** ✓**Twin Rooms**
Individual Guest Rate: $33.75 ✓**Includes 3 Meals Daily**
✓**Reservations Required** ✓**Advance Deposit:** $25.00 non-refundable
Guest Rules: No alcohol. Contemplative lifestyle with active involvement with
one's family, job, society.
On Site Attractions/Nearby Points of Interest: Nearby is Palo Duro Canyon State
Park; to the north is the expansive Lake Meredith National Recreation Area; and to
the south, Buffalo Lake.
Additional Information: No children. Non-profit groups welcomed.

5. **Christian Renewal Center, 1515 Hughes Rd., Dickinson, TX 77539**
   (713) 337-1312 ✤ Contact: Rosemary Munoz
✓**Single Rooms** ✓**Twin Rooms** ✓**Other:** Dormitory-style cottages
Individual Guest Rate: $25.00 to $40.00 ✓**Includes 3 Meals Daily**
✓**Reservations Required** ✓**Advance Deposit:** 25%
Guest Rules: Respect each others' needs and the spiritual mission of the Center.
On Site Attractions/Nearby Points of Interest: The Center, with its 50﹎beautiful
acres of woods and fields, is situated on waterfront property on the Dickinson Bayou.
Hiking trails, recreational areas, swimming pool on the premises. Just 30 minutes
from Houston and nearby to the Center are Galveston Island (Gulf of Mexico), the
NASA Manned Spacecraft Center, the Pirates and Stewart Beach along the Gulf
shores, and Houston's Zoological Gardens featuring small mammals, hippopotami,
and alligators.
Additional Information: Children 7 years and older OK with parental supervision.
Groups welcomed.

6. **St. Joseph Retreat House, 127 Oblate Dr., San Antonio, TX 78216**
   (512) 349-4173 ✤ Contact: Peggy Beck or Steve Saldana
✓**Single Rooms** ✓**Twin Rooms**
Individual Guest Rate: $25.00 single; $35.00 total cost for double room
✓**Self-Catering Kitchenette**
✓**Reservations Required** ✓**Advance Deposit:** $20/room
Guest Rules: Plan arrival before 5:00 p.m.
On Site Attractions/Nearby Points of Interest: The House is on 10 acres of lovely

shaded grounds, a quiet refuge in the central San Antonio region. For those interested in Southwestern history, remnants of the Alamo still stand, a tour of four missions along the San Antonio River leaves daily, and behind the city hall is the Spanish governor's former palace. The Riverwalk is lined with shops, cafes, gardens and connects downtown hotels. Sea World, the Zoo, Fiesta Texas add to San Antonio's appeal.

Additional Information: Children OK with adult supervision. Groups welcomed, and full meal service provided for groups of 16 or more. Open to all faiths. 10 minutes from San Antonio International Airport.

7. Christ the King Retreat Center, 802 Ford St., San Angelo, TX 76902
   (915) 651-5352 ❖ Contact: M.A. Lewis
✓**Single Rooms** ✓**Twin Rooms**
Individual Guest Rate: $28.75 ✓**Includes 3 Meals Daily**
✓**Reservations Required** ✓**Advance Deposit: 10%**
On Site Attractions/Nearby Points of Interest: San Angelo, in west central Texas is in a triangular direction, 185 miles NW of San Antonio, 230 miles SW of Dallas, and 100 miles south of Abilene. The Center is located on 19 green acres that border the Concho River. Nature trails wind along the riverbanks. A retrospective of the Wild West can be seen at Fort Concho Historical Site with 20 buildings restored to their 1867 period. At Fisher Lake and Lake Nasworthy there is fishing, boating, water skiing, golf, nature trails and swimming.
Additional Information: No children, groups welcomed. Full-time cook and meals served cafeteria style.

8. Presbyterian Mo-Ranch Assembly, Rt. 1 Box 158, Hunt, TX 78024
   (210) 238-4455 Ext. 346/"0" ❖ Contact: Registration Services
✓**Twin Rooms**
✓**Other:** 82 conventional private rooms with bath, 4 apartments, dormitories
Individual Guest Rate: $29.50 and up, depending on choice of accommodation
✓**Includes 3 Meals Daily** ✓**Reservations Required**
✓**Advance Deposit:** Call in
Guest Rules: No smoking in buildings. No use of alcohol in common or public areas.
On Site Attractions/Nearby Points of Interest: Hunt is 90 miles NW of San Antonio International Airport, and 23 miles west of Kerrville. Mo-Ranch is on 434 acres of scenic Texas hill country at the headwaters of the Guadalupe River. The Ranch, part of the 6,000 acre estate of the late multimillionaire Dan Moran, offers everything to refresh the body and spirit: swimming, canoeing, tennis courts, children's playground, book shop, library, nature trails that reveal deer, armadillo, wild turkey; Indian museum and sculptures. All around are picturesque red-roofed buildings, bridges, riverfront views, citrus trees, and arching catwalks across the canyons.
Additional Information: Children OK. Groups of 5 to 500 welcomed. AV equipment available — meeting spaces complimentary or at nominal charge.

VERMONT

1. Monastery of the Immaculate Heart of Mary
   HCR Box 11, Westfield, VT 05874
   (802) 744-6525 ❖ Contact: Sr. Marie Catherine Lavalles
✓**Single Rooms** **Individual Guest Rate: $25.00** ✓**Includes 3 Meals Daily**
✓**Reservations Required** ✓**Advance Deposit: None**

Guest Rules: Women only. Respect the quiet of those who desire it. No smoking in rooms. 15-day stay maximum.

On Site Attractions/Nearby Points of Interest: The monastery is located about 1 hour north of Montpelier near Lowell, less than an hour south of the Canadian border. The 400 acres of grounds are in the Lowell Mountains, near the Missisquoi River. The gift shop features postcards (painted by the local chaplain) depicting scenes of the picturesque surroundings.

Additional Information: No children. No groups.

2. Karmê-Chöling, Barnet, VT 05821

(802) 633-2384 ❖ **Contact:** Front Office

✓**Single Rooms** ✓**Double Rooms** ✓**Other:** Dormitories, cabins, shrine rooms

Individual Guest Rate: $25 dormitory, $45 private room, $55 double room

✓**Includes 3 Meals Daily**

✓**Reservations Required** ✓**Advance Deposit:** $50.00 for groups

Guest Rules: Lights out at 10:30 p.m. Guests are invited to share in the work of the Center. Delicious vegetarian and non-vegetarian meals served.

On Site Attractions/Nearby Points of Interest: Karmê-Chölung is a Tibetan Buddhist meditation center located 35 miles east of Montpelier and an hour north of White River Junction. Situated on 540 acres of wooded countryside, the Center, with its pond and gardens, is a hiker's paradise. Nearby Harvey's Lake offers boating and waterfront activities. The beautiful fall foliage surrounds the Center. In Montpelier, the state capital, nature paths in preserved wilderness coil through the Hubbard Park and Fitness Trails. The Karmê Center also owns and operates a charming hotel in the city of Barnet.

Additional Information: Children 3 years and older OK. Groups welcomed.

3. Milarepa Center, Barnet Mountain, Barnet, VT 05821

(802) 633-4136 ❖ **Contact:** Martha Tack

✓**Single Rooms** ✓**Twin Rooms** ✓**Other:** Camping spaces

Individual Guest Rate: $25-45 *(meals can be provided: $25 per day)*

✓**Includes 3 Meals Daily** ✓**Self-Catering Available**

✓**Reservations Required** ✓**Advance Deposit:** 10%

Guest Rules: No smoking or alcohol. Cooperative work experience, vegetarian meals.

On Site Attractions/Nearby Points of Interest: The Center is situated on a 270 acre farm located in Vermont's scenic Northeast Kingdom, northeast of Montpelier and 8 miles south of St. Johnsburg. One can visit the Athenaeum Gallery of early American artists and the Fairbanks Museum and Planetarium in the immediate area. The scenic village of Peacham is an oasis for city dwellers and artists searching for peace and inspiration.

Additional Information: Children OK; groups welcomed with advance approval of Director. Milarepa is a residential center for study and retreat in the Tibetan Buddhist tradition, one of 30 centers worldwide belonging to the Foundation for Preservation of the Mahayana Tradition. Advisable to send for brochure.

4. Institute for Spiritual Development

Trinity College, 208 Colchester Ave., Burlington, VT 05401

(802) 658-0337, ext. 410 ❖ **Contact:** Sr. Elaine Dessy or Sr. Judy Fortune

✓**Twin Rooms** **Individual Guest Rate:** $35.00 ✓**Includes 3 Meals Daily**

✓**Reservations Required** ✓**Advance Deposit:** Call in or write

Guest Rules: Quiet atmosphere to prevail.

On Site Attractions/Nearby Points of Interest: The retreat house itself is located about 60 miles south of Burlington, in the village of Benson, 20 miles NW of Rutland,

Vermont's second largest city. The center sits amid 40 acres of pasture, pond and woods of pine, hemlock and yellow birch. The 340,000 acre Green Mountain National Forest is just to the north. The Norman Rockwell Museum in Rutland exhibits 2000 of the famed artist's pictures, and close by the New England Maple Museum satisfies the sweet tooth of all who visit.
Additional Information: No children. Groups up to 20 welcomed. Reservations and information through the Burlington Institute above.

VIRGINIA

1. Holy Family Retreat House, 1414 N. Mallory Rd., Hampton, VA 23663
   (804) 722-3997 ✤ **Contact:** Retreat Office
✓**Single Rooms** ✓**Twin Rooms**
Individual Guest Rate: $40.00 ✓**Includes 3 Meals Daily**
✓**Reservations Required** ✓**Advance Deposit:** Varies with length of stay
Guest Rules: Smoking allowed only in outside areas.
On Site Attractions/Nearby Points of Interest: The House is on 10 acres of tree-shaded grounds, close to the historical centers of colonial America. Within an hour's drive is Yorktown, its museum replete with "living history" and items from the Revolutionary War; Jamestown Festival Park, site of the first landing of English settlers in the New World; Williamsburg Colonial National Historic Park, with its restored gardens, craft shops, costumed actors in the historic district, and the decorative arts museum.
Additional Information: Children over 16 OK. Groups of 40 persons minimum for the weekends, 25 minimum for mid-week.

2. The Well Retreat Center, 18047 Quiet Way, Smithfield, VA 23430
   (804) 255-2366 ✤ **Contact:** Diane Weymouth
✓**Single Rooms** ✓**Twin Rooms**
Individual Guest Rate: $30.00 ✓**Includes 3 Meals Daily**
✓**Reservations Required** ✓**Advance Deposit:** 50%
Guest Rules: No smoking or alcohol. The Center is strictly for making a retreat, not to be used as a motel.
On Site Attractions/Nearby Points of Interest: The Well Center is located at the southeastern tip of Virginia, a short distance northwest of Norfolk in a corner of Isle of Wight County. The grounds of the Center include 13 acres in a serene wooded setting near a spring-fed lake. The region is rife with historical sites: Colonial Williamsburg, a restored 18th century village; and Jamestown Island/Settlement, the first English colony in North America. Museums abound and Virginia Beach all within easy driving distance.
Additional Information: No children; groups welcomed. Special membership with the Suffolk YMCA allows retreat guests to use the exercise room and pool for a nominal fee.

3. Richmond Hill, 2209 E. Grace St., Richmond, VA 23223
   (804) 783-7903 ✤ **Contact:** Program Director
✓**Single Rooms** ✓**Twin Rooms**
Individual Guest Rate: $30.00 ✓**Includes 3 Meals Daily**
✓**Reservations Required** ✓**Advance Deposit:** None
Guest Rules: No alcohol, pets, smoking in buildings.
On Site Attractions/Nearby Points of Interest: Richmond Hill is an ecumenical urban retreat center open seven days a week to all those who decide to learn, work,

study, and seek spiritual renewal. Located on the crest of Church Hill, just east of downtown, the site includes St. John's Church, and has a panoramic view of southern Richmond. Within walking distance are parks, James River canoeing, bicycle trails, Annabel Lee paddlewheel dining cruises, historic capital buildings, museums and a wildlife sanctuary.
Additional Information: Groups welcomed.

WASHINGTON, D.C.

1. St. Anselm's Abbey, 4501 So. Dakota Ave. NE, Washington, DC 20017
  (202) 269-2300 ✤ Contact: Guestmaster
✓**Single Rooms   Individual Guest Rate: $25.00   ✓Includes 3 Meals Daily**
✓**Reservations Required   ✓Advance Deposit:** None
Guest Rules: Men only. Quiet observed in rooms and chapel. The Abbey extends its hospitality to men who seriously seek a time for quiet reflection and a contemplative environment. Those who desire to visit the many historical sights in the nation's capital should plan such time either before or after their retreat experience.
On Site Attractions/Nearby Points of Interest: The English Tudor-style monastery and its grounds are a restful oasis in urban Washington, D.C. In Washington, D.C. the many historical buildings — Capitol, Supreme Court, White House, Lincoln and Jefferson Memorial; gardens, museums, parks, zoos, theaters, concerts, night life.
Additional Information: No children. No groups.

WASHINGTON

1. Immaculate Retreat House, S 6910 Ben Burr Rd., Spokane, WA 99223
  (509) 448-1224
✓**Single Rooms   ✓Other:** Apartments with kitchenettes available
Individual Guest Rate: $50.00
✓**Includes 3 Meals Daily   ✓Self-Catering Kitchenette**
✓**Reservations Required   ✓Advance Deposit:** $10.00
On Site Attractions/Nearby Points of Interest: Spokane, in eastern Washington, the city of 2 dozen parks, has arboretums, gardens, outdoor recreational activities and spectacular bridges spanning the Spokane River and Falls. At Manito Park are 2000 species of trees, flowers and shrubs, and the Museum of Native American Culture has primitive art and relics from the Western Hemisphere. Free concerts are given during the weekdays in summer and the Gondola Skyride over the Falls gives a bird's-eye view of distant mountains.
Additional Information: No children. Groups welcomed.

2. Still Point, 2333 13th Ave. East, Seattle, WA 98102
  (206) 322-8006 ✤ Contact: Buz Stuart — Registration
✓**Single Rooms   ✓Twin Rooms**
Individual Guest Rate: $40.00   ✓**Includes 3 Meals Daily**
✓**Reservations Required   ✓Advance Deposit:** None
Guest Rules: No smoking in the House. A quiet atmosphere prevails. Still Point is for individuals who wish a peaceful retreat milieu, not a temporary stopover.
On Site Attractions/Nearby Points of Interest: Centrally located in Seattle, the spacious old home is in a quiet park-like residential area. From the House is a picture-postcard view of the snow-capped Cascade Mountains and Lake Washington.

Nearby is a beautifully tended park for strolling, and an arboretum with exotic plants and ferns. Seattle offers: cultural performances at the University, the Japanese Gardens, Pioneer Square, Gold Rush Park, the Henry Art Gallery, the Center for Wooden Boats, where sailboats and rowboats can be rented.
Additional Information: No children or groups.

3. St. Martin's Abbey Guest House
5300 Pacific Ave. S.E., Lacey, WA 98503
(206) 438-4457 ✥ **Contact:** Br. Edmund Ebbers, O.S.B.
✓**Single Rooms** ✓**Twin Rooms**
Individual Guest Rate: $25.00 ✓**Includes 3 Meals Daily**
✓**Reservations Required** ✓**Advance Deposit:** None
Guest Rules: No-smoking facility. Quiet and peaceful atmosphere maintained.
On Site Attractions/Nearby Points of Interest: Attractively located at the south end of Puget Sound, St. Martin's House shares a campus with coeducational St. Martin's College. Lacey, 60 miles south of Seattle, is the gateway to Olympic National Park and an hour from scenic Gray's Harbor on the Pacific coast. The uniquely styled wooden Guest House is surrounded by Douglas fir, cedar, and hemlock trees. 14,400-foot Mt. Ranier is visible from many points, and the Park itself is 70 miles to the east.
Additional Information: No children. Groups welcomed. Provide own director.

4. Convent of St. Helena, 1114 21st Ave. E., Seattle, WA 98112-3513
(206) 325-2830 ✥ **Contact:** Guest Mistress
✓**Twin Rooms** **Individual Guest Rate:** $25.00 or according to means
✓**Includes 3 Meals Daily**
✓**Reservations Required** ✓**Advance Deposit:** None
Guest Rules: Silence in bedrooms from 9:00 p.m. until breakfast. Remake beds with clean linens prior to departure. Maximum length of stay is normally 7 days. Meals served family-style.
On Site Attractions/Nearby Points of Interest: The Convent is located in a quiet residential area in the Capital Hill district of Seattle. Pike Place Market, a Seattle highlight, packs in produce stalls, fishmongers, bakeries, craft bins, and boutiques in a covered 3-block area. A short walk then takes you to the waterfront, the street lined with fancy shops and ethnic restaurants. Nearby is the Maritime Museum and the Water Link, which sells harbor tours to Coast Guard stations and marinas. At Kelly's Landing you can rent canoes and paddle among the houseboats moored in Lake Union.
Additional Information: Guests of all faiths welcomed. Children must be over 12 years of age, able to respect the silence of others and must be adequately supervised. Groups welcomed.

5. The Priory Spirituality Center, 500 College St. NE, Lacey, WA 98516-5338
(206) 438-2595 ✥ **Contact:** Hospitality Coordinator
✓**Single Rooms** ✓**Twin Rooms** **Individual Guest Rate:** $25.00-$45.00
✓**Includes 3 Meals Daily** ✓**Self-Catering Kitchenette**
(Guests may prepare own meals if desired)
✓**Reservations Required** ✓**Advance Deposit:** $10.00
Guest Rules: No smoking or alcohol.
On Site Attractions/Nearby Points of Interest: Lacey is ten minutes from downtown Olympia which is at the southernmost tip of Puget Sound, 60 miles south of Seattle. The Center is in a dense forest setting of tall firs with many wooded trails; an ideal setting for life giving and liberating growth. Olympia, Washington's state

capitol, has created an authentic bamboo-studded Japanese Garden; and in nearby Wolfhaven, a 60 acre refuge for wolves and canines, the public can participate in a Friday and Saturday night "howl-in." The Pacific Ocean is a 45 minute drive west of the Center.
Additional Information: No children. Groups welcomed, and can provide own meals or negotiate for service. Many excellent programs are offered throughout the year.

6. Cloud Mountain Retreat Center, 373 Agren Rd., Castle Rock, WA 98611
 (206) 286-9060 ❖ **Contact:** Northwest Dharma Association
✓**Single Rooms** ✓**Twin Rooms**
✓**Other:** 6 rooms accommodate 3-5 people each
Individual Guest Rate: No charge (work retreat) to $35.00
✓**Includes 3 Meals Daily**
✓**Reservations Required** ✓**Advance Deposit:** Varies with stay
Guest Rules: No pets, alcohol or radios. Earphones OK. No smoking in buildings. Guests asked to bring sleeping bags or bedding and necessary toilet articles.
On Site Attractions/Nearby Points of Interest: Cloud Mountain, a rural Buddhist retreat center near the Cowlitz River, is approximately 2 hours south of Seattle and one hour north of Portland, Oregon. Situated on 5 acres of woodland, the Center has views of snow-capped Mount Ranier and Mt. St. Helens from a nearby country road. On the land are a sauna, small lake, organic garden, greenhouse, fish pond, resident cats, chickens and peacocks. The Center is visually rustic, lighted and heated with propane, but warm and comfortable. Healthy vegetarian meals; tea, fruit snacks available all day.
Additional Information: Children OK; depends on individual basis. Groups welcomed. While the emphasis of the Center focuses on Tibetan, Zen, and Vispassana tradition, all faiths interested in meditation or study are welcome.

WISCONSIN

---

1. St. Benedict's Abbey, Benet Lake, WI 53102
 (414) 396-4311 ❖ **Contact:** Fr. Quentin Koplinka, OSB
✓**Single Rooms** ✓**Twin Rooms**
Individual Guest Rate: $30.00 ✓**Includes 3 Meals Daily**
✓**Reservations Required** ✓**Advance Deposit:** None
Guest Rules: Minimum length of stay: 1 week.
On Site Attractions/Nearby Points of Interest: Benet Lake is close to the midway point between Milwaukee and Chicago along Lake Michigan. In Milwaukee, 45 minutes to the north, there is an abundance of festivals: Summerfest, in late June and early July, a melange of music, arts and crafts, food stands, watershow; the Rainbow Summer gives a series of free lunchtime concerts; the Grand Circus Parade in mid-July. The Milwaukee County Zoo provides a natural setting for native and African wildlife.
Additional Information: No children. Groups cannot be accommodated.

2. Siena Retreat Center, 5635 Erie St., Racine, WI 53402
 (414) 639-4100 ❖ **Contact:** Sr. Grace Smith
✓**Single Rooms** ✓**Twin Rooms**
Individual Guest Rate: $37.00 ✓**Includes 3 Meals Daily**
✓**Reservations Required** ✓**Advance Deposit:** $5.00 per person
Guest Rules: Smoke-free facility.
On Site Attractions/Nearby Points of Interest: Siena Center is a short 30 minute

Lighthouse in Door County, Wisconsin

drive south of Milwaukee's city center and 90 minutes north of Chicago. The Center, located on the shores of Lake Michigan, has spacious grounds for walking and jogging — as well as a gift shop and large and small chapels. The abundant attractions of Milwaukee include professional sporting events, ballet, theatre, and the strikingly beautiful Performing Arts Center. Racine itself ("little Denmark") is noted for its Zoological Gardens, Harbor Park and Reefpoint Marina for boating, picnicking, and fishing contests.

Additional Information: No children, groups welcomed. Emphasis on hospitality.

3. St. Bede Retreat Center
   1190 Priory Rd., P.O. Box 66, Eau Claire, WI 54702-0066
   (715) 834-8642 ❖ Contact: Mary or Sister Michaela Hedican, OSB
✓**Single Rooms** ✓**Twin Rooms** ✓**Other:** Triple rooms
Individual Guest Rate: $30.00-$35.00 ✓**Includes 3 Meals Daily**
✓**Reservations Required** ✓**Advance Deposit:** None
Guest Rules: General respect for individuals and groups using the facility.
On Site Attractions/Nearby Points of Interest: Eau Claire is on the Chippewa River in western Wisconsin, about 60 miles from the Minnesota border. There are wooded trails, numerous parks, the Paul Bunyan Logging Camp Museum. The beauty of the Chippewa Valley is reflected in the exhibits of the Valley Museum and in the many perimeter lakes around Eau Claire.
Additional Information: Children OK with adequate parental supervision. Groups welcomed; registration fee and deposit required.

4. St. Benedict Center, 4200 County Hwy. M, Middleton, WI 53562
   (608) 836-1631 ❖ Contact: Guest Coordinator
✓**Single Rooms** ✓**Twin Rooms**
Individual Guest Rate: $36.00 ✓**Includes 3 Meals Daily**
✓ **No Reservations Required**
Guest Rules: No smoking.
On Site Attractions/Nearby Points of Interest: Situated on 135 acres that include an orchard, woods, pond, and hillsides, the Center is just 15-20 minutes west of

Madison, the state capital. An outdoor swimming pool, hiking trails, and tennis courts are on the premises, which lie close to the recreational boating activities on Lake Mendota. Madison can boast of 135 city parks, four sparkling lakes, an arboretum, art museum, and the performing artists series at the University of Wisconsin. A favorite jogging trail extends by the lake from the Memorial Student Union building to Picnic Point.
Additional Information: Children OK. Groups welcomed.

5. Sinsinawa Mound Center, Sinsinawa, WI 53824
(608) 748-4411 ❖ Contact: Arrangements Office
✓**Single Rooms**   **Individual Guest Rate:** $35.00   ✓**Includes 3 Meals Daily**
✓**Reservations Required**   ✓**Advance Deposit:** $10 individuals; $25 groups
Guest Rules: Brochure sent upon request.
On Site Attractions/Nearby Points of Interest: The Center is set on a geological mound on 450 acres in the rolling hills of southwest Wisconsin. The model farm produces most of the food the Center needs to sustain itself, and emphasizes natural and organic agriculture. The Center is a large complex, with a library, bookshop, lounges, museum, and archival artifacts. There are nature trails, farm tours, and a short distance away are Dubuque, Iowa and Galena, Illinois; also nearby are the waterfront scenes along the Mississippi River.

6. Christine Center for Unitive Planetary Spirituality
RR 1, Box 245, Willard, WI 54493
(715) 267-7507 ❖ Contact: Sr. Johanna Seubert
✓**Single Rooms**   ✓**Twin Rooms**
Individual Guest Rate: $29.00   ✓**Includes 3 Meals Daily**
✓**Reservations Required**   ✓**Advance Deposit:** 1/3 of total amount
On Site Attractions/Nearby Points of Interest: The Center is located near Wausau, almost in the middle of the state, 3½ hours northwest of Milwaukee. The Sandhill School of Natural Healing and the Gaia (Mother Earth) Community are very close by. Tucked between farmland and wilderness area, the region is famous for the production of red granite. Wausau itself lies at the foot of a solid mountain of granite: Rib Mountain, 1940 feet high.
Additional Information: Schedule of seminars sent upon request. Body energetics services are available. Children OK and groups welcomed.

7. Monte Alverno Retreat Center
1000 N. Ballard Rd., Appleton, WI 54911
(414) 733-8526 ❖ Contact: Secretary
✓**Single Rooms**   ✓**Twin Rooms**
Individual Guest Rate: $25.00   ✓**Includes 3 Meals Daily**
✓**Reservations Required**   ✓**Advance Deposit:** $10.00
Guest Rules: Silent and contemplative environment.
On Site Attractions/Nearby Points of Interest: The Center is beautifully located on the Fox River, a short distance from Lake Winnebago. The wooded surroundings are unexcelled for walking, and in spring the white and pink blossoms from the apple and cherry orchards dazzle the eyes. Lush forests and tributaries of the Wolf River frame the picture. Lawrence University, rated as one of the top 10 private liberal arts institutions in the US, contains the Worcester Art Center and Conservatory of Music. Paper making from inception to finished product is shown at the Dard Hunter Paper Museum.
Additional Information: No children. Cannot accommodate retreat groups.

8. Convent of the Holy Nativity
   101 E. Division St., Fond du Lac, WI 54935
   (414) 921-2560 ❖ Contact: Guest Mistress
✓Single Rooms   ✓Twin Rooms
Individual Guest Rate: $20.00 minimum   **✓Includes 3 Meals Daily**
✓Reservations Required   ✓Advance Deposit: None
Guest Rules: Quiet environment. No smoking or alcohol. Various quiet hours observed during the day and after 8:00 p.m.
On Site Attractions/Nearby Points of Interest: Fond du Lac is on the south shore of 215-square-mile Lake Winnebago, and a center of the Anglo-Catholic movement in the Episcopal Church. The city's Cathedral Church of St. Paul is listed in the National Register of Historic Places. Rich in agricultural produce, the region has produced corn, beans, potatoes, squash, onions, beets and cucumbers. The food served is a vegetarian's delight.
Additional Information: No children. Groups welcomed.

9. Lasalle Spiritual Center, 522 Second St., Menasha, WI 54952
   (414) 722-8918 ❖ Contact: Thomas Craig
✓Twin Rooms   ✓Other: Bedrooms for 3
Individual Guest Rate: $10.00   **✓Self-Catering Kitchenette**
✓Reservations Required   ✓Advance Deposit: None
Guest Rules: Spiritual director available if requested.
On Site Attractions/Nearby Points of Interest: The Center is located near a spacious tree-shaded park just 5 minutes from Appleton and about 35 miles south of Green Bay. Situated at the north end of Lake Winnebago, the twin cities of Menasha-Neenah form the focal point of the nation's wood products industry. 1½ hours north is the breathtaking Door Peninsula, forty miles long and encompassing 5 state parks, 8 inland lakes, and 250 miles of shoreline. At Whitefish Dunes State Park are 10 miles of hiking trails in a wildlife preserve; and at Peninsula State Park, 20 miles of shoreline biking paths.
Additional Information: Inquire about children's accommodations. Groups welcomed. Minimal linen charge.

10. Ministry and Life Center, St. Norbert Abbey, De Pere, WI 54115
   (414) 337-4315 ❖ Contact: Bonnie Simonar
✓Single Rooms   ✓Twin Rooms
Individual Guest Rate: $33.00   **✓Includes 3 Meals Daily**
✓Reservations Required   ✓Advance Deposit: $25.00
Guest Rules: Quiet atmosphere respected.
On Site Attractions/Nearby Points of Interest: De Pere is about 120 miles north of Milwaukee, along the west coast of Lake Michigan, 3 miles south of Green Bay. Set among the beautiful 100 acres of courtyard gardens and fields are a tennis court, indoor swimming pool, walking trails, book shop and prayer rooms. The Weidner Center for Performing Arts is at the University of Wisconsin's 700-acre campus in Green Bay. 75 locomotives are on display at the National Railroad Museum, and the Bay Beach and Wildlife Sanctuary offers a natural habitat and water sports recreation on the lakefront.
Additional Information: Young people must be 16 years of age and over. Groups welcomed. Seven meeting rooms.

11. Jesuit Retreat House, 4800 Farhnwald Rd., Oshkosh, WI 54901
   (414) 231-9060 ❖ Contact: Resident House Director
✓Single Rooms   ✓Twin Rooms   ✓Other: Separate guest houses

Individual Guest Rate: $5.00-$10.00   ✓**Self-Catering Kitchenette**
✓**Reservations Required**   ✓**Advance Deposit:** None
Guest Rules: Prepare own food.
On Site Attractions/Nearby Points of Interest: Oshkosh, on the west shore of Lake Winnebago, largest freshwater lake in the state, is 80 miles north of Milwaukee, just south of Appleton. The EAA Air Adventure Museum displays aircraft of every vintage, with a special World War II collection. The Paine Art Center has exhibitions of oriental rugs, sculpture, furniture. Water sports of every kind at Menominee Park on the lakefront. The University of Wisconsin/Oshkosh has many programs open to the community.

WYOMING

---

1. **Thomas the Apostle Center, 45 Road 3 CX-5, Cody, Wyoming**
   (307) 587-6068 ✣ **Contact:** Ann Wafer
✓**Single Rooms**   ✓**Twin Rooms**   ✓**Other:** Two guest houses
Individual Guest Rate: $18.00   ✓**Self-Catering Kitchenette**
✓**Reservations Required**   ✓**Advance Deposit:** 10%
Guest Rules: No smoking in buildings. No pets.
On Site Attractions/Nearby Points of Interest: The Center is located on a high hill, Dinosaur Ridge, overlooking the city of Cody, the Bighorn Basin and the north fork of the Shoshone River. The Center has a library, recreation room, and access to 90 acres of open grounds and trails. Cody serves as the East Gate to Yellowstone National Park; within an hour's drive are Bighorn Lake, the 12,000-foot peaks of the Rockies, the Bear Tooth and Big Horn Mountain Range.
Additional Information: Groups welcomed. No children. Group rate of $15 per person — use of kitchen for small charge, or option for catered meals. Meeting rooms and staff support available.

The Grand Tetons, Wyoming

84

Canada

1. **King's Fold Retreat Centre, Box 758, Cochrane, AB Canada T0L 0W0**
   (403) 932-3174 ❖ Contact: Gwen Nienkirchen
   ✓**Single Rooms** ✓**Twin Rooms**
   Individual Guest Rate: $40.00 US; $72.00 US for couples
   ✓**Includes 3 Meals Daily**
   ✓**Reservations Required** ✓**Advance Deposit:** $45.00 US
   Guest Rules: No smoking indoors. No alcohol. A place for reflection, healing, and growth.
   On Site Attractions/Nearby Points of Interest: Situated on the banks of the Ghost River 15 miles northwest of Calgary in the foothills of the Rockies, King's Fold is a center offering warm hospitality, peaceful surroundings, and qualified resource people. 1½ hours from Banff National Park and the filmmakers' favorite Alpine subject, Lake Louise. Nearby Calgary, with more than its world-famous midsummer Stampede, is proud of its Zoo, the Glenbow Museum, Olympic Park and Devonian Gardens. Worth visiting nearby is the Tyrrell Museum of Paleontology.
   Additional Information: No children. Groups welcomed (minimum of 25 persons).

2. **Martha Retreat Centre, Box 914, Lethbridge, AB Canada T1J 3Z8**
   (403) 328-3422 ❖ Contact: Sister Therese LeBlanc, CSM
   ✓**Single Rooms** **Individual Guest Rate:** $35.00 US ✓**Includes 3 Meals Daily**
   ✓**Reservations Required** ✓**Advance Deposit:** None
   Guest Rules: No smoking in the House. Quiet in bedroom area after 10:00 p.m.
   On Site Attractions/Nearby Points of Interest: Lethbridge is in the far south of the Province of Alberta, about a 2½ hour drive north of Glacier National Park in Montana. The Centre sits on the edge of a viewpoint ravine, where indescribable sunrises and sunsets bathe the landscape. Nearby are the harmonious Japanese Gardens. Waterton Lakes National Park in Alberta and Glacier National Park unite two of the most unspoiled natural wilderness areas on the continent. The parks have all the outdoor recreational activities imaginable, and provide a sanctuary for bighorn sheep, moose, and mountain goats.
   Additional Information: No children. Groups welcomed.

3. **FCJ Christian Life Centre**
   219-19 Ave. S.W., Calgary, AB Canada T2S 0C8
   (403) 228-4215 ❖ Contact: FCJ Christian Life Centre
   ✓**Single Rooms** ✓**Twin Rooms**
   Individual Guest Rate: $36.00 US ✓**Includes 3 Meals Daily**
   ✓**Reservations Required** ✓**Advance Deposit:** None
   Guest Rules: Workshops on socially significant topics throughout the year. Open to all who wish to foster human growth and an active faith.
   On Site Attractions/Nearby Points of Interest: The Centre is a 10-minute walk from downtown Calgary and adjacent to the Lindsay Park Sports Centre. The Elbow River flows through the Centre's grounds, adding to the tranquility of its tree-shaded paths. 5 blocks away is the Calgary Stampede Grounds, where in July there is steer-wrestling, bull riding, chuckwagon racing, and a free pancake breakfast. Also in Calgary: the Devonian Gardens, a 2.5-acre garden with fountains, waterfalls, and 20,000 plants; the Alberta Planetarium; and the Calgary Zoo on St. George's Island.

Additional Information: Children OK. Groups welcomed. Very positive evaluations on the facility.

4. Stillpoint House of Prayer
   10647 81st Ave., Edmonton, AB Canada T6E 1Y1
   (403) 433-1342 ❖ **Contact:** Germaine Walchuk
✓**Single Rooms   Individual Guest Rate:** $37.00 US   ✓**Includes 3 Meals Daily**
✓**Reservations Required   ✓Advance Deposit:** None
Guest Rules: Respect for quiet. Calendar of seminars and events seeks to inform participants of the need for social justice throughout the world.
On Site Attractions/Nearby Points of Interest: Although located in the heart of Edmonton, the House nevertheless harbors a peaceful garden courtyard where one can find peace, rest, and strength. Close by are the University of Alberta's Ring House Art Gallery and the Strathcoma Science Park, where an actual anthropological "dig" retrieves artifacts from 3000 BC. Plays presented at the Citadel Theater are rated at the top of Canada's repertory performances.
Additional Information: No children. Groups welcomed.

5. St. John's Priory, 11717 93rd St., Edmonton, AB Canada T5G 1E2
   (403) 474-7465 ❖ **Contact:** Sister in charge
✓**Single Rooms   ✓Twin Rooms**
Individual Guest Rate: Negotiable   ✓**Includes 3 Meals Daily**
✓**Reservations Required   ✓Advance Deposit:** None
Guest Rules: Brochure sent upon request. Desire to have guests who may need time for renewal, study, special projects, a rethinking of goals, or to be near someone who is hospitalized.
On Site Attractions/Nearby Points of Interest: In Edmonton, the North Saskatchewan River flows through the city, thereby keeping the 17 miles of parks green year round. The Provincial Museum has dinosaur and native craft exhibits, while the Muttart Conservatory with its five glass conical pyramids encloses three different climatic zones to sustain different plant forms. Throughout the year, the city presents folk music festivals, rodeos, Klondike Days and Summerfest.
Additional Information: No children. Groups of up to 25 persons welcomed.

6. Star of the North Retreat Centre
   3 St. Vital Ave., St. Albert, AB Canada T8N 1K1
   (403) 459-5511 ❖ **Contact:** Mary Smith (Administrator)
✓**Single Rooms   Individual Guest Rate:** $45.00 US   ✓**Includes 3 Meals Daily**
✓**Reservations Required   ✓Advance Deposit:** 10%

Peyto Lake, Banff National Park, Alberta, Canada

On Site Attractions/Nearby Points of Interest: The Centre is perched on a hill with a sweeping view of all of historic St. Albert and its environs. On the grounds is a man-made lake circled by walking and bicycle paths. Located on the outskirts of Edmonton, there is easy access to the Edmonton Mall, billed as the world's largest indoor shopping center: 800 retail stores, an ice palace, indoor beach and waterslides, theaters, gardens, and 24 different ethnic restaurants. The Mayfield Inn has dinner theater, and the Ukrainian Museum traces one of the major immigrant group's contribution to Canada.
Additional Information: Children OK. Groups welcomed.

7. Providence Retreat Centre
   3005 119th St., Edmonton, AB Canada T6J 5R5
   (403) 436-7250, Ext. 226 ✤ **Contact:** Reservations Coordinator
✓**Single Rooms** ✓**Twin Rooms**
Individual Guest Rate: $32.00 US ✓**Includes 3 Meals Daily**
✓**Reservations Required** ✓**Advance Deposit:** None
On Site Attractions/Nearby Points of Interest: The Centre is able to provide peace and rest with proximity to accessible transportation and city services. In Edmonton, the Canadian Aviation Hall of Fame honors the heritage of bush pilots who pioneered surveys of Alberta. At Fort Edmonton Park, a reconstructed 1846 fort stands on part of the 178 acres, where a steam locomotive puffs around a farm and "living town" that traces the city's history. The Muttart Conservatory and Devonian Gardens deliver summertime flora and blossoms in mid-winter weather.
Additional Information: Children OK. Groups welcomed.

BRITISH COLUMBIA

1. Mount St. Nicholas Priory
   4655 Westside Rd., Kamloops, BC Canada V2C 1Z3
   (604) 579-9150 ✤ **Contact:** Fr. Ephrem
✓**Single Rooms** ✓**Twin Rooms**
Individual Guest Rate: $49.00 US ✓**Includes 3 Meals Daily**
✓**Reservations Required** ✓**Advance Deposit:** $15.00 US
Guest Rules: Observe community quiet times.
On Site Attractions/Nearby Points of Interest: Kamloops is 4 hours east of Vancouver by auto in the lower end of the Cariboo Mountains on the Fraser Plateau. The Priory is adjacent to lakes, pine forests, parks, and hiking trails. Fishing and boating are in the immediate vicinity on the North Thompson River that flows through Kamloops.
Additional Information: Children may be accommodated (negotiable). Day groups of up to 15 and overnight groups of up to 6 persons welcomed.

2. Queenswood, 2494 Arbutus Rd., Victoria, BC Canada V8N 1V8
   (604) 477-3822 ✤ **Contact:** Sandra or Sr. Christopher Marie
✓**Single Rooms** ✓**Twin Rooms** ✓**Other:** Rollaways available
Individual Guest Rate: $36.00 US; $23.00 US for room only
✓**Includes 3 Meals Daily**
✓**Reservations Required** ✓**Advance Deposit:** None
Guest Rules: No-smoking facility. Ecumenical, and a peaceful atmosphere prevails.
On Site Attractions/Nearby Points of Interest: The Centre is situated in a wooded area a short walking distance from Cadboro Bay beach and village, close to the

University of Victoria. Guests have access to a 7,000-volume library, an indoor heated swimming pool, and quiet trails through the pines. Victoria is a walker's city, but horse-drawn carriages and double-decker buses can show you the majestic Empress Hotel, the Crystal Gardens Aviary, the Royal London Wax Museum and 5,000 marine specimens in the Pacific Undersea Garden. Take a look at turn-of-the-century Market Square and quaint Fan Tan Alley in Chinatown for a fascinating contrast of cultures.
Additional Information: No children. Groups welcomed.

3. **Marywood, RR 2 Site 13-68, Cranbrook, BC Canada V1C 4H3**
   (604) 426-8117 ❖ **Contact:** Director
✓**Single Rooms   Individual Guest Rate:** $32.00 US   ✓**Includes 3 Meals Daily**
✓**Reservations Required   ✓Advance Deposit:** None
Guest Rules: Respect the quiet of the home. Staff willing to assist in every way possible.
On Site Attractions/Nearby Points of Interest: Cranbrook is lcoated in the far southeastern corner of British Columbia, about 2½ hours northwest of Glacier National Park and Waterton-Glacier International Peace Park. The Home provides a spectacular view of the Rockies, and the nearby woods and mountains beckon one to hike the numerous forest trails.
Additional Information: No children. Small groups welcomed.

4. **Salt Spring Center, Box 1133, Ganges, BC Canada V0S 1E0**
   (604) 537-2326 ❖ **Contact:** Pamela Thornley
✓**Single Rooms   ✓Twin Rooms**
Individual Guest Rate: $60.00 US   ✓**Includes 2 Meals Daily**
✓**Reservations Required   ✓Advance Deposit:** None
Guest Rules: Vegetarian meals, quiet after 11:00 p.m. Minimum stay, 2 nights.
On Site Attractions/Nearby Points of Interest: The Center is located on Salt Spring Island, midway between and a short ferry ride from either Vancouver or Victoria, BC. The Center rests in the heart of 69 acres of cedar forest, wild meadows, organic gardens and apple orchards. The community supports the creative arts and health sciences (saunas, herbal baths) within the framework of spiritual growth and discovery. Various rejuvenation programs are presented throughout the year.
Additional Information: No children, groups welcomed.

5. **Other Dimensions Center, Box 2269, Salmon Arm, BC Canada V1E 4R3**
   (604) 832-8483 ❖ **Contact:** Marlene or Bonnie
Rooms: Dormitory-style in separate rooms
Individual Guest Rate: $16.00 US   ✓**Self-Catering Kitchenette**
✓**Reservations Required   ✓Advance Deposit:** Call in
Guest Rules: No smoking or alcohol. Quiet atmosphere. Those staying overnight should bring sleeping bags and toiletries.
On Site Attractions/Nearby Points of Interest: Salmon Arm is 65 miles east of Kamloops, near the Trans-Canada Highway in the southeast corner of British Columbia. Surrounded by woods, the Center provides a peaceful setting near scenic Shuswap Lake. The facilities include a library, bookstore, sauna, volleyball court, therapy room, and nearby beaches for swimming. Nature walks around bird sanctuaries and McGuire Lake. Programs focus on spiritual, personal, and psychological growth.
Additional Information: No children. Groups doing workshops or conferences welcomed.

MANITOBA

1. **St. Charles Retreat House, 323 St. Charles St., Winnipeg, MB Canada R3K 1T6**
   (204) 885-2260 ❖ Contact: Sr. Rita Hamel
   ✓Single Rooms ✓Twin Rooms
   Individual Guest Rate: $30.00 US ✓Includes 3 Meals Daily
   ✓Reservations Required ✓Advance Deposit: $10.00
   On Site Attractions/Nearby Points of Interest: St. Charles House is a large one story facility in a peaceful area at the far end of the city. Public transportation can take you to the Portage Place (the indoor mall with 120 stores), the Planetarium's Cosmic Theatre, and St. Boniface Cathedral. Winnipeg is proud of its symphony, ballet and opera companies. A variety of adventures are offered on the Prairie Dog Central Steam Train and the dining cruises on the Red and Assiniboine Rivers.
   Additional Information: No children. Groups of 15 or less welcomed.

NEW BRUNSWICK

1. **Villa Madonna Retreat House**
   P.O. Box 2321, St. John, NB Canada E2L 3V6
   (506) 847-5150
   ✓Single Rooms ✓Twin Rooms
   Individual Guest Rate: $35.00 US ✓Includes 3 Meals Daily
   ✓Reservations Required ✓Advance Deposit: None
   On Site Attractions/Nearby Points of Interest: St. John, which has an open harbor year round, is a shipping center for eastern Canada. The New Brunswick Museum displays replicas of two centuries of shipbuilding, and at the Market Slip is a restoration of 18th-century shops. In August, the Festival by the Sea draws more than 1,000 performers from all over Canada. At Old City Market, the stalls show an array of lobster, freshly-caught fish, handicrafts, antiques, gifts, and international foods.
   Additional Information: No children. Groups welcomed.

NOVA SCOTIA

1. **Carmel Centre**
   3208 Mt. Carmel Ave., New Waterford, NS Canada B1H 1T7
   (902) 862-3370/862-2062 ❖ Contact: Sister Sadie Henneberry
   ✓Single Rooms ✓Twin Rooms ✓Other: Suites
   Individual Guest Rate: $27.00 US
   ✓Includes 3 Meals Daily ✓Self-Catering Kitchenette
   ✓Reservations Required ✓Advance Deposit: None
   Guest Rules: Respect for quiet atmosphere.
   On Site Attractions/Nearby Points of Interest: Carmel Centre is located at the far eastern tip of Cape Breton Island in Nova Scotia. Close by are swimming beaches, Cabot Trail National Park, Louisberg National Museum, Brus d'Or Lake and Cape Breton Highlands National Park.
   Additional Information: No children. Groups welcomed.

2. **Society of Our Lady Saint Mary**
   Bethany Place, P.O. Box 762, Digby, NS Canada B0V 1A0
   (902) 245-4841 ❖ Contact: Sister Barbara, S.L.S.M.

✓**Single Rooms**   ✓**Other:** Fully-equipped cottage (Sandy Cove)
Individual Guest Rate: $25.00 US suggested donation
✓**Includes 3 Meals Daily**
✓**Reservations Required**   ✓**Advance Deposit:** None
Guest Rules: Quiet observed from 9:30 p.m. until 9:00 a.m.
On Site Attractions/Nearby Points of Interest: Digby is a town serviced by ferries from St. John, New Brunswick, near the southwestern end of the Nova Scotia peninsula. Its popular location between St. Mary's Bay and the Annapolis Basin provides canoeing, deep sea fishing, whale watching, and swimming in Lake Medway. Also at Digby are the Pines Golf Course and the Upper Clements Theme Park and Bird Sanctuary. At nearby Sandy Point are the scallop draggers, old churches, and sheep farms.
Additional Information: No children. No groups.

3. Spirituality Centre, 150 Bedford Hwy., Halifax, NS Canada B3M 3J5
   (902) 453-3434 ✤ **Contact:** Centre Office
✓**Single Rooms**   **Individual Guest Rate:** $16.00 US *(dining costs extra)*
✓**Reservations Required**   ✓**Advance Deposit:** $16.00 US
Guest Rules: No smoking in buildings. Entrance closes at 11:00 p.m.
On Site Attractions/Nearby Points of Interest: Halifax is the largest city in the maritime provinces. The Centre is located in a setting of natural beauty overlooking Bedford Basin, adjacent to the broad greenbelt campus of Mt. St. Vincent University. Cobblestone streets meander through Historic Properties, a restored city section from the year 1800, replete with boutiques, shops, and restaurants. Sailing tours leave from Privateers Wharf; first rate productions can be seen at Dalhousie University Performing Arts Center.
Additional Information: No children. Groups welcomed. The Centre's programs strive to develop a sensitivity toward those whom the world oppresses, and to right injustices.

ONTARIO

1. Crieff Hills Community, RR 2, Puslinch, ON Canada N0B 2J0
   (519) 824-7898 ✤ **Contact:** Crieff Hills Community
✓**Single Rooms**   ✓**Twin Rooms**
Individual Guest Rate: $20.00 US   ✓**Self-Catering Kitchenette**
✓**Reservations Required**   ✓**Advance Deposit:** $20.00 US
Guest Rules: Smoking restricted in some areas.
On Site Attractions/Nearby Points of Interest: A former country estate with 250 acres of rolling countryside in the heart of Ontario farmland with two modern lodges — this is the picture of Crieff Hills Community. There are hiking and nature trails, tennis courts, cross-country ski paths, and meditation sites all on the premises. Located west of Toronto about 5 miles south of Guelph.
Additional Information: Children OK. Groups welcomed. Meals can be provided for groups of 10-80 people. Small linen charge.

2. Notre Dame Centre, 1921 Snake Rd., Waterdown, ON Canada L0R 2H0
   (416) 689-6646 ✤ **Contact:** Notre Dame Centre
✓**Single Rooms**   ✓**Twin Rooms**
Individual Guest Rate: $43.00 single, $40.00 shared, $48.00 suites (all US)
✓**Includes 3 Meals Daily**   ✓**Self-Catering Kitchenette**
✓**Reservations Required**   ✓**Advance Deposit:** $25.00 US

Guest Rules: Respect for property. Smoking restricted to one room.
On Site Attractions/Nearby Points of Interest: The Centre is situated a few miles north of Hamilton on 52 acres of land near Bruce Trail. In Hamilton one finds the library, campus, cultural arts and theater presentations at McMaster University, which has recently been the recipient of the papers of Bertrand Russell. The Whitehorn Estate, overlooking Hamilton Harbor, shows a classic combination of Georgian-Canadian architecture. A 45-minute drive from Toronto and also 45 minutes from the unique lifestyles of Mennonite country.
Additional Information: Children OK with parental supervision. Groups with their own facilitator welcomed.

3. St. Michael's House, 127 Burgundy Dr., Oakville, ON Canada L6J 6R1
   (416) 844-9511 ❖ **Contact:** Sister Michael
✓**Single Rooms   Individual Guest Rate:** $32.00 US   ✓**Includes 3 Meals Daily**
✓**Reservations Required   ✓Advance Deposit:** 25% of total amount
Guest Rules: No smoking in the House. No pets. Quiet observed from 9:00 p.m. to 8:00 a.m.
On Site Attractions/Nearby Points of Interest: The House is located on lovely, spacious grounds midway between Hamilton and Toronto. Lake Ontario, a short walk from the house, bristles with yachts and motor cruisers. Oakville is an affluent area with stately homes, a bedroom community of the Ford Motor Co. Bronte Creek Provincial Park offers tractor tours, miles of bicycle paths and hiking trails. Just half an hour away, Toronto can provide the visitor with music, art, parks, and sporting events of all types.
Additional Information: No children. Maximum overnight group allowed is 15 persons; 25-30 for day programs. Closed July and August.

4. St. Joseph's Centre of Spirituality
   P.O. Box 155, Station "A", Hamilton, ON Canada L8N 3A2
   (416) 528-0138 ❖ **Contact:** Sr. Barbara Graf, Director
✓**Single Rooms   Individual Guest Rate:** $44.00 US   ✓**Includes 3 Meals Daily**
✓**Reservations Required   ✓Advance Deposit:** $15.00 US
On Site Attractions/Nearby Points of Interest: Hamilton's Royal Botanical Gardens treats one to 2000 acres of plants, flowers and parkland, and serves up snacks at the South Tea House. Hess Village, a central farmers market, is a feast to savor, and a "sugaring-off" festival in March celebrates maple sugar production with a free pancake breakfast. An hour to the south is Niagara Falls.
Additional Information: No children. Groups welcomed.

5. Canterbury Hills
   Fiddlers Green, P.O. Box 81089, Ancaster, ON Canada L9G 4X1
   (416) 648-2712 ❖ **Contact:** Jackie Hayes, Registrar
✓**Single Rooms   ✓Twin Rooms   ✓Other:** 9 log cabins with showers
Individual Guest Rate: $35.00 US *(can vary)*   ✓**Includes 3 Meals Daily**
✓**Reservations Required   ✓Advance Deposit:** None
Guest Rules: No smoking. Restricted use of alcohol.
On Site Attractions/Nearby Points of Interest: Ancaster is located about 12 miles southeast of Hamilton. In Hamilton, historic Dundurn Castle, built in 1835, is now used as a concert hall and children's theater. Dundas Valley and Bruce Trails are scenic hiking areas; nearby is the Cootes Paradise Wildlife Sanctuary, a migratory stopover for many species of waterfowl. Hamilton is the home of the Canadian Football Hall of Fame.

Additional Information: Children 6 years and older OK with adult supervision. Groups welcomed, with staff assistance available.

6. **Queen of Apostles Renewal Centre**
   1617 Blythe Rd., Mississauga, ON Canada L5H 2C3
   (416) 278-5229 ✤ **Contact:** Rev. Sr. J. Smith
   ✓**Single Rooms** ✓**Twin Rooms**
   Individual Guest Rate: $32.00-$40.00 US ✓**Includes 3 Meals Daily**
   ✓**Reservations Required** ✓**Advance Deposit:** None
   On Site Attractions/Nearby Points of Interest: The Centre is located on the southern outskirts of Toronto on 12 beautifully landscaped acres overlooking the Credit River Valley. There is an outdoor swimming pool, lounges, private bedrooms (each with bath), and quiet paths for strolling. In nearby Toronto, one can visit the polyglot Kensington Market, Kew Gardens, Queens Park, or shop along urban Yonge Street, the 5th Avenue of Canada.
   Additional Information: No children. Groups welcomed. Groups should reserve early as 90% of weekends are full.

7. **Holy Family Retreat House, RR 1, Harrow, ON Canada N0R 1G0**
   (519) 726-6545
   ✓**Single Rooms** ✓**Twin Rooms**
   Individual Guest Rate: $32.00 US ✓**Includes 3 Meals Daily**
   ✓**Reservations Required** ✓**Advance Deposit:** None
   Guest Rules: Appreciate guests who wish to relax, enjoy, and restore themselves in a quiet atmosphere. Not to be used as a temporary stopover, however.
   On Site Attractions/Nearby Points of Interest: Harrow is situated by Lake Erie in a country setting about 35 miles south of the Windsor/Detroit area. Nearby is Amherstburg, with the National Historic Park at Fort Malden, and the North American Black Historical Museum. Holiday Beach Provincial Park has picnic and jogging areas and a well-stocked fishing pond.
   Additional Information: No children. Groups welcomed.

8. **Medaille House Retreat Centre, 485 Windermere Rd., London, ON**
   Canada N5X 2T1
   ˊ**(519) 432-9379** ✤ **Contact:** Receptionist
   ✓**Single Rooms** ✓**Twin Rooms**
   Individual Guest Rate: $35.00 US ✓**Includes 3 Meals Daily**
   ✓**Reservations Required** ✓**Advance Deposit:** Depends on stay (50%)
   Guest Rules: No smoking, respect for quiet atmosphere.
   On Site Attractions/Nearby Points of Interest: The university town of London is about midway between Toronto and Detroit, Michigan in the southwest corner of Ontario. The Centre is situated on 13 acres of beautiful groomed grounds located on the north side of the James River. London offers first rate performances at the Grand Theatre, swimming, sailing, paddle-boats at Fanshawe Park, opera, a respected regional art gallery, and recreation at Storybook Gardens.
   Additional Information: No children. Groups welcomed. Nourishing meals; laundry facilities.

9. **Holy Spirit Centre, 88 Fennell Ave. W., Hamilton, ON Canada L9C 1E7**
   (905) 385-1222 ✤ **Contact:** Mrs. Joan Faria
   ✓**Single Rooms** ✓**Twin Rooms**
   Individual Guest Rate: $42.00 US ✓**Includes 3 Meals Daily**
   ✓**Reservations Required** ✓**Advance Deposit:** 15%

Medaille House Retreat Center, Hamilton, Ontario, Canada

Holy Spirit Centre, Hamilton, Ontario, Canada

Guest Rules: Smoke-free environment. Guests must be in by 11:00 p.m. Quiet atmosphere appreciated.

On Site Attractions/Nearby Points of Interest: Hamilton is 40 miles south of Toronto and about 50 miles west of Niagara Falls. The Centre lies on 10 magnificent acres of natural grounds, with two chapels and 44 single bedrooms with adjoining bathrooms. Hamilton is the home of Mohawk College and McMaster University — cultural centerpieces of this city on the shores of Lake Ontario. Sixteen different attractions are found in Hamilton, from African Lion Safariland to 7000 acres of regional conservation areas.

Additional Information: No children. Groups welcomed. Small and large meeting rooms with technical facilities available.

10. **Loyola Retreat House, P.O. Box 245, Guelph, ON Canada N1H 6J9**
    (519) 824-1250, ext. 266 ❖ **Contact:** The Secretary
✓**Single Rooms   Individual Guest Rate:** $28.00 US   ✓**Includes 3 Meals Daily**
✓**Reservations Required   ✓Advance Deposit:** Varies
Guest Rules: Facilities are for directed retreats in an atmosphere of silence.

On Site Attractions/Nearby Points of Interest: Guelph is an hour's drive southwest of Toronto. The House is on the beautiful farmland campus of Ignatius College, and is a center where a retreatant is guided by a personal director through reflection toward judgement and action. An hour to the west is the world-class Shakespearean Theatre Festival at Stratford, along with rare bookshops, tasteful gift stores and an experimental theatre in-the-round.
Additional Information: No children. Groups welcomed. Many programs and workshops available throughout the year.

11. The Wyebridge Centre, 74 Madison Ave., Toronto, ON Canada M5R 2S4
    (416) 924-9070 ❖ **Contact:** June Zelonka
✓**Single Rooms**   ✓**Twin Rooms**
Individual Guest Rate: $40.00 US   ✓**Self-Catering Kitchenette**
✓**Reservations Required**   ✓**Advance Deposit:** Call in
Guest Rules: Minimum stay 2 days.
On Site Attractions/Nearby Points of Interest: The Centre has accommodations in a tastefully restored historic lodge on parklike grounds; in addition, a cottage stands on a sandy beach with excellent swimming in Lake Huron. The Centre features a health spa program, along with meditation, movement and music therapy. Toronto, with a reputation as a dynamic and exciting city, has attractions equal to those in major world capitals.
Additional Information: No children. Groups welcomed. Delicious vegetarian meals served at an extra charge.

12. Loretto Christian Life Centre
    6881 Stanley Ave., Niagara Falls, ON Canada L2G 7B6
    (905) 354-2775 ❖ **Contact:** Sr. Marianna or Sr. Mary Kay
✓**Single Rooms**   ✓**Twin Rooms**
✓**Other:** 6 dorms — 60 beds, separate floors for men/women
Individual Guest Rate: $38.00 US   ✓**Includes 3 Meals Daily**
✓**Reservations Required**   ✓**Advance Deposit:** For groups
Guest Rules: Respect for quiet.
On Site Attractions/Nearby Points of Interest: The Centre, 45 minutes from the Buffalo, NY airport, is located on the Niagara River overlooking Horseshoe Rapids and Niagara Falls. On the spacious grounds are break-out rooms, Chapel, reading lounges, conference room, gymnasium, indoor pool. Along the 35 mile stretch of parks range many attractions: the Aero Cable Car stretching high across the river rapids, the Cave of the Winds tour, Maid of the Mist boat cruise (raincoats provided), the 240´ scenic tunnel, part of the Great Gorge Adventure. "Beside Niagara's sounding deeps,/Dark wooded isles and vine-clad steeps,/Like incense ride the clouds of spray,/Where rainbows shine at close of day . . . ."
Additional Information: No children. Non-denominational. Individuals and groups of all faiths welcomed. The Centre is not to be thought of as a tourist stopover. Retreatants must be educationally or spiritually oriented.

United Kingdom

(telephone country code number: 44)

INTERNATIONAL DIALING INSTRUCTIONS
(Station-to-Station Calls)

Dial in sequence:
1. 011 — the International Access Code.
2. The Country Code.
3. The City Code.
4. The local telephone number.
5. The "#" button — if using a touch-tone phone (this step saves additional time).
6. If you cannot complete your call, dial "00" for assistance in order to obtain proper city code.

Note: After dialing any international call, allow at least 45 seconds for the ringing to begin.

ENGLAND

---

1. Ammerdown Renewal House, Radstock, Bath, England BA3 5SW
(0761) 433709 ✦ **Contact:** Melvyn Matthews, Director
✓**Single Rooms** ✓**Twin Rooms** **Individual Guest Rate:** £35.00 + VAT
✓**Includes 3 Meals Daily** ✓**Self-Catering Kitchenette** *(for refreshments)*
✓**Reservations Required** ✓**Advance Deposit:** None
Guest Rules: The aim of Ammerdown is to promote individual peace within, social peace and reconciliation without through study themes and courses.
On Site Attractions/Nearby Points of Interest: The House is located 8 miles southwest of Bath. Bath, founded in the 1st century A.D. by the Romans, was changed in the 18th century to a well-planned city of beautiful streets and buildings. Nearby is Glastonbury, the acknowledged birthplace of Christianity in England and the seat of Arthurian legend. There are breathtaking views of the Avon Valley from several vantage points in the hills.
Additional Information: No children. Groups accepted. Conference facilities.

2. Launde Abbey, East Norton, England LE7 9XB
(0572) 86254 ✦ **Contact:** The Warden
✓**Single Rooms** ✓**Twin Rooms** **Individual Guest Rate:** Will vary; call in
✓**Reservations Required** ✓**Advance Deposit:** £5.00 per person
Guest Rules: Quiet atmosphere observed where guests are welcome for a rest or retreat.
On Site Attractions/Nearby Points of Interest: East Norton is about 45 miles northeast of Birmingham, 13 miles east of Leicester. Launde Abbey is an Elizabethan manor built on the site of an 1119 A.D. Augustinian priory. The Abbey is surrounded by 50 acres of private gardens, parks and woods. Nearby Leicester has the earliest remains of a Roman town and pleasure baths, the Jewry Wall (site of a former Jewish ghetto), museums and art galleries.
Additional Information: Children OK. Groups welcomed, but must reserve far in advance for weekends.

3. St. Margaret's Convent
St. John's Rd., East Grinstead, England RH19 3LE
(0342) 323497 ✦ **Contact:** Rev. Mother Superior
✓**Single Rooms** ✓**Twin Rooms** ✓**Other:** Silent retreat houses

95

Chapel at Ammerdown, Bath, England

Individual Guest Rate: Free-will donation ✓**Includes 3 Meals Daily**
✓**Reservations Required** ✓**Advance Deposit:** None
Guest Rules: No smoking in the House. Quiet observed after 9:30 p.m. Punctuality for meals. Spiritual resources provided.
On Site Attractions/Nearby Points of Interest: East Grinstead is about 20 miles south of London and close to public transport — a market town lying on rolling green English countryside. Nearby are interesting river scenes, historic towns and villages, the Ashdown forest, and the rebuilt St. Swithin's Church, constructed entirely out of local sandstone.
Additional Information: No children. Small groups welcomed on occasion.

4. Winchester House, Old Alresford Pl., Alresford, England SO24 9DH
    (0962) 732518 ✤ **Contact:** The Warden
✓**Single Rooms** ✓**Twin Rooms**
Individual Guest Rate: £23.00 ✓**Includes 3 Meals Daily**
✓**Reservations Required** ✓**Advance Deposit:** £23.00
Guest Rules: Guests are asked to help at mealtimes, make their own beds on the day of departure with fresh linen provided. A comfortable place "to be on your own."
On Site Attractions/Nearby Points of Interest: The large Georgian house is set in

five acres of gardens. 65 miles southwest of London and nine miles from Winchester. Winchester Cathedral is the largest medieval church in Europe. The remains of William the Conqueror's 11th-century castle and King Arthur's Round Table are displayed here. Nearby is Portsmouth, Britain's chief naval base, with its magnificent harbor, Nelson's flagship, the Victory Museum, City Museum, and Charles Dickens' birthplace.

Additional Information: Children OK. Groups accepted.

5. Castlerigg Manor, Keswick, Cumbria, England CH12 4AR
    07687 72711 ✤ Contact: Bill Duncan
✓Single Rooms ✓Twin Rooms ✓Other: 3- to 6-bed rooms
Individual Guest Rate: £20.00 **✓Includes 3 Meals Daily**

Winchester House, Alresford, England

Castlerigg Manor, Keswick, England

✓**Reservations Required**   ✓**Advance Deposit:** £10.00
Guest Rules: No smoking upstairs. Consideration for others in the house.
On Site Attractions/Nearby Points of Interest: Keswick is located about 100 miles north of Liverpool in the heart of the Lake District, one of England's most beautiful tourist spots. The city is the hikers' springboard for the central and northern lakes of the District. The Druids Circle (c. 2000 BC) and Wordsworth's cottage are 20 minutes away. Tennis, miniature golf, pony trekking, cycle hire, sailing, boating at Derwentwater Lake, are all available in the area.
Additional Information: Children OK. Groups accepted. Must supply own towels. Meeting and conference rooms available.

6. **Burford Priory, Priory Lane, Burford, Oxon, England OX18 4SQ**
   (0993) 823605 ❖ **Contact:** Guest Brother OSB
✓**Single Rooms**   ✓**Twin Rooms**
Individual Guest Rate: Call ahead   ✓**Includes 3 Meals Daily**
✓**Reservations Required**   ✓**Advance Deposit:** Call ahead
Guest Rules: No smoking or radios. Atmosphere of quiet. Silence after 9:00 p.m. Minimum stay two days.
On Site Attractions/Nearby Points of Interest: Burford, 20 miles west of Oxford, is a gem set in the beautiful Cotswold Hills. The Priory occupies an historic building on landscaped grounds with outstanding views of the Cotswolds. The unique Cotswold villages have stores and homes with traditional tile or thick thatch roofs; surrounding them are the ruins of historic Roman settlements. Oxford, the city with 800 years of history and tradition, is half an hour away.
Additional Information: Guest House completely refurbished in 1993. Children OK. Groups accepted.

7. **Alton Abbey, Alton, Hampshire, England GU34 4AP**
   (0420) 62145 ❖ **Contact:** The Guestmaster
✓**Single Rooms**   ✓**Twin Rooms**   **Individual Guest Rate:** £22.50
✓**Includes 3 Meals Daily**   ✓**Self-Catering Kitchenette**
✓**Reservations Required**   ✓**Advance Deposit:** Varies with stay
Guest Rules: Quiet observed after night prayer and ends after Mass the following day.
On Site Attractions/Nearby Points of Interest: Alton is 44 miles southwest of London, next to Chawton Park Manor House and the Jane Austen Museum. One of the most pristine and unspoiled cities of England, Winchester, is half an hour away. The Cathedral there ranks second only to Westminster. Alton Abbey has extensive gardens, woods, and pathways.
Additional Information: Children OK. Groups accepted.

8. **Abbey House, Chilkwell St., Glastonbury, Somerset, England BA6 8OH**
   (0458) 31112 ❖ **Contact:** The Warden
✓**Single Rooms**   ✓**Twin Rooms**
Individual Guest Rate: £22.00   ✓**Includes 3 Meals Daily**
✓**Reservations Required**   ✓**Advance Deposit:** Varies with stay
Guest Rules: Quiet when a silent retreat is in progress. Minimum stay two days.
On Site Attractions/Nearby Points of Interest: Glastonbury is about 23 miles south of Bath and Bristol. The House is a large Victorian mansion that overlooks the original Abbey founded in 601 A.D. The city is the acknowledged birthplace of Christianity in England and the seat of Arthurian myth. It is believed that the cup of the Last Supper (the Holy Grail) is buried here in Chalice Hill. Cycling and walking trails through Somerset countryside circle Wearyall Hill.

Abbey House, Glastonbury, Somerset, England

Additional Information: Children 10 and older OK. Groups welcomed; mini-mum of 16 persons. Guests must provide own towels and soap.

9. The Friars, Maidstone, Aylesford, England ME20 7BX
    (0622) 717272 ✤ **Contact:** The Guestmaster
✓**Single Rooms** ✓**Twin Rooms** ✓**Other:** Family rooms (3-4 beds)
Individual Guest Rate: £21.50 double, £23.50 single   ✓**Includes 3 Meals Daily**
✓**Reservations Required** ✓**Advance Deposit:** £10.00
Guest Rules: Quiet after 11:00 p.m.
On Site Attractions/Nearby Points of Interest: Aylesford is about 40 miles south-east of London. Nearby are the Rochester and Canterbury cathedrals, Leeds Castle, the Chatham Maritime Museum, and the Palaces of the Archbishop at Canterbury. The Maidstone Museum and Bentliff Art Gallery are stopover points on the way to Allyngton Castle, which is surrounded by 13th-century moats. A tea room and book store are on the grounds of The Friars.
Additional Information: Children and groups welcomed. Provide own towels.

10. Belmont Abbey, Belmont, England HR2
    (0432) 277 475 ✤ **Contact:** The Guestmaster
✓**Single Rooms** ✓**Twin Rooms**
Individual Guest Rate: £17.00   ✓**Includes 3 Meals Daily**
✓**Reservations Required** ✓**Advance Deposit:** £7.00 per day
Guest Rules: Relaxed atmosphere, but respect for other guests' quiet time. Maxi-mum stay 9 days.
On Site Attractions/Nearby Points of Interest: Belmont is about 30 miles south of Birmingham in a countryside of exceptional beauty. Belmont, with its own unique historical sites, is within easy access to the cultural centers of Shakespeare's Stratford-on-Avon, Cardiff's National Museum of Wales, and Birmingham's Museum of Sci-

ence and Industry.
Additional Information: Children OK. Groups of up to 100 persons acceptable.

11. The Old Vicarage, Christchurch, Coleford, England GL16 7NS
(0594) 35330 ✤ **Contact:** Rev. John Grover
✓**Single Rooms** ✓**Twin Rooms**
Individual Guest Rate: £17.00 ✓**Includes 3 Meals Daily**
✓**Reservations Required** ✓**Advance Deposit:** Varies
On Site Attractions/Nearby Points of Interest: Coleford is about 40 miles north of Bristol and the scene of one of William the Conqueror's hunting preserves, the Forest of the Dean. A walk through the forest to the River Wye and Symond's Yat Rock reveals one of the most remarkable beauty spots in all of England. Close to Coleford are Monmouth, Tintern and Gloucester. Among the extensive woods and hills, there is trout and salmon fishing in the Wye and Monnow Rivers.
Additional Information: No children. Groups welcome.

12. Diocesan Retreat House, Pleshey, Chelmsford, England CM13 1HA
(0245) 37251 ✤ **Contact:** The Warden
✓**Single Rooms** ✓**Twin Rooms** ✓**Other:** Cottages
Individual Guest Rate: £20.00 ✓**Includes 3 Meals Daily**
✓**Reservations Required** ✓**Advance Deposit:** £10.00
Guest Rules: Quiet observed in main house.
On Site Attractions/Nearby Points of Interest: The House is located about 45 miles north of London and 8 miles northwest of Chelmsford. Chelmsford is divided by two rivers into three parts; on one part is the site of an ancient Norman castle and a 15th-century pub. The Chelmsford and Essex Museums have an excellent collection of birds, butterflies, moths, beetles, fossils and Romano-British weapons. Beautiful gardens, fruit trees, and wandering ducks on the premises.
Additional Information: No children. Groups accepted; minimum of 12 persons.

The Old Vicarage, Christchurch, Coleford, England

13. The Retreat House, 11 Abbey Sq., Chester, England CH1 2HU
    (0244) 321801 ✤ Contact: The Warden
✓Single Rooms ✓Twin Rooms
Individual Guest Rate: £20.00 ✓Includes 3 Meals Daily
✓Reservations Required ✓Advance Deposit: 50%
Guest Rules: Smoking restricted. Respect other's quiet time. Welcome to individuals serious about spiritual renewal.
On Site Attractions/Nearby Points of Interest: Chester is 15 miles south of Liverpool and probably the most picturesque old town in England. Surrounded by Roman walls, the old streets date from the middle ages. Rows of shops border the street on two levels, and the exposed wooden criss-cross patterns add a unique charm to the busy town. The grounds of Chester Castle open up to post-card views of rural scenery.
Additional Information: No children. Groups accepted. Provide own towels.

14. Lamplugh House, Thwing, Driffield, England YO25 0DY
    (0262) 87282 ✤ Contact: Conference Dept.
✓Twin Rooms Individual Guest Rate: Negotiable ✓Includes 3 Meals Daily
✓Reservations Required ✓Advance Deposit: Varies with stay
Guest Rules: No smoking or alcohol. Courses and conferences offered.
On Site Attractions/Nearby Points of Interest: The House is 8 miles north of Driffield. Driffield is itself 34 miles east of York and 12 miles from Skipsea, a seaside resort in the North Yorkshire Moors. York, a city of narrow medieval streets, is surrounded by a 13th-century wall. York Minster is the largest Gothic cathedral in England and famous for its medieval stained glass. Castles, Museum Gardens, the Jarvik Viking Museum, and art galleries are all part of York, one of the historic centers of Western civilization.
Additional Information: Children OK. Groups by prior arrangement.

15. Priory of Our Lady
    Sayers Common, Hassocks, West Sussex, England BN6 9HT
    (0273) 832901 ✤ Contact: The Retreat Secretary
✓Single Rooms ✓Twin Rooms ✓Other: 4-bedded room
Individual Guest Rate: £20.00 ✓Includes 3 Meals Daily
✓Reservations Required ✓Advance Deposit: £15.00 per person
Guest Rules: Prefer more than 1 night stay.
On Site Attractions/Nearby Points of Interest: Hassocks is located 47 miles south of London, 12 miles from Brighton. Brighton is one of the most popular seaside resorts in the British Isles, with a 6 mile frontage on the sea — and at Brunswick Lawns the esplanade continues for another 2 miles. In West Sussex are numerous country lanes for walking, leading to gardens and parks.
Additional Information: Children OK. Groups welcome. Conference rooms available.

16. St. John's Priory Guesthouse
    Victoria Road, Castle Cary, Somerset, England BA7 7DF
    (0963) 50429 ✤ Contact: Guest Mistress
✓Single Rooms ✓Twin Rooms
Individual Guest Rate: £17.00 ✓Includes 3 Meals Daily
✓Reservations Required ✓Advance Deposit: £10.00
Guest Rules: Women only.
On Site Attractions/Nearby Points of Interest: Castle Cary is a small, quiet town between Wells and Glastonbury. Nearby is the mysterious Stonehenge, its 22-foot-

St. John's Priory Guesthouse, Somerset, England

high stones built over hundreds of lifetimes between 2100 and 1500 BC, with no consensus explanation of how they were lifted and put into place. Close by are the historic Roman spas at Bath, and the 13th-century cathedral at Wells, the subterranean caves at Wookey Hole, and the birthplace of Christianity in England and seat of Arthurian myth, Glastonbury.

Additional Information: For reservations, send a self-addressed envelope with deposit. Children OK upon occasion; call ahead. Groups welcomed.

17. Hampton Manor, Stoke Climsland, Callington, England PL178LX
   (0579) 870494 ❖ **Contact:** Mrs. B.A. Ferguson
✓**Single Rooms** ✓**Twin Rooms**
Individual Guest Rate: £25.00 ✓**Includes 3 Meals Daily**
Guest Rules: No smoking indoors. Guests asked to spend two hours a day help-ing in home or garden. Guests are welcome to stay either for a holiday or for a quiet retreat.
On Site Attractions/Nearby Points of Interest: Callington is located on the Devon/Cornwall border, about 30 miles north of Plymouth. Close by are the strange and beautiful 90,000 acres of Dartmoor National Park, where ravens still fly and monkey trees are silhouetted against a foreboding sky. The Manor House is on 2 acres of gardens adjacent to lovely country lanes. The north and south Cornish coasts are alive with resorts, commercial shipping, theater, and art films.
Additional Information: Children OK. Groups welcomed. Groups of only 5 or less for overnight stays; larger groups for daily retreats. Reduced rates for couples and weekly stays. Discounts for children.

18. Oblate Retreat House, 89 Broughton Lane, Crewe, England CW2 8JS
   (0270) 68653 ❖ **Contact:** Father Director O.M.I.
✓**Single Rooms** ✓**Twin Rooms** ✓**Other:** Triple rooms
Individual Guest Rate: £19.00 (£34.00 Fri.-Sun.) ✓**Includes 3 Meals Daily**

Hampton Manor, Callington, England

✓**Reservations Required** ✓**Advance Deposit:** £10.00
On Site Attractions/Nearby Points of Interest: Crewe is about 25 miles south of
Manchester, near to Nantwich, a center of the Cheshire salt industry, and known for
its medicinal brine baths. Just half an hour to the west is Chester, one of the most
picturesque old towns in England. The town walls of 2 miles follow the line of the
Roman walls of 68 A.D. Fashionable shops are tucked away in half-timbered med
ieval houses, and the Chester Summer Music Festival recruits choral and orchestral
groups from all of Britain.
Additional Information: Children OK. Groups welcomed. Large gardens, conference and bar facilities, library. Overnight accommodations for 40 people.

19. Sacred Passion Convent, Lower Rd., Effingham, England KT24 5JP
   (0372) 457091 ❖ **Contact:** The Guest Sister
✓**Single Rooms** **Individual Guest Rate:** Free-will donation
✓**Includes 3 Meals Daily** ✓**Self-Catering Kitchenette** *(breakfast and tea time)*
✓**Reservations Required** ✓**Advance Deposit:** None
Guest Rules: Prompt attendance and quiet at mealtimes are appreciated.
On Site Attractions/Nearby Points of Interest: Effingham is southwest of London.
Enroute, one travels through the cities of Kingston-on-Thames, where Anglo-Saxon
kings had a riverside palace; and Esher, Cardinal Wolsey's palace. London is easily
accessible (20 miles), and in nearby Wisley are 250 acres of the Royal Horticultural
Society, with exotic plants from around the world. Sutton Place, a fine Tudor man-
sion built in 1532, belongs to the estate of American J. Paul Getty.
Additional Information: No children. No groups.

20. Trelowarren Fellowship, Mawgan, Helston, England TR12 6AD
   (0326) 22366 ❖ **Contact:** Warden
✓**Single Rooms** ✓**Twin Rooms**

103

Individual Guest Rate: £18.00 ✓**Includes 3 Meals Daily**
✓**Reservations Required** ✓**Advance Deposit:** £5.00 per day
Guest Rules: No smoking. Quiet after 10:30 p.m. An ecumenical center for a time to be "away from it all." Interesting program series throughout the year.
On Site Attractions/Nearby Points of Interest: The Fellowship site is just 4½ miles from Helston, a market town on the southwestern tip of Cornwall. The region of the Lizard Peninsula has some of the most magnificent cliff scenery in Cornwall. Loe Pool is a freshwater lake, separated from the Atlantic Ocean by a sand bar. Nearby, the beautiful Penrose estate shows the patina of the old tin and copper mines, now wrapped in ivy and moss. Trelowarren itself is an ancient manor house in the heart of viewpoint country.
Additional Information: Children OK. Christian groups welcome.

21. Massingham St. Mary
   Little Massingham, Kings Lynn, England PE32 2JU
   (0485) 520245 ❖ **Contact:** Retreat Secretary
✓**Single Rooms** ✓**Twin Rooms**
Individual Guest Rate: £22.00 ✓**Includes 3 Meals Daily**
✓**Reservations Required** ✓**Advance Deposit:** £10 short stay; £20 long stay
Guest Rules: Smoking limited to specific areas. Quiet atmosphere to be observed. For individuals seeking a "place away" for meditation.
On Site Attractions/Nearby Points of Interest: Kings Lynn is a seaport town located about 60 miles northwest of Norwich, in The Wash off of the North Lea. Several handsome buildings adorn the town: the two-gabled Guildhall, the octagonal Red Mount Chapel, the wood carvings in the Custom House. The House itself is a quiet, comfortable country residence of 30 acres near the university town of Cambridge, and Ely, whose cathedral rises from the base like "the sky-tipped peaks of the Alps."
Additional Information: Children OK. Groups welcomed. Provide own towels.

22. St. Philip's Priory, Springhill Rd., Begbroke, Oxford, England OX5 1RX
   (0867) 52149 ❖ **Contact:** The Prior
✓**Single Rooms** ✓**Twin Rooms**
Individual Guest Rate: £18.00 ✓**Includes 3 Meals Daily**
✓**Reservations Required** ✓**Advance Deposit:** None
Guest Rules: Guests join the community at St. Philip's for meals and prayer. Respect for a general atmosphere of quiet.
On Site Attractions/Nearby Points of Interest: Begbroke is 6 miles from Oxford, home of famed Oxford University (founded in the 12th century), and now comprising 31 colleges. Walking tours of Oxford take in the Sheldonian Theatre (Wren, 1667), the Bodleian Library (2.5 million volumes), and the Ashmolean Museum (oldest in the country). In nearby Woodstock, the magnificent park and mansion of Blenheim Palace, birthplace of Winston Churchill. 40 minutes to Shakespeare's Stratford-on-Avon.
Additional Information: No children. Small groups welcomed.

23. St. Katherine Foundation, 2 Butcher Row, London, England E14 8DS
   071-790 3450 ❖ **Contact:** Bookings Secretary
✓**Single Rooms** ✓**Twin Rooms**
Individual Guest Rate: £18.00 ✓**Includes 3 Meals Daily**
✓**Reservations Required** ✓**Advance Deposit:** Varies with stay
On Site Attractions/Nearby Points of Interest: St. Katherine's is just minutes

outside of central London. London has something for everyone: Westminster Abbey, the burial place of the great figures of Western civilization; Buckingham Palace, residence of British sovereigns; the Houses of Parliament; the British Museum, with its unrivalled collection of ancient manuscripts; the Tate Gallery, containing the national collection of British art from the 17th century; Hyde Park — 350 acres of grass, lake, gardens . . . the list goes on, but in addition, London offers a rich melange of theater, music, dance, an excellent variety of entertainment and dining.
Additional Information: No children. Groups welcomed.

24. Maryvale Pastoral Centre
   Snowdenham Lane, Bramley, Surrey, England GU5 0DB
   (0483) 892765 ❖ **Contact:** Jean Tugwell, Secretary
✓**Single Rooms** ✓**Twin Rooms** **Individual Guest Rate:** £24.00
✓**Includes 3 Meals Daily** ✓**Self-Catering Kitchenette**
✓**Reservations Required** ✓**Advance Deposit:** Varies with length of stay
Guest Rules: Smoking only in specified areas. Considerate use of property and respectful toward others' needs.
On Site Attractions/Nearby Points of Interest: The Centre, located 30 miles southwest of London, is a large structure on acres of gardens and lawns, adjoining a lake with waterfalls cascading down into the valley. On the River Wey is Guildford, just 3 miles away in the midst of the scenic walking trails of Surrey Valley. Between the ruins of a Norman castle and the Cathedral on Stag Hill are the interesting inns of literary fame: the Crown, the White Hart, and the Lion.
Additional Information: Children OK. Groups welcomed.

25. The Abbey, Sutton Courtenay, Abingdon, England OX14 4AF
   (0235) 847401 ❖ **Contact:** The Warden
✓**Single Rooms** ✓**Twin Rooms**
✓**Other:** Dormitory-style (provide own sleeping bag)
Individual Guest Rate: £18.00 and up
✓**Includes 3 Meals Daily** ✓**Self-Catering Kitchenette**
✓**Reservations Required** ✓**Advance Deposit:** None
On Site Attractions/Nearby Points of Interest: The Abbey is located just 7 miles south of Oxford in the historic market town of Abingdon. The Abbey itself was first built in the 13th century and is situated in a quiet rural area on the banks of the Thames River. The old gatehouse still survives and the granary contains an Elizabethan theatre where performances are given every summer. At nearby Oxford, the university town *par excellence*, are the ancient college quadrangles, stone-built walls, the punts poling on the river, the fascinating public houses, restaurants and shops.
Additional Information: Children OK with prior approval. Groups welcomed.

26. St. Julian's Community, Coolham, Horsham
   West Sussex, England RH13 8QL
   0403-741-220 ❖ **Contact:** The Warden
✓**Single Rooms** ✓**Twin Rooms**
Individual Guest Rate: £26.00 ✓**Includes 3 Meals Daily**
✓**Reservations Required** ✓**Advance Deposit:** None
Guest Rules: No smoking in public rooms. No pets.
On Site Attractions/Nearby Points of Interest: Coolham is located 36 miles south of London (via Worthing) and six miles beyond Horsham. St. Julian's has extensive grounds and woodlands, a conservation area, a 5 acre lake and private bird sanctuary. Breakfast is served to guests in their bedrooms, and while there is quiet for the

two main meals, people are free to assemble, talk, and join in with the community as much as they please. The main house is very large, with log fires, and a well-stocked library.
Additional Information: No children. No groups. The community's aim is to provide a quiet space for refreshment and renewal, not serve as a holiday base.

27. St. Augustine's Abbey
St. Augustine's Road, Ramsgate, Kent, England CT11 9PA
(0843) 593045 ✤ Contact: Fr. Stephen Holford, OSB
✓**Single Rooms   Individual Guest Rate:** According to means
✓**Includes 3 Meals Daily**
✓**No Reservations Required   ✓Advance Deposit:** None
Guest Rules: For men only.
On Site Attractions/Nearby Points of Interest: Ramsgate is about 70 miles east of London, between Canterbury and Margate on the Kent coast. The Abbey looks out directly to the Straits of Dover and perches on the West Cliff, close to the Royal Esplanade. The Guest House was the former estate house of the architect Pugin. Canterbury Cathedral is about a 20 minute drive away.
Additional Information: No children, no groups.

28. Burrswood
Burrswood, Groombridge, Tunbridge Wells, Kent, England TN3 9PY
(0892) 863637 or 863818 ✤ Contact: Mrs. J. O'Keefe
✓**Single Rooms   ✓Twin Rooms**
Individual Guest Rate: £40.00 *(discount for stays of 7 days or longer)*
✓**Includes 3 Meals Daily   ✓Reservations Required   ✓Advance Deposit:** £40
On Site Attractions/Nearby Points of Interest: Burrswood is about 30 miles SE of London and 4 miles SW of the spa town of Tunbridge Wells. Set on 290 acres of lovely countryside, the large country mansion has a glorious view of the valley of the River Medway. Breakfast is served in the bedrooms; other meals in the main

Burrswood, Kent, England

dining room. All the time in the world to rest, read, write, walk — swimming in the hydrotherapy pool, a tennis court on the grounds. Extensive footpaths through park-like surroundings.
Additional Information: No children. 40% discount for ordained people in active ministry with their spouses. Can cater to special diets. Interdenominational.

SCOTLAND

1. St. Ninian's Centre
   Comrie Rd., Crieff PH7 4BG, Scotland, United Kingdom
   (0764) 3766 ✤ Contact: The Warden
   ✓Single Rooms ✓Twin Rooms ✓Other: Dormitory accommodations
   Individual Guest Rate: £21.00 **✓Includes 3 Meals Daily**
   ✓Reservations Required ✓Advance Deposit: £5.00
   Guest Rules: Smoking only in the lounge. No alcohol. Doors close at midnight. The modern residential center welcomes all who seek rest and refreshment.
   On Site Attractions/Nearby Points of Interest: The Centre is located about 50 miles northwest of Edinburgh and 16 miles west of Perth. A nearby parkland offers riding, fishing, water sports, tennis and golf. To the north of the crystal glass factories are beautiful nature trails that wind along the river and through heather moors. Tours of Scotland's oldest distillery, pottery factories, fish farm are conducted during the seasons.
   Additional Information: Children welcomed. Groups accepted. Small linen charge. Provide own towels.

2. Gillis College
   115 Whitehouse Loan, Edinburgh EH3 1BB, Scotland, United Kingdom
   031-447-2807 ✤ Contact: Rev. P. Kerr
   ✓Single Rooms ✓Twin Rooms
   Individual Guest Rate: £10.00 *(includes breakfast)*
   ✓Reservations Required ✓Advance Deposit: None
   On Site Attractions/Nearby Points of Interest: Gillis College is just 10 minutes from one of the finest thoroughfares in Europe, Princes Street. On the hill across the lush park ravine stands the stately Edinburgh Castle. The Royal Mile is of historic fascination, with cobblestone alleyways, Holyrood Palace, well-preserved 16th-century houses, St. Giles Cathedral and Parliament House. The International Festival in August features theater, music, mime, opera, revues, and exhibitions. A military tattoo with bagpipes and drum corps performs in the Castle Esplanade.
   Additional Information: Children OK. Individuals and groups can be accommodated during the period when the seminary is not in session (*i.e.,* summer months). Inquire about Easter and Christmas vacation periods.

3. St. Peter's Retreat House
   33 Briar Rd., Glasgow G43 2TU, Scotland, United Kingdom
   041-637-5363 ✤ Contact: Administrator
   ✓Single Rooms ✓Twin Rooms ✓Other: Triple-bed family rooms
   Individual Guest Rate: £20.00 **✓Includes 3 Meals Daily**
   ✓Reservations Required ✓Advance Deposit: None
   Guest Rules: Smoking in designated areas
   On Site Attractions/Nearby Points of Interest: The House is situated on extensive park grounds. Glasgow, Scotland's largest city and third largest in Britain, recently celebrated the honor of being the cultural capital of Europe. Among its treasures: the

40,000-student University population, the art nouveau of Glasgow School of Art, the Museum of Transport, Kibble Palace with statuary and ornamental ponds; Peoples Palace, with artifacts of working class life, Botanic Gardens, and the Barras, called the largest open-air flea market in the world. Add to this theater, music, folk festivals and you begin to scratch the surface.
Additional Information: Children OK. Groups welcomed. Audio visual backup.

4. The Abbey, Fort Augustus PH32 4DBn, Scotland, United Kingdom
    0320-6232 ❖ **Contact:** Abbot or Guestmaster
✓**Single Rooms** ✓**Twin Rooms**
Individual Guest Rate: By arrangement ✓**Includes 3 Meals Daily**
✓**Reservations Required** ✓**Advance Deposit:** None
On Site Attractions/Nearby Points of Interest: Fort Augustus is about 40 miles southwest of Inverness, bordering the Caledonian Canal, and close to Loch Ness, the legendary haunt of the "monster." Nearby are the Urquhart Castle, the moors of Culloden Battlefield, Cawdor Castle of Macbeth fame, numerous distilleries and majestic scenery.
Additional Information: Groups welcomed. No children.

5. Kinharvie House, Dumfries, Scotland, United Kingdom
    (0387) 85433 ❖ **Contact:** Administrator
✓**Single Rooms** ✓**Twin Rooms** ✓**Other:** Family rooms
Individual Guest Rate: £20.00 ✓**Includes 3 Meals Daily**
✓**Reservations Required** ✓**Advance Deposit:** £20.00
Guest Rules: Restricted smoking areas.
On Site Attractions/Nearby Points of Interest: Dumfries is about 80 miles south of Edinburgh, on the river Nith. The area is rife with Robert Burns' literary references, as well as the inn where he drank and the house where he died. This section of southern Scotland is part of the Galloway Forest Park — 240 square miles of valleys, rocky shores, and peaks over 2,000 feet. Nearby is Caerlaverock Castle, the first triangular castle built in the British Isles. Witchcraft documents can be read at the restored windmill museum in Dumfries.
Additional Information: Children OK. Groups accepted.

6. Scottish Churches House
    Dunblane FK15 0AJ, Scotland, United Kingdom
    (0786) 823588 ❖ **Contact:** The Booking Secretary
✓**Single Rooms** ✓**Twin Rooms** **Individual Guest Rate:** £23.50 + 15%
✓**Includes 3 Meals Daily** ✓**Self-Catering Kitchenette**
✓**Reservations Required** ✓**Advance Deposit:** £5.00
Guest Rules: Guests discouraged from bringing alcohol into the House. There is a pub nearby.
On Site Attractions/Nearby Points of Interest: Dunblane is 30 miles northeast of Glasgow and four miles north of Stirling, the gateway to the region of the Trossach Mountains, an area loved by Sir Walter Scott and Queen Victoria. Buses link the Trossachs with the exciting city of Glasgow. Placid Loch Katrine, in the heart of the Trossachs, was the setting for Scott's "The Lady of the Lake." Amidst the breathtaking scenery, historical tours and boat cruises are available. The House itself is a series of beautifully converted cottages.
Additional Information: Children OK. Groups welcome.

7. Bishop's House, Isle of Iona, Argyll PA76 6SJ, Scotland, United Kingdom
    44-06817-306 ❖ **Contact:** The Warden

✓Single Rooms   ✓Twin Rooms
Individual Guest Rate: £26.00   ✓Includes 3 Meals Daily
✓Reservations Required   ✓Advance Deposit: $30.00
Guest Rules: Quiet hours from 11:00 p.m. to 7:00 a.m. No pets.
On Site Attractions/Nearby Points of Interest: The Isle of Iona is off the west coast of Scotland, 70 miles NW of Glasgow as the crow flies, in the county of Argyll. Travel to Iona and hopscotching to the scores of islands in the Argyll is by ferries, which transport both cars and pedestrians. Iona, just 3 miles long and 1½ miles wide, had its monastic beginnings in 563 AD. The island remains as it was: beaches of silver sand, heather-covered hills, rugged cliffs and caves, with seals and otters inhabiting the rocky shoreline. Nearby tours take in the canals, castles, whiskey distilleries, and restored cloisters.
Additional Information: Children OK over 9 years of age. Groups welcomed.

8. Sancta Maria Abbey, Nunraw, Garvald
   Haddington, Scotland, United Kingdom EH41 4LW
   44-062-083-228   ✤   Contact: Guest Master
✓Single Rooms   ✓Twin Rooms
Individual Guest Rate: Free will donation   **✓Includes 3 Meals Daily**
✓Reservations Required   ✓Advance Deposit: None
Guest Rules: Guests check in by 8:30 p.m.
On Site Attractions/Nearby Points of Interest: Haddington is 24 miles east of Edinburgh on the River Tyne. The town has one of the best preserved medieval street plans in the country. Much of nearby Edinburgh can be viewed on a walking tour: stroll up the Royal Mile in Old Town, past Edinburgh Castle to the Palace of Holyroodhouse (hear the cannons thunder the traditional one o'clock hour), then wind back to Princess Street's new town and see the Castle perched high on the cliff. Several different tours show the richness and beauty of the capital city.
Additional Information: Children OK, groups welcomed.

9. Craig Lodge, Dalmally, Argyllshire, Scotland PA 13 1AR
   08382-216   ✤   Contact: Calum Macfarlane
✓Twin Rooms   ✓Other: 1 cottage with 4 twin rooms
Individual Guest Rate: £10.00-£20.00
✓Includes 3 Meals Daily   ✓Self-Catering Kitchenette
✓Reservations Required   ✓Advance Deposit: 10%
On Site Attractions/Nearby Points of Interest: Craig Lodge is located on the west coast of Scotland, 2 hours northwest of Glasgow at the headwaters of Loch Ewe on the Orchy River. Beautiful walking trails wind along the wooded shores of Arve, all within sight of Kilchurn Castle. On a tiny islet off Port Appin is Castle Stalker; nearby are clan burial grounds and Chapel Inchail, dating back to the 13th century. A climb to the summit of Ben Cruachan gives a panoramic view of Ardanaisey Gardens and the sailboats below plying the serpentine waters of Loch Ewe.
Additional Information: Children OK. Retreat groups welcomed.

WALES

1. Ty Mam Duw Monastery
   Upper Ashton Lane, Hawarden CH5 3EN, Wales, United Kingdom
   (0244) 531029   ✤   Contact: Mother Francesca
✓Single Rooms   ✓Twin Rooms   ✓Other: Flat with shower and kitchenette
Individual Guest Rate: Free-will donation   **✓Self-Catering Kitchenette**

✓**Reservations Required** ✓**Advance Deposit:** None
Guest Rules: Guests are asked to be in by 8:30 p.m. Welcome those who seek quiet and reflection; not a holiday house as such.
On Site Attractions/Nearby Points of Interest: Hawarden is a few miles west of Chester, an hour or so south of Liverpool. Nearby, towns of Cheshire and Upton, with their fine timber and plaster houses with checkerboard patterns. The Dee River flows down from the Welsh Mountains, adding to lush rural scenery. A zoo is in Upton, and Hawarden Castle, the home of the longtime Prime Minister William Gladstone, rises above the ruins of an old castle in the park.
Additional Information: Children OK. Cannot accept groups.

2. **Llangasty Retreat House**
   Llangasty, Brecon LD3 7PJ, Wales, United Kingdom
   (0874) 84250 ❖ **Contact:** Sister Rosalie
✓**Single Rooms** ✓**Twin Rooms**
Individual Guest Rate: £16.00 ✓**Includes 3 Meals Daily**
✓**Reservations Required** ✓**Advance Deposit:** £2.00
Guest Rules: Smoking only on the first floor. Individual stays not encouraged during winter months.
On Site Attractions/Nearby Points of Interest: The House is located about 40 miles north of Cardiff and seven miles east of Brecon. Situated on the shores of Llangorse Lake, the solid stone house is surrounded by the beauty of Brecon Beacons National Park of South Wales. Miles from main roads, views from the House gaze at inspirational peaks of the Black Mountains and Brecon Beacons. The Brecon Museum in the Wye Valley contains prehistoric Celtic artifacts and furnishings.
Additional Information: Children OK. Groups accepted. Home-grown fruits and vegetables are served at mealtimes.

3. **St. Deiniol's Library**
   Deeside, Hawarden CH5 3DF, Wales, United Kingdom
   (0244) 532350 ❖ **Contact:** The Booking Secretary
✓**Single Rooms** ✓**Twin Rooms** ✓**Other:** Double-bedded rooms
Individual Guest Rate: £30.00 ✓**Includes 3 Meals Daily**
✓**Reservations Required** ✓**Advance Deposit:** £25/person for week-long stays
Guest Rules: Smoking restricted. Usual minimum stay is 2 nights.
On Site Attractions/Nearby Points of Interest: Hawarden is about 30 miles south of Liverpool, six miles west of Chester, and near to the Vale of Clwyd, one of the loveliest districts in Northern Wales. Swimming, ice skating nearby; croquet on the lawns in summer. Hawarden Castle was the home of Prime Minister William Gladstone, and the library and park are part of his legacy. Upton Zoo nearby is noted for its lions, and boating on the Dee River takes you to Eaton Hall, home of the Duke of Westminster.
Additional Information: Children OK. Groups welcome. £1 linen charge. Extensive technical facilities for groups. On-site laundromat.

Ireland

(telephone country code number: 353)

1. Borrisoleigh Retreat House, Borrisoleigh, Ireland
(0504) 51109 ❖ **Contact:** Sister Emmanuel Casey
✓**Single Rooms** ✓**Twin Rooms** ✓**Other:** Dormitory
Individual Guest Rate: £20.00 IR ✓**Includes 3 Meals Daily**
✓**Reservations Required** ✓**Advance Deposit:** Depends on length of stay
Guest Rules: Unpretentious, but takes pride in hospitality and homespun atmosphere. Women only.
On Site Attractions/Nearby Points of Interest: Borrisoleigh is just a half hour from Tipperary. Nearby is the striking Rock of Cashel, a hill that supports an elaborate complex of medieval buildings; the Brú Boru Cultural Center in Cashel; tours can take you to Cahir Castle, which is built on a rock in the middle of the Suir River, limestone caves and the 30-ft. Tower of Babel stalagmite.
Additional Information: Children OK. Groups welcomed.

2. St. Anthony's Retreat Centre, Dundrean, Burnfoot, Co. Donegal, Ireland
(077) 68370
✓**Single Rooms** ✓**Twin Rooms**
Individual Guest Rate: £18.00 IR ✓**Includes 3 Meals Daily**
✓**Reservations Required** ✓**Advance Deposit:** None
Guest Rules: Reasonable quiet. Simple lifestyle.
On Site Attractions/Nearby Points of Interest: Burnfoot is 4 miles from Derry (British name Londonderry, not popular) with a commanding view of Lough Swilly. The garden of the Centre borders on the frontier of Northern Ireland. Letterkenny, Donegal's largest city, is south of the indescribable coastal scenery of Donegal's four peninsulas, each of which is crossed by narrow roads that poke along the river and up the hillsides.
Additional Information: No children. Groups of up to 6 for overnight stays; larger groups for days.

3. All Hallows Centre, Drumcondra, Dublin 9, Ireland
373-745 ❖ **Contact:** The Secretary
✓**Single Rooms** ✓**Twin Rooms**
Individual Guest Rate: £13.00 IR *(includes breakfast)*
✓**Reservations Required** ✓**Advance Deposit:** None
On Site Attractions/Nearby Points of Interest: The Centre is 10 minutes from downtown Dublin. Dublin's attractions: Trinity College, founded by Queen Elizabeth I; the historic Old Library, which houses the Book of Kells. Fascinating walks of the city conducted by Trinity College students include stops at the National Museum, the National Gallery, Dublin Castle, Kilmainham Jail, a tribute to those who died for Irish independence; the Abbey Theater, which provides music and drama year-round.
Additional Information: Inquire for children. Groups welcome with their own director. Full board available. Ideal for groups on their way to or coming from the airport, or who want quiet surroundings within easy access to Dublin.

4. Dominican Retreat House, Tallaght, Dublin 24, Ireland
515-002 ❖ **Contact:** Rev. Adrian Farrelly O.P.
✓**Single Rooms** ✓**Twin Rooms**
Individual Guest Rate: £18.00 IR ✓**Includes 3 Meals Daily**

✓**Reservations Required** ✓**Advance Deposit:** £10.00 IR
Guest Rules: Quiet atmosphere.
On Site Attractions/Nearby Points of Interest: The House, six miles from Dublin city center, is on acres of extensive green grounds. Dublin Castle, the old and new houses of Parliament, and the Gallery of Modern Art offer a varied aspect of architectural styles. The names of Swift, Wilde, Yeats, Joyce, Beckett, and Shaw are associated with the city's literary tradition. Leading cultural events take place at Dublin's dozen or so theaters, and one can always hear folk music at scores of pubs around town.
Additional Information: Children OK. Groups welcomed.

5. Gort Mhuire Centre, Ballinteer, Dublin 16, Ireland
  984-014 ✤ **Contact:** Yvonne Malone
✓**Single Rooms** ✓**Twin Rooms**
Individual Guest Rate: £18.00 IR ✓**Includes 3 Meals Daily**
✓**Reservations Required** ✓**Advance Deposit:** None
On Site Attractions/Nearby Points of Interest: The Centre is 20 minutes from Dublin city center. On the beautiful grounds are nature trails, tennis courts, and a billiard room in the lounge. Popular day trips are a visual feast, encompassing the rocky headland of Howth at Dublin Bay, the valley of ruins at Glendalough, the Bayne River castle towns, and Ye Olde Abbey Tavern, where traditional music is played every night in the summer.
Additional Information: Children OK. Groups welcomed.

6. Esker Retreat House, Esker, Alhenry, Ireland
  44007 ✤ **Contact:** Fr. Tommy Byrne, Director
✓**Single Rooms** ✓**Twin Rooms**
Individual Guest Rate: £20.00 IR ✓**Includes 3 Meals Daily**
✓**Reservations Required** ✓**Advance Deposit:** 20% of total
Guest Rules: Common courtesy.
On Site Attractions/Nearby Points of Interest: Alhenry is near the west coast of Ireland, just 16 miles east of Galway city and Galway Bay. The House borders nice "wild" grounds, with trails among the trees and over rolling sand hills. The 500-year-old city of Galway has tiny cobblestone streets and lanes, a waterside promenade called the Long Walk on the banks of the Corrib River, and Lynch's Castle, a 15th-century townhouse with carved gargoyles. Nearby is the seaside resort of Salthill, with its amusement park and scores of pubs with nighttime "singalongs."
Additional Information: Children OK with adult supervision. Groups welcomed.

France

(telephone country code number: 33)

1. **Notre-Dame du Cénacle, 23 Rue Deville, 31000 Toulouse, France**
   61.23.15.92 ✤ Contact: Secrétariat
   ✓**Single Rooms**   ✓**Twin Rooms**
   Individual Guest Rate: 130-150 Fr.F.   ✓**Includes 3 Meals Daily**
   ✓**Reservations Required**   ✓**Advance Deposit:** None
   On Site Attractions/Nearby Points of Interest: Toulouse, at the doorstep to the Pyrenees Mountains, is France's fourth-largest city, and as cosmopolitan as any in Europe. This is where the Concorde and Airbus are built, where 40,000 students attend university, where sidewalks and downtown cafes echo with Spanish, German, French and English languages. The city sits astride the Garonne River, and shows off Basilica of St. Sernin, the richest in relics of Romanesque churches. As a music center, Toulouse presents summer concerts in the old courtyards on the banks of the river.
   Additional Information: Children OK with supervision of parents. Groups welcomed. Small linen charge.

2. **Grand Séminaire, 15 rue Eugène-Varlin, Limoges Cedex 87036, France**
   55.30.39.79 ✤ Contact: Soucr Madeleine
   ✓**Single Rooms**   ✓**Twin Rooms**   ✓**Other:** Triple rooms
   Individual Guest Rate: Free-will donation
   ✓**Reservations Required**   ✓**Advance Deposit:** None
   On Site Attractions/Nearby Points of Interest: Directly on the rail and highway route from Paris, Limoges is the porcelain and enamel capital of France. The Municipal Museum has samples of Limoges china from the 12th century to the present and tours of the factories and workshops are conducted throughout the summer. In the region are a wealth of river valleys, quaint villages, prehistoric relics, and lonely castles resting on sheer cliffs.
   Additional Information: Older, supervised children OK. Groups welcomed.

3. **Prieure Notre Dame, Bouchard, Arles 13200, France**
   90.97.00.55 ✤ Contact: Frère Hôtelier
   ✓**Single Rooms**   ✓**Twin Rooms**
   Individual Guest Rate: 130 Fr.F.   ✓**Includes 3 Meals Daily**
   ✓**Reservations Required**   ✓**Advance Deposit:** None
   Guest Rules: Atmosphere of quiet solitude.
   On Site Attractions/Nearby Points of Interest: The Prieure is 5 miles from Arles, once a Roman colony under Julius Caesar. The Roman amphitheater, a stone circle seating 20,000 spectators, is still used for Sunday bullfights, without the slaughter of the bulls. The Reascu Museum of Paintings, beautifully situated on the banks of the Rhône River, exhibits 58 of Picasso's donated paintings. The tree-shaded boulevards, open-air cafes, and street musicians are the sights and sounds of Arles. Tours to Les Baux, Montmajour, St. Rémy leave daily and shouldn't be missed.
   Additional Information: No children. Groups welcomed.

4. **Abbaye St. Michel de Frigolet, Tarascon 13150, France**
   90.95.70.07 ✤ Contact: Mr./Mme. Bernard
   ✓**Single Rooms**   ✓**Twin Rooms**   ✓**Other:** Triple rooms
   Individual Guest Rate: 165 Fr.F. *(135 Fr.F. for one-meal-only)*
   ✓**Includes 3 Meals Daily**

✓Reservations Required   ✓Advance Deposit: Depends on length of stay.
Guest Rules: Punctuality at mealtime. Doors close at 10:00 p.m. in summer, 9:30 p.m. in winter.
On Site Attractions/Nearby Points of Interest: Tarascon is in the heart of Vincent Van Gogh's Provence, the southern paradise of France with its deep-green cypresses and magical hues and lush, verdant countryside. Nearby are Arles, steeped in Roman history; Les Baux, a town built into the side of a cliff overlooking the blazing-red Valley of the Inferno; the thermal springs of Aix; and Avignon, the palace of the Popes. Music and drama festivals add to the excitement of this perfumed region.
Additional Information: Children welcome. Groups welcome with qualified leader. Discount on price for longer stays. Closed from January 15 until the end of February.

5. **Accueil des Frères Carmes, 1 rue Père Jacques, Avon Cedex 77215, France**
   60.72.28.45 ❖ Contact: Accueil des Frère Carmes
✓Single Rooms   ✓Twin Rooms
Individual Guest Rate: 165 Fr.F.   **✓Includes 3 Meals Daily**
✓Reservations Required   ✓Advance Deposit: 120 Fr.F.
Guest Rules: Silence observed in the main chapel. Appreciate joining in meditation with the host community.
On Site Attractions/Nearby Points of Interest: Avon is 10 miles south of Fontainebleau, the palace of a successive generation of French kings. The celebrated 40,000 acres of forest surrounding the palace feature aged oak and beech trees, stag and boar runs, and hunts with hounds and horns. The magnificent Renaissance palace (compared favorably to Versailles) is resplendent with Gobelin tapestries, marble staircases, crystal chandeliers and priceless paintings. Nearby on the shores of the Loing River is the village of Moret, which attracts Parisians seeking bread and wine picnic parks.
Additional Information: No children. Groups welcomed. Small linen charge.

6. **Abbaye Saint Martin, Liguge 86240, France**
   49.55.21.12 ❖ Contact: Père Hotelier
✓Single Rooms   ✓Twin Rooms
✓Other: arrangements for double-bedded rooms in the annex
Individual Guest Rate: Free-will donation *(suggested rate: 110 Fr.F.)*
✓Includes 3 Meals Daily   ✓Self-Catering Kitchenette
✓Reservations Required   ✓Advance Deposit: None
Guest Rules: Respect for the quiet required by others.
On Site Attractions/Nearby Points of Interest: Poitiers, six miles to the north, is one of the most charming small towns of France. Its history, visible in the Romanesque church that still stands, reaches back to the 4th century of St. Jean and to the 12th century of Richard the Lion Heart. From the ramparts of Angouléme, the panorama of the Charente Valley lies hundreds of feet below. Close by is Cognac, the town famous for its brandy from the cellars of Hennessy and Martel. Museums and ceramic stores on site.
Additional Information: Children OK. Groups welcomed.

7. **Villa Sainte Anne, 21 Rue Jules Alain, 72300 Solesmes, France**
   43.95.45.05 ❖ Contact: Souer Hôtelière
✓Single Rooms   ✓Twin Rooms
Individual Guest Rate: 170 Fr.F.   **✓Includes 3 Meals Daily**
✓Reservations Required   ✓Advance Deposit: None

Chateau Chambord, Loire Valley, France

Guest Rules: Meals served at fixed hours. Attendance requested at services.
On Site Attractions/Nearby Points of Interest: The Villa is located 30 miles north of Angers, at the northern end of the Loire Valley. This is the gateway to vineyards, medieval ruins, old chateaux and elegant country mansions. Behind the Angers Gothic chapel is Les Halles, the busy, noisy covered marketplace. Nearby is the sandy lakeside beach at Lac de Maine.
Additional Information: Children OK. No groups.

8. Abbaye St. Marie, S Leger F-89630, France
    86.32.21.23 ❖ **Contact:** Père Hôtelier
✓**Single Rooms**   ✓**Twin Rooms**   ✓**Other:** Dormitory-style accommodations
Individual Guest Rate: Free-will donation   ✓**Includes 3 Meals Daily**
✓**Reservations Required**   ✓**Advance Deposit:** None
Guest Rules: Welcome participation in monastic services. Ideal for those seeking spiritual focus.
On Site Attractions/Nearby Points of Interest: The Abbaye is situated in the heart of a beautiful forest area, about 15 miles north of Sens, and 60 miles southeast of Paris. Sens, for centuries the ecclesiastical center of France, has one of the oldest Gothic cathedrals in the country, and is the repository of gold and silver robes of archbishops and 15th-century tapestries. From April to November, dance and drama festivals are held, attracting name performers from Paris.
Additional Information: Children 16 years and older OK. Groups welcomed. Languages spoken: English, German, French, Italian, Spanish, Swedish. Camping sites available to youth groups.

9. Abbaye Notre-Dame et Saint Pierre, 77515 Faremoutiers, France
   64.04.20.37
✓**Single Rooms** ✓**Twin Rooms** ✓**Other:** Dormitory; also, cots can be added
Individual Guest Rate: Free-will donation ✓**Includes 3 Meals Daily**
✓**Reservations Required** ✓**Advance Deposit:** None
On Site Attractions/Nearby Points of Interest: Faremoutiers is 45 miles east of
Paris, near the Aubetin and Vienne Rivers. Faremoutiers is in the Champagne district of France, where one can drive along Champagne Road and view thousands of
acres of vineyards scattered over a beautiful countryside of hills and valleys. A
plains area contains chalk deposits up to 2000 feet deep left by a prehistoric inland
sea. The soil adds the unique taste to the grapes and storage caves underground keep
the sparkling wine at a constant temperature.
Additional Information: Children 15 and older OK. Groups welcomed. Provide
own towels. Youth groups (ages 15-25) invited; cooking facilities available; bring
sleeping bags if convenient.

10. Monastère de la Visitation
   68 Av. Denfert-Rochereau, Paris 75014, France
   43.27.12.90 ✤ **Contact:** Mère Superieure
✓**Single Rooms**
Individual Guest Rate: 120-130 Fr.F. ✓**Includes 3 Meals Daily**
✓**Reservations Required** ✓**Advance Deposit:** None
Guest Rules: Women only. Welcome those who seek solitude and quiet for meditation. Maximum stay of 8 days.
On Site Attractions/Nearby Points of Interest: The Gothic Nôtre Dame Cathedral, the steel lacing of the Eiffel Tower, the Grande Galerie of the Louvre, concerts
in the Palais des Congress, the excitement of the Champs-Elysées, the student-filled
Left Bank, the Arc de Triomphe from which 12 avenues radiate, the statuary and
obelisk in the spacious Place de la Concorde — this amd more make Paris one of the
most beautiful cities in the world.
Additional Information: No children. Groups welcomed, but no more than 5 at one
time.

11. Prieure Saint-Benoît de Chauveroche
   Lepuix, 90200 Giromagny, France
   84.29.01.57 ✤ **Contact:** Père Hôtelier
✓**Single Rooms** ✓**Twin Rooms**
Individual Guest Rate: 130 Fr.F. ✓**Includes 3 Meals Daily**
✓**Reservations Required** ✓**Advance Deposit:** None
Guest Rules: Respect the quiet of the Benedictine community. Maximum stay of 6
days.
On Site Attractions/Nearby Points of Interest: Giromagny is about 50 miles north-
west of Basle, Switzerland, and 12 miles north of Belfort. The Lion of Belfort, a superb
statue carved by Bartholdi — who also made New York's Statue of Liberty — is 72
feet long, 35 feet high, and placed in a striking pose at the foot of an ancient citadel.
A short distance west of Belfort, in Ronchamp, is one of the most modern and famous chapels of postwar Europe. Resembling a ship, the structure designed by Le
Corbusier has a rolled-back roof and sun-breaker windows.
Additional Information: No children or groups.

12. Le Chatelard, B P 4, Francheville 69340, France
    78.59.2752 ❖ **Contact: Accueil** *(reception desk)*
✓Single Rooms   ✓Twin Rooms
Individual Guest Rate: 160 Fr.F.   ✓Includes 3 Meals Daily
✓Reservations Required   ✓Advance Deposit: 80 Fr.F.
On Site Attractions/Nearby Points of Interest: The Center is a few miles from Lyon, France's second-largest city, and in the Rhône valley with its hundreds of churches, chateaux, abbeys, and magnificent scenery. Le Chatelard is surrounded by over 100 acres of wooded parkland. Lyon is an industrial and commercial center, and has a modern civic complex and a university campus in the suburbs. Nearby are varied sights: old Renaissance mansions, a textile museum, a host of special restaurants and cafés, an aviary with over 400 species of birds, and the walled village of Pérouges.
Additional Information: Children OK. Groups welcomed.

13. St. Joseph-de-Mont-Rouge, 34480 Puimisson, France
    67-37-07-85 ❖ **Contact: Fr. René Granier**
✓Single Rooms   ✓Twin Rooms   ✓Other: Many cabins
Individual Guest Rate: 150-170 Fr.F.   ✓Includes 3 Meals Daily
✓Reservations Required   ✓Advance Deposit: None
Guest Rules: Minimum stay 8-15 days.
On Site Attractions/Nearby Points of Interest: Puimisson is in the center of the southern French wine district, a village south of Montpellier and eight miles west of Béziers. A view to the south is the Mediterranean Sea, to the west the Pyrenées, to the north the Cevennes — all these views converge on the center of Mont-Rouge. The Center has an extensive library, amphitheater, and shaded promenade walkways. Close by is the sandy beach of Narbonne, and in the wild valleys are Romanesque churches, archbishops' palaces, art museums, Roman ruins and wine festivals.
Additional Information: Children OK with supervision. Small linen charge. Ample parking space.

14. Aumônieres Recontre Paris
    3-5 Rue de la Source, 91310 Longpont-sur-Orge, France
    69-01-01-15 ❖ **Contact: Yvonne LePrince**
✓Single Rooms   ✓Twin Rooms   ✓Other: Six residence halls with showers
Individual Guest Rate: 106 Fr.F.
✓Includes 3 Meals Daily   ✓Self-Catering Kitchenette
✓Reservations Required   ✓Advance Deposit: None
On Site Attractions/Nearby Points of Interest: The Center is a half hour south of Paris, 10 miles from Orly Airport, and situated in a vast wooded park. Easy rail/bus access to all the sights of the world's most beautiful city; to the grand boulevard of the Champs Elysées, with its high fashion, elegant shops, cinemas, cafes, to the splendid square of the Place de la Concorde. The world-famous art museums of the Louvre, Cluny, the Cathedral of Nôtre Dame, the Arch of Triumph, and the Sacre Coeur, are all visible from the Eiffel Tower. Near to the Center are the terraced gardens and park of the largest and most magnificent palace ever built, Versailles.

Belgium

(telephone country code number: 32)

1. Monastder Benedictin, Chevetogne (Ciney) 5590, Belgium
   (083) 211763 ❖ **Contact:** P. Hôtelier
✓**Single Rooms** ✓**Twin Rooms** **Individual Guest Rate:** 800 Be.Fr.
✓**Reservations Required** ✓**Advance Deposit:** None
On Site Attractions/Nearby Points of Interest: Ciney is 70 miles southeast of Brussels, near to Dinant and Namur, historic Roman cities in the Meuse Valley and birthplace of Charlemagne's empire. Namur is a city of 17th-century pink brick houses, rich baroque churches, and numerous gardens. Boat trips on the Meuse River offer beautiful scenery and views of the ancient palace fortifications. The Convent of Sisters of Notre Dame houses some of the finest silverwork in the world, created by the famous silversmith Hugo d'Oignies.
Additional Information: Children OK. Groups up to a maximum of 15 welcomed. Small linen charge.

2. Abdij Nazareth, Abdijlaan 9, Brecht 2160, Belgium
   031/313-92-50 ❖ **Contact:** Sr. Haskuyh
✓**Single Rooms** ✓**Twin Rooms**
Individual Guest Rate: 650 Be.Fr. ✓**Includes 3 Meals Daily**
✓**Reservations Required** ✓**Advance Deposit:** None
Guest Rules: Certain hours of quiet observed.
On Site Attractions/Nearby Points of Interest: Brecht is located in pleasant surroundings 15 miles northeast of Antwerp. Antwerp, the fifth largest port in the world, is known for its 500-year tradition of diamond cutting. Tours can be arranged to visit the diamond center and the Maritime Museum, which displays models of East India clipper ships, early steamships, and a diorama of the port's history. Paintings by the great Flemish artist Rubens hang in the city's cathedral, and his home and studio with souvenirs and *objets d'art* are open for visitations.
Additional Information: No children. Groups welcomed.

3. Beguinage of Bruges, Oud-Begijnhof 30, Brugge 8000, Belgium
   050/ 33.00.11 ❖ **Contact:** Mère Prieure
✓**Single Rooms** ✓**Twin Rooms**
Individual Guest Rate: 1,000 Be.Fr. ✓**Includes 3 Meals Daily**
✓**Reservations Required** ✓**Advance Deposit:** None
Guest Rules: Doors close at 6:30 p.m. Quiet time until breakfast.
On Site Attractions/Nearby Points of Interest: Brugge is a city interlaced with canals, hunch-backed bridges, buildings with medieval façades, narrow streets, elegant spires. A view of old Europe by boat along the Napoleon Canal takes you to the nearby town of Damme. In Brugge is the College of Europe (cultural and scientific departments for contemporary Europe), the Groeninge Museum, the fascinating fish market, the octagonal turrets of the Stadhuis; often called "the Venice of the North."
Additional Information: Children OK. Groups of up to 25 persons welcomed. Small linen charge.

4. Abbaye Notre-Dame de Clarefontaine
   Cordemoy-Sur-Semois, Bouillon 6830, Belgium
   061/46.61.59 ❖ **Contact:** Souer Hôtelière
✓**Single Rooms** ✓**Twin Rooms**
Individual Guest Rate: 750 Be.Fr. ✓**Includes 3 Meals Daily**

✓Reservations Required   ✓Advance Deposit: None
Guest Rules: Observe quiet hours. For individuals who desire rest and reflection; not suitable for those who are passing through.
On Site Attractions/Nearby Points of Interest: Bouillon is close to the northern border of France, about 120 miles southeast of Brussels and 70 miles northwest of Luxembourg. The city is a sheer delight for castle lovers, with medieval fortifications still intact, and prisons and gallows hollowed into solid rock. The historic city and castle are situated on a picturesque bend of the Semois River, a strategic vista in the Ardennes Hills. At night the castle is bathed in floodlights, and by day one can view the Semois flowing past houses and fields.
Additional Information: No children. Groups welcomed. Small charge for linens and towels.

5. Stella Matutina, Rue des Fusillés 5, Banneux-Louveigné 4141, Belgium
   041.608329 ❖ **Contact:** Denonne Bernadette
✓Single Rooms   ✓Twin Rooms
Individual Guest Rate: 750 Be.Fr.   **✓Includes 3 Meals Daily**
✓Reservations Required   ✓Advance Deposit: 200 Be.Fr.
On Site Attractions/Nearby Points of Interest: The House is in park-like surroundings with beautiful walkways. Banneux is located 18 miles southeast of Liège, near the northwest border of Luxembourg. The region of Liège is set under the protective hills of the Haute Range in the Meuse Valley. In Liège, the Meuse River sprawls and glides along islands, lagoons, and under shop-filled bridges. Though it's a city of industry and factories, the people and lifestyle make it one of the loveliest cities of Belgium. The river trips show off the esplanade gardens of Avroy Park and the Park of Birds.
Additional Information: Children OK with supervision. Groups welcomed.

6. Abbaye Notre Dame, Rue Val Dieu 227, Aubel 4580, Belgium
   0871687381 ❖ **Contact:** Pére Hotelier
✓Single Rooms   ✓Twin Rooms
Individual Guest Rate: $25.00   **✓Includes 3 Meals Daily**
✓Reservations Required   ✓Advance Deposit: None
Guest Rules: Quiet observed. Guests may provide own linens or the abbey can provide them at a small charge.
On Site Attractions/Nearby Points of Interest: Aubel is located 20 miles NE of Liege, west of Aachen, Germany, and 18 miles north of Verviers. In nearby Liege are lagoons, shop-lined bridges, the Theatre Royal, and majestic St. Paul's Cathedral. The green hills surrounding the Lake of Gileppe paint Verviers with an idyllic beauty.
Additional Information: No children. Groups welcomed.

7. Monastère Notre Dame
   Rue de Monastère 1, Ermeton Sûr Biert 5644, Belgium
   071 / 72.72.04 ❖ **Contact:** Souer Bénédicte
✓Single Rooms   ✓Twin Rooms
✓Other: Larger rooms with 6 beds (self-catering)
Individual Guest Rate: 700 Be.F. *(600 Be.F. for students)*
✓Includes 3 Meals Daily
✓Reservations Required   ✓Advance Deposit: None
Guest Rules: Observe silent times. Maximum stay of 15 days. Guides will be happy to take you to visit nearby cities, castles and abbeys.
On Site Attractions/Nearby Points of Interest: This beautiful monastery is lo-

Monastère Notre Dame, Ermeton Sur Biert, Belgium

cated about 65 miles southeast of Brussels and about 20 miles southwest of Namur. Surrounded by trees and pastureland, the community produces its own farm produce and provides opportunities for participation in serving the community. Namur is located on the Meuse River, which snakes its way between high cliffs. It's a 17th-century city of pink brick houses, Baroque churches, gardens and outdoor theater.

Additional Information: Children OK and groups welcomed. Provide own linens or pay a minimum charge for bed covers.

8. De Karmelitaanses, Schuttersstraat 5-7, Brugge 8000, Belgium
   050 / 34.31.42 ✤ **Contact:** Sister Marie-Theresa Troy
✓**Single Rooms**   **Individual Guest Rate:** 800 Be.F. *(inquire about food service)*
✓**Reservations Required**   ✓**Advance Deposit:** None
Guest Rules: Women only. Guests are welcomed to participate in the liturgy. No planned activities.

On Site Attractions/Nearby Points of Interest: Being in Bruges is stepping back into time, for in this medieval city there is not a street or canal that is not a vision of the past. Strict building regulations have preserved its merchant houses with their gabled frontages and the Italian Renaissance influence found in the Groeninge Museum and the Brangwin Museum. The waters of the Reie River flow through Bruges, and 50 bridges interconnect the winding cobblestone streets.

Additional Information: Generally no children; however, exceptions are possible. No groups.

Netherlands

(telephone country code number: 31)

1. St. Willibrordusabdij, Abdijlaan 1, Doetinchem 7004 jl, Netherlands
   31-0359-0268 ✤ **Contact:** Dom Gerard Helwig OSB
✓**Single Rooms   Individual Guest Rate:** $20.00   ✓**Includes 3 Meals Daily**
✓**Reservations Required   ✓Advance Deposit:** None
Guest Rules: Observe quiet hours. Request attendance at services.
On Site Attractions/Nearby Points of Interest: Doetinchem is a small market
town 20 miles east of Arnhem, about 80 miles south of Amsterdam. The Center is
located in beautiful surroundings. In nearby Otterlo at the Rijksmuseum are 110
works by Van Gogh, hundreds of Delftware porcelain pieces, and sculptures by
Moore, Rodin, and Lipchutz. Two zoos close by give African wildlife a natural
habitat setting. Several magnificent parks are in Arnhem, and an open-air museum
shows farms, windmills, thatched cottages, flower gardens and peaceful lakes.
Additional Information: Children 17 and older OK. No groups.

2. St. Adelbertusabdij, Abdijln 26, Egmund-Binnen 1935 BH, Netherlands
   02206-1415 ✤ **Contact:** Gastenpater
✓**Single Rooms   Individual Guest Rate:** $21.00   ✓**Includes 3 Meals Daily**
✓**Reservations Required   ✓Advance Deposit:** $10.00
Guest Rules: Quiet observed. Men only on individual basis. Men and women for
group attendance (limited to 12 persons).
On Site Attractions/Nearby Points of Interest: The Guest House is located just 5
miles south of Alkmaar and 25 miles northeast of Amsterdam. Alkmaar is world-
famous for its Friday morning cheese market, where scores of trucks unload the
4-14 lb. balls of cheese. Very traditional ceremony during the marketing time — the
bell tower rings, trumpets blow, and horsemen burst out of the clock tower. Nearby
is Bergen, on the edge of sand dunes and beside a forest; an artist's market is on the
square and carillon chimes ring out the hour.
Additional Information: No children. Small groups welcomed.

3. Zusters Benedictinessen
   Herenweg 85, Egmond-Binnen 1935 AH, Netherlands
✓**Single Rooms   ✓Twin Rooms   Individual Guest Rate:** $30.00
✓**Includes 3 Meals Daily   ✓Self-Catering Kitchenette**
✓**Reservations Required   ✓Advance Deposit:** None
Guest Rules: Minimum stay of 5 days. Request presence in the guest quarters by
9:00 p.m. Guests are welcome to celebrate church ceremonies.
On Site Attractions/Nearby Points of Interest: Egmond-Binnen is about 20 miles
northwest of Amsterdam, just minutes from the North Sea. Nearby Limmen is the
center of the tulip, narcissus and hyacinth industry, and features a unique outdoor
tulip museum. Also close by is the windmill village of De Zaanse Schans, featuring
an historic grocery shop, bakery museum, clock museum, and wooden clog workshop. A short drive takes you to the De Reef Bird Sanctuary and the famous Alkmaar
Friday morning cheese market, where hundreds of pounds of cheese are auctioned
off in a traditional ceremony dating back two centuries.
Additional Information: No children. Groups welcomed.

Switzerland

(telephone country code number: 41)

1. Hotel Viktoria, Hasilberg Reuti CH-6086, Switzerland
036/71-11-21
✓**Single Rooms** ✓**Twin Rooms** ✓**Other:** Dormitories and family rooms
Individual Guest Rate: 68-103 Sw.Fr.
✓**Includes 3 Meals Daily** ✓**Self-Catering Kitchenette**
✓**Reservations Required** ✓**Advance Deposit:** 30%
Guest Rules: No alcohol.
On Site Attractions/Nearby Points of Interest: Hasilberg, southeast of Bern near Interlaken, is in the Bernese Oberland, one of the world's most celebrated winter sports areas. Jungfraujoch, close by, is the highest train terminus in Europe (11,400 feet), and the "Inns-above-the-Clouds" the highest restaurant. There is an open-air museum in neighboring Baffenberg and cascading waterfalls in Reichenbach. Cross-country ski trails take in sights of Aletach, Europe's highest glacier, and on clear days one can see the Jura and Vosges Rivers and Black Forest. Summer forest walks throughout the twin lakes area bordering Hasilberg.
Additional Information: Children OK. Groups welcomed, special rates available.

2. Erholungsheim und Famlienhotel Artos
Alpenstrasse 45, Interlaken 3800, Switzerland
036/23-34-34 E Contact: K. Glur
✓**Single Rooms** ✓**Twin Rooms** ✓**Other:** 1 apartment for 5 persons
Individual Guest Rate: 35-65 Sw.Fr. ✓**Includes 3 Meals Daily**
✓**Reservations Required** ✓**Advance Deposit:** 20%
Guest Rules: No smoking in rooms. No alcohol.
On Site Attractions/Nearby Points of Interest: Interlaken, about 65 miles southeast of Bern, is surrounded by a breathtaking panorama of the Alps. The city's 19th-century atmosphere is evident in the tree-lined streets with horse-drawn carriages and the majestic Hotel Victoria. Classical music concerts, modern operetta numbers, and yodeling contests are performed in the huge casino. Mountain excursion trains depart from the city, traversing lakes and hills at 2,000 feet to the Jungfraujoch at 11,400 feet. Sailing and water sports are found at Lake of Thoune and Lake Brienz.
Additional Information: Children OK. Small groups welcomed in the summer, larger groups in the winter.

The Matterhorn, Switzerland

Germany
(telephone country code number: 49)

1. Gästehaus der Nazarethschwestern
Nicodéstraße 1, Dresden, Germany 8053
35210
✓Single Rooms   ✓Twin Rooms
Individual Guest Rate: 45 DM.   ✓Includes 3 Meals Daily
✓Reservations Required   ✓Advance Deposit: None
On Site Attractions/Nearby Points of Interest: The Guest House is located in a suburb of Dresden, a lovely, quiet spot on the River Elbe, 10 to 15 minutes from downtown. Dresden is the capital of Saxony, and its beauty is shown in the National Gallery, the Zwinger Palace, the Cathedral and other outstanding baroque buildings. There are riverboat excursions on the Elbe, and tours to Meisen, famed for its porcelain, and the Moritzburg Castle, former hunting lodge of the Saxon kings.
Additional Information: Children OK with supervision. Groups welcomed.

2. Abtei Frauenwörth im Chiemsee, Frauenchiemsee, Germany D-8211
08054/521 ✣ Contact: Guestmistress
✓Single Rooms   ✓Twin Rooms
Individual Guest Rate: 56 DM.   ✓Includes 3 Meals Daily
✓Reservations Required   ✓Advance Deposit: None
Guest Rules: No smoking. Quiet after 9:30 p.m. Conservative attire.
On Site Attractions/Nearby Points of Interest: Frauenchiemsee and Herrenchiemsee are on the shores of the largest lake in Bavaria, in the heart of the Bavarian Alps. Frauenchiemsee has a 1200-year-old castle and church. Ferrys shuttle visitors to King Ludwig II's extravagant castle on the island of Herrenchiemsee, where on Saturday nights thousands of lighted candles shine while classical chamber music is performed. Nearby is Traunstein, an historic marketplace and health spa, and gateway to the most scenic section of the German Alpine Road.
Additional Information: Children OK. Groups welcomed from January to June and September to December.

3. Benediktinerabtei Ottobeuren
Seb.-Kneipp-Str. 1, 8942 Ottobeuren, Germany
08332/7980 Abbey; 79870 Office ✣ Contact: P. Thomas Greiter
✓Single Rooms   ✓Twin Rooms   ✓Other: Rooms for 3 persons
Individual Guest Rate: 50 DM. single, 44 DM. twin   ✓Includes 3 Meals Daily
✓Reservations Required   ✓Advance Deposit: None
On Site Attractions/Nearby Points of Interest: Ottobeuren is a gateway town to the Alpine Mountains, about 70 miles west of Munich and 5 miles south of Memmingen in the Schwaben region. Situated on a tributary of the Gunz River, Ottobeuren has moonlight concerts during the summer. Within an hour's drive are many beautiful baroque churches, famous Bavarian castles (such as Neuschwanstein), and inspiring views from the Alpine highway. The Abbey itself is one of the finest rococo churches in Europe, with 6 courtyards, 20 halls, and 250 rooms.
Additional Information: Children OK. Groups welcomed.

4. OASE Benediktinerabtei Königsmünster
Postfach 11 61, Klosterberg 10, 5778 Meschede, Germany
0291/2995-211 ✣ Contact: P. Guido Hügen OSB
✓Single Rooms   ✓Twin Rooms

Benediktinerabtai Ottobeuren, Ottobeuren, Germany

Individual Guest Rate: 45 DM. ✓**Includes 3 Meals Daily**
✓**Reservations Required** ✓**Advance Deposit:** None
On Site Attractions/Nearby Points of Interest: The Center is located almost at the midpoint between Essen and Kassel in castled Westphalia. The city is situated on the Ruhr River in a valley of the Rothaar Mountains. Nearby is Dortmund (25 miles northwest), which has the largest congress and sports hall in Europe, a glass-looking structure that holds 230,000 persons. Dortmund is the greatest brewing center in Germany after Munich, and tours of several breweries are available throughout the year. The Saarland provides hiking and skiing areas, as well as water sports on Lakes Hennesee and Mihnesee.
Additional Information: Children OK. Groups welcomed. Discount for youth groups.

5. Landvolkschochschule
   Bischof-Sproll-Straße 9, 7970 Leutkirch, Germany
   07561-82122 ✤ **Contact:** Frau Schwarz/Frau Wunn
✓**Single Rooms** ✓**Twin Rooms**
Individual Guest Rate: $25.00 including breakfast; other meals by arrangement
✓**Reservations Required** ✓**Advance Deposit:** None
Guest Rules: Meals at specific hours.
On Site Attractions/Nearby Points of Interest: Leutkirch is about 95 miles southwest of Munich, 30 miles northwest of Kempten, capital of the Allgäu region. This is the gateway to Lake Constance, the winter sports resort of Isny, the Bregence Forest, the German Alpine Road, and to Three Corners, where Austria, Switzerland and Germany meet at one point. In Kempten, one of the most remarkable sights in Germany is the square which has medieval buildings on all sides — the Kornhaus, St. Lorenz and the extended Residenz.
Additional Information: No children. Groups welcomed.

6. Haus Maria-Immaculata, Mallinkrodt Str. 1, 4790 Paderborn, den, Germany
   05 251/697-154 ✤ **Contact:** Sr. M. Carita Meyer
✓**Single Rooms Individual Guest Rate:** 55 DM ✓**Includes 3 Meals Daily**
✓**Reservations Required** ✓**Advance Deposit:** None
On Site Attractions/Nearby Points of Interest: Paderborn is located about midway between the cities of Dortmund and Hanover in the Teutoberger Forest area of North Rhine Westphalia. The 1,000-year-old city, with its impressive cathedral and imperial palace, is a western gateway to the fairytale highway of the Brothers Grimm, and the city of Hamelin, of Pied Piper fame. To the north are the famous spas: Bad Driburg, Bad Lippspringe, and Höxter, described by some as "the Rome of the North," lies between the wooded heights of Solling and the Weser River.
Additional Information: No children. Groups welcomed.

Sweden

(telephone country code number: 46)

1. **Birgittasystrarna, Burevägen 12, Djursholm S-182-63, Sweden**
   08-7551785 ✤ **Contact:** Birgittasystrarna (Kloster med Gästhem)
   ✓**Single Rooms** ✓**Twin Rooms** ✓**Other:** Annex for 3 persons with kitchen
   Individual Guest Rate: 500 Sw.Kr. ✓**Includes 3 Meals Daily**
   ✓**Reservations Required** ✓**Advance Deposit:** None
   Guest Rules: Quiet observed after 9:30 p.m. No smoking. Minimum length of stay 3 days.
   On Site Attractions/Nearby Points of Interest: The Briggetine Convent, with 14 sisters from different nations, is located just 6 miles from Stockholm city center, and a 5-minute walk to the sea. Golf and tennis are nearby. Stockholm is a city built on 14 islands, a city of bridges, towers, broad boulevards, parks. The Stadshuset (city hall) is reputed to be one of the finest examples of modern architecture in Europe. An open-air museum has 150 dwellings from the 18th and 19th centuries constructed on 75 acres of park. The Royal Palace has 600 rooms and contains the invaluable crown jewels of Europe.
   Additional Information: No children. Small groups welcomed.

Malta

(telephone country code number: 356)

1. **Mount Saint Joseph, Targa Gap, Mosta, Malta**
   411110 ✤ **Contact:** Fr. Godwin Preca SJ
   ✓**Single Rooms** ✓**Twin Rooms**
   Individual Guest Rate: $20.00 ✓**Includes 3 Meals Daily**
   ✓**Reservations Required** ✓**Advance Deposit:** None
   Guest Rules: Respect for others, for property and cleanliness.
   On Site Attractions/Nearby Points of Interest: The island of Malta in the Mediterranean displays a rich and eventful past in its ruins of Neolithic temples and stone megaliths left by prehistoric inhabitants. Malta was ruled by Phoenicians, Carthaginians, and Romans, and their legacy has been left in ornate palaces and museums: the National Museum of Archaeology, Museum of Fine Art, the Government Kraft Museum, to mention a few. Easy access to any point in Malta by public transport, taxi, or boat (20 minutes).
   Additional Information: No children. Groups welcomed.

Australia

(telephone country code number: 61)

1. **Benedictine Abbey, New Norcia, Western Australia 6509, Australia**
   096548018 ❖ Contact: Mrs. Debbie Smith, Guest House Secretary
   ✓**Single Rooms** ✓**Twin Rooms**
   Individual Guest Rate: $40.00 Australian ✓**Includes 3 Meals Daily**
   ✓**Reservations Required** ✓**Advance Deposit:** None
   On Site Attractions/Nearby Points of Interest: New Norcia is 80 miles north of
   Perth on the Great Northern Highway. From the river walks, one can arrive at the
   Abbey, situated on the New Norcia Heritage Trail, which takes one to the monastery
   and the historic buildings of old town. In addition to the city's museum and art
   gallery is a small college, home to more than 200 students.
   Additional Information: No children. Groups welcomed.

2. **Blackfriars Priory**
   P.O. Box 900, Dickson, New South Wales 2602, Australia
   06-2488253 ❖ Contact: Coordinator
   ✓**Single Rooms** ✓**Twin Rooms**
   Individual Guest Rate: $35.00 Australian ✓**Includes 3 Meals Daily**
   ✓**Reservations Required** ✓**Advance Deposit:** $20.00 Australian
   Guest Rules: Quiet atmosphere.
   On Site Attractions/Nearby Points of Interest: Dickson is 4 miles south from the
   center of Canberra, the capital of Australia. In the center of a parkland with an inner
   cloister garden is the Priory, close to two tree-studded nature reserves ideal for
   walking. Public transport is close by, and in 10 minutes one is viewing the capital's
   parks and gardens brimming with fauna and flora. From Telecom Towers on Black
   Mountain are breathtaking views of the entire city and the mountain ranges to the
   south.
   Additional Information: Children OK with supervision. Groups welcomed.

3. **Retreat House, 29 Gloucester Ave., P.O. Box 188, Belair, 5052 Australia**
   08-278-1631 ❖ Contact: Jacqui May
   ✓**Single Rooms** ✓**Twin Rooms**
   Individual Guest Rate: $20.00 Australian *(includes breakfast)*
   ✓**Reservations Required** ✓**Advance Deposit:** None
   Guest Rules: Minimum length of stay — 8 days.
   On Site Attractions/Nearby Points of Interest: This lovely Retreat House with
   ample accommodations is just 15 minutes from the capital city of Adelaide, in South-
   ern Australia. Adelaide, often called "the city of churches," is a veritable Eden, on a
   saucer-like plain between the Mount Lofty Mountains and the Gulf of St. Vincent.
   Surrounding Adelaide are the Barossa Valley vineyards, the orchards of Adelaide
   Hills, and the towering cliffs and lakes bordering the Murray River. Fifteen miles of
   beaches stretch along the area facing the seals at play on Kangaroo Island.
   Additional Information: No children; groups of up to 45 welcomed. Small linen
   charge.

New Zealand

(telephone country code number: 64)

1. Sisters of the Sacred Name
   181 Barbados Street, Christchurch, New Zealand
   (03) 3668-245 ❖ **Contact:** Reverend Mother
✓Single Rooms   ✓Twin Rooms
Individual Guest Rate: $20.00 NZ   **✓Includes 3 Meals Daily**
✓Reservations Required   ✓Advance Deposit: $10.00 NZ
Guest Rules: Quiet observed at stated times.
On Site Attractions/Nearby Points of Interest: The lovely landscaped Center has modern, comfortable accommodations with lounges, meeting and dining rooms, all within easy walking distance of the city center. Christchurch is a compact walking city. Along the way you see punts drifting on the Avon River, children playing cricket, groups entering the very English Botanic Gardens. Christchurch Cathedral (Anglican and Roman Catholic), artisans at the Galleria, Victoria Lake near the Tea Kiosk in North Hagley Park add to the beauty of this South Island capital.
Additional Information: Children OK with supervision. Groups welcomed, ample facilities for seminars and conferences. Group prices are negotiable.

2. Frederic Wallis House, 12 Military Rd., Lower Hutt, New Zealand
   (04) 5676876 ❖ **Contact:** Registrar
Individual Guest Rate: $45.00 NZ   **✓Includes 3 Meals Daily**
✓Reservations Required   ✓Advance Deposit: $20.00 NZ
Guest Rules: No smoking in building.
On Site Attractions/Nearby Points of Interest: The Wallis House is situated at the end of a tree-lined lane in a spacious garden setting of shade foliage and flowers. The House is close to public bus service which can take you to the Dowse Art Museum, Huia Pool, and the Queensgate Shopping Center. Tennis, golf, and squash are within easy walking distance. Nearby Wellington has cable cars, a maritime museum, parliament buildings, ballet and a symphony orchestra.
Additional Information: No children. Groups welcomed. Ecumenical, and operated by the Pilgrim Community.

Frederic Wallis House, Lower Hutt, New Zealand

Japan

(telephone country code number: 81)

Temple Lodgings in Kyoto, Japan

Kyoto, once Japan's capital city, was founded 1,200 years ago. Its long history under feudal lords and Buddhist priests, at war and at peace, is now the sixth largest city in Japan.

An excursion around Kyoto shows eleven centuries of history — 1600 temples and hundreds of shrines and gardens — yet a modern industrialized city with an efficient subway and bus network that covers the entire city.

The eastern section of Kyoto is a treasure house of Japanese culture. The exquisite blending of Chinese and Japanese architectural carvings in the 15th-century Gunkakiji Temple is across a canal from a quiet villa and tea house at Hakusasonso Garden. The cherry blossom walk along the Path of Philosophy leads to the Momura Art Museum, with a vast collection of scrolls, calligraphy, lacquerware, ceramics, dolls, and antiques.

In the western section is the Uzumasa Eigamura Movie Village, the "Hollywood of Japan" with its stage sets of traditional Japanese scenes. Nearby is Daitakiji Temple, not one but a complex of 24 temples.

The central business and geisha district is also the site of the restored Imperial Palace, home of past emperors. Throughout Nijojo Castle is "bird walk floor," a squeaky warning system to guard emperors against would-be assassins.

In the north a cable car ride takes you to Mt. Hiei. Here, close to the cedar trees surrounding Enryakiji Temple, is an observatory with a panoramic view of the mountains and Lake Biwa.

Information

Those wishing to stay at the temples listed below should apply in writing as far in advance as possible, listing names, nationality, ages, and approximate dates. Tentative reservations may be made by phone, but a letter should be sent requesting confirmation (include return postage fee).

Recent exchange rates give 120-130 yen to the dollar. Using those figures, a typical temple stay with breakfast at ¥4,000 would run approximately $32.00 in U.S. funds. A less-expensive temple hostel offering lodging and two meals for ¥3,200 would run about $26.00.

Buses depart from the bus terminal, which is across the street from the main exit of the Japanese National Railroad Station.

MYORENJI TEMPLE　妙運寺
Omiya Higashi-iru, Teranouchi　上京区寺の内大宮
Kamigyo-ku, Kyoto
(075) 451-3527 ❖ ¥2,500 without meals; ¥3,000 with breakfast
Take Bus #9 to "Horikawa Teranouchi" bus stop. A beautiful Japanese garden is attached to the temple compound. No bath at the facility, but a public bath is available in the neighborhood of the temple.

MYOKENJI TEMPLE　妙顕寺
Horikawa Higashi-iru, Teranouchi　上京区寺の内通り堀川東入ル
Kamigyo-ku, Kyoto
(075) 414-0808 or (075) 431-6828 ❖ ¥3,500 with breakfast

Take Bus #9 to "Teranouchi" bus stop (a 25-minute ride from Kyoto Station). A beautiful garden.

HIDEN-IN TEMPLE 悲田院
Sennyuji Yamauchicho
Higashiyama-ku, Kyoto 東山区泉涌寺山内町35
(075) 561-8781 ❖ ¥4,000 with breakfast
Take Bus #6 to "Sennyuji-michi" bus stop; the Temple is a 10-minute walk from the stop. In the neighborhood of the Temple, Tofukuji Temple is a 5-minute walk and Sanjusangendo Temple is a 20-minute walk.

DAISHIN-IN OF MYOSHINJI TEMPLE 妙心寺内 大心院
(in the precincts of Myoshinji Temple)
Myoshinji-nai, Hanazono
Ukyo-ku, Kyoto 右京区花園妙心寺内
(075) 461-5714 ❖ ¥3,800 with breakfast
Take Bus #26 to "Myoshinji Kita-mon" (North Gate of the Temple) bus top. Myoshinji Temple is the Great Head Temple of the Rinzaishu Myoshinjiha sect. It was founded by Muso Daishi in 1337. There is a beautiful garden attached to the Daishin-in.

ENRYAKUJI KAIKAN ON MT. HIEI 延暦寺会館.比叡山西
Sakamoto, Otsu City, Shiga Pref.
(adjacent to Kyoto) 滋賀県大津市阪本
(0775) 78-0047 ❖ ¥8,000 with two meals
Mt. Hiei is situated in the northeast part of the city, and the Enryakuji Temple is on its summit. The Enryakuji Kaikan is an accommodation facility belonging to the

temple. The Enryakuji Temple is the Grand Head Temple of the Tendai sect. It was founded by Saicho (Dengyo Daishi) in 788. The present building of Kompon-chudo Hall is designated as a National Treasure.

Take Bus #51 from the front of Kyoto Central Post Office (near to JNR Kyoto Station) to the "Enryakuji" bus stop (about 70 minutes and ¥650 one-way). The bus runs very infrequently, most often in the morning.

From Yase-Yuen (a gateway to Mt. Hiei), take the cable car to the halfway point on the mountain, and transfer to the ropeway to the summit (about 15-20 minutes in all).

INARI-TAISHA SANSHU-DEN　稲荷大社参集殿
OF FUSHIMI INARI TAISHA SHRINE
Yabuuchicho, Fukukasa　伏見区深草薮内町68
Fushimi-ku, Kyoto
(075) 641-7331 ❖ ¥2,700-¥3,700 without meals
(if requested, meals can be served)
Take Bus #56 or #83 to "Inari Taisha-me" bus stop (about 20 minutes). The building is of modern construction.

OHARA NENBUTSUJI KAIKAN　大原念仏寺会館
(across from Sanzen-in Temple, at Ohara)　左京区大原来迎院町270
Raigoincho, Ohara, Sakyo-ku, Kyoto
(075) 744-2540 ❖ ¥3,700 with breakfast; ¥3,000 without meals
Take Bus #1 to "Ohara" bus stop (about 1 hour). Many foreigners stay here. The lodging is located in a rural area.

Temple Hostels

There are many temple youth hostels throughout Japan. Contrary to the name, all ages are welcomed. At these temples, visitors can stay overnight for 1900-2000 yen. Breakfast is available for 400 yen, and supper for 700 yen.

For the lowest rates, one should possess an International Youth Hostel identity card. For prices and information, call (800) 777-0112, (213) 208-3551, or (212) 986-9470. It is possible to buy a guest pass at the temple hostel for a short stay. For more information on Japanese temple youth hostels, call or write the Japan National Tourist Organization, 624 So. Grand Ave., 1 Wilshire Bldg. #1611, Los Angeles, CA 90017; telephone (213) 623-1952.

Listed below are the numbers of temple youth hostels open to all ages in the following cities:

Aomori. 1	Osaka 3	Yamaguchi. 1
Niigata 4	Hyogo. 10	Tokushima 2
Toyama. 2	Nara 2	Kochi 5
Gifu. 2	Wakayama 2	Mie 4
Shizokua. 2	Tottori. 1	Nagasaki. 1
Kyoto 1	Okayama. 2	Oita. 1

Appendix A
Map Locations

Map numbers correspond to listing numbers.

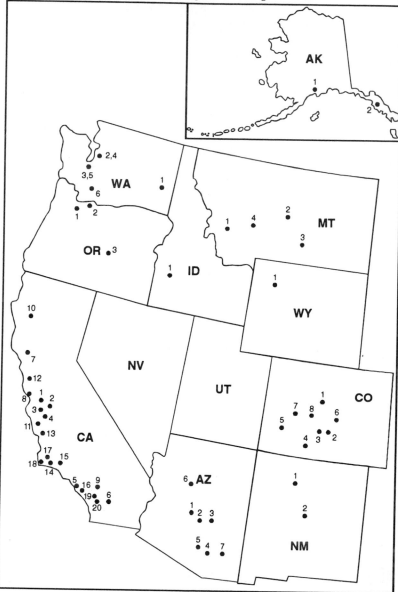

Western United States

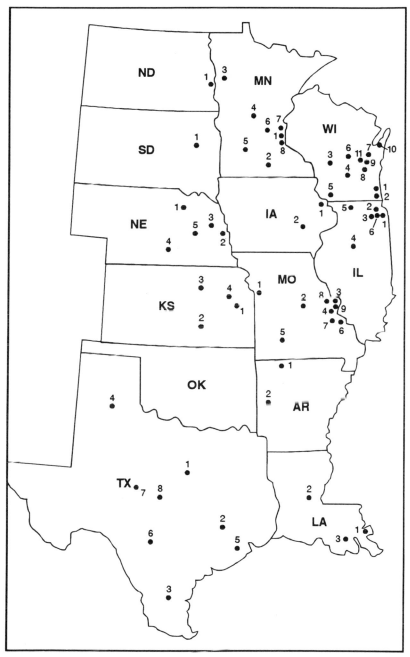

Central United States

133

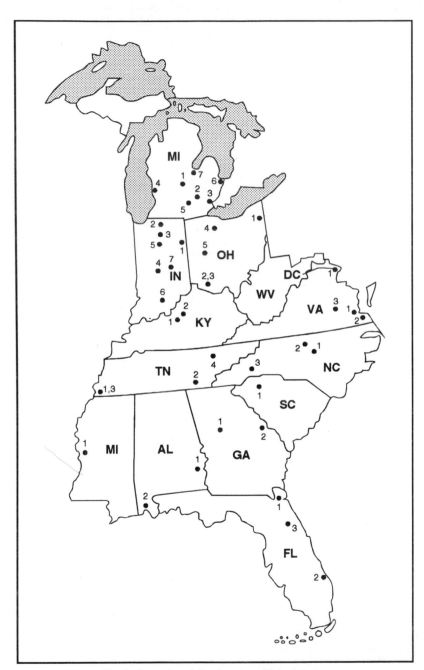

North Central and Southeastern United States

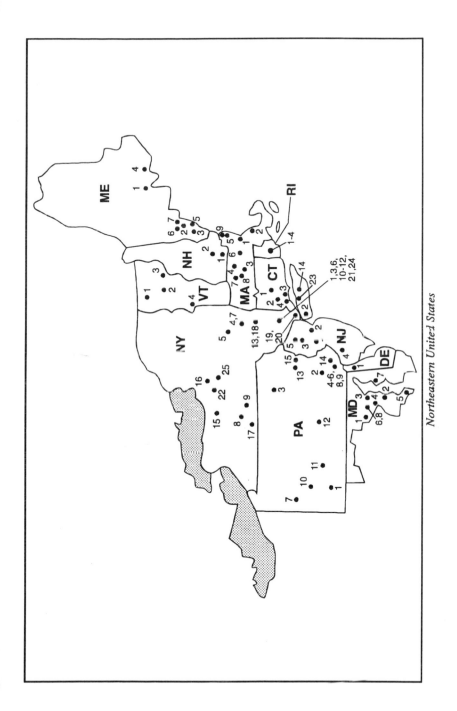

Northeastern United States

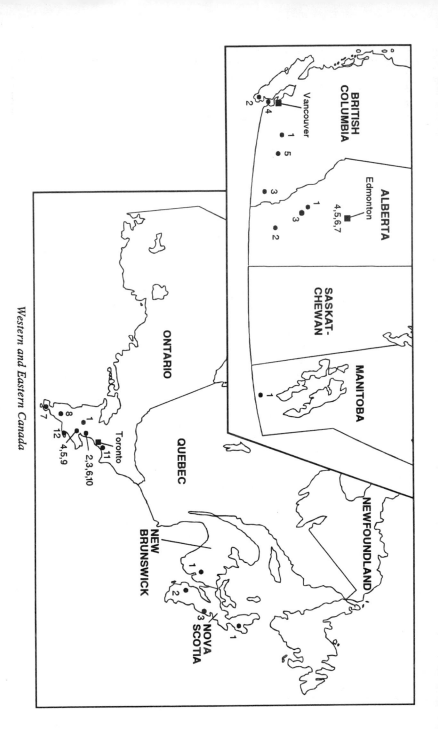

Western and Eastern Canada

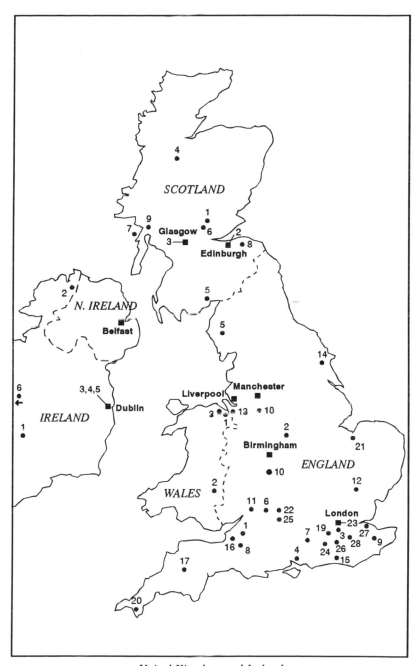

United Kingdom and Ireland

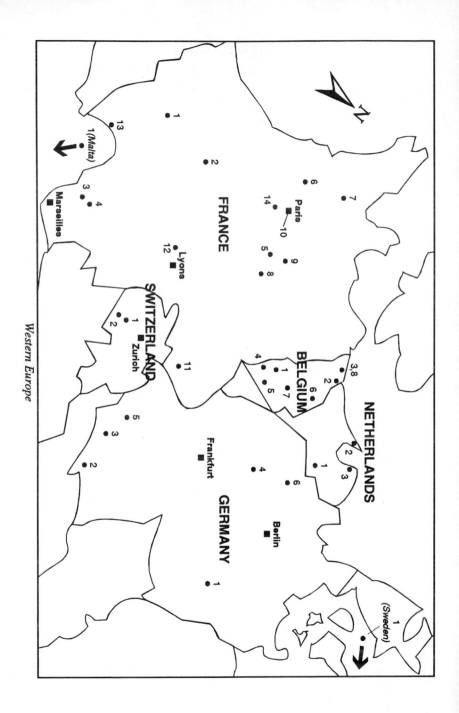

Western Europe

138

Appendix B

Supplementary Retreat Guest House Addresses

In addition to the retreat center guest houses described in the Guide, the following list of other locations presents promising possibilities for excellent retreat experiences. Call or write for information. Please enclose a self-addressed stamped envelope.

United States

ALABAMA

Benedictine Sisters Conference Center
916 Convent Rd.
Cullman, AL 35056
(205) 734-4622

Monastery of the Visitation
2300 Spring Hill Ave.
Mobile, AL 36607
(205) 473-2321

ARKANSAS

St. Scholastica Center
Box 3489
Fort Smith, AR
(501) 783-1135

CALIFORNIA

Center for Spiritual Development
434 S. Batavia
Orange, CA 92668-3995
(714) 744-3175

Christ the King Retreat Center
6520 Van Maren Lane
Citrus Heights, CA 95621
(916) 969-4706

El Carmelo Retreat House
926 E. Highlands Ave. POB 446
Redlands, CA 92373
(714) 792-1047

Holy Spirit Retreat Center
4316 Lanai Rd.
Encino, CA 91436
(818) 784-4515

Manresa Jesuit Retreat House
801 E. Foothill Blvd.
Azusa, CA 91702-1330
(818) 969-1848

Marianist Center
22622 Marianist Way
Cupertino, CA 95014-2668
(408) 253-6279

Mary and Joseph Retreat Center
5300 Crest Rd.
Rancho Palos Verdes, CA 90274
(310) 377-4867

Mater Dolorosa Retreat Center
700 N. Sunnyside Ave.
Sierra Madre, CA 91024
(818) 355-7188

Mercy Center
2300 Adeline Dr.
Burlingame, CA 94010
(415) 340-7474

Mount Mary Immaculate
Retreat Center
3254 Gloria Terrace
Lafayette, CA 94549-2025
(510) 934-2411

Poverello of Assissi Retreat House
1519 Woodworth St.
San Fernando, CA 91340
(818) 365-1071

St. Anthony Retreat Center
43816 Sierra Dr. Hwy. 198
Three Rivers, CA 93271-0249
(209) 561-4595

St. Clare's Retreat House
2381 Laurel Glen Rd.
Soquel, CA 95073
(408) 423-8093

St. Francis Retreat Center
P.O. Box 1070
San Juan Bautista, CA 95045
(408) 623-4234

Vallombrosa Center (Diocesan)
250 Oak Grove Ave.
Menlo Park, CA 94025
(415) 325-5614

Villa Maria Del Mar
2-1918 E. Cliff Dr.
Santa Cruz, CA 95062
(408) 475-1236

COLORADO

Holy Cross Abbey
P.O. Box 351
Canon City, CO 81212
(719) 275-8631

Queen of Peace Oratory
5360 Columbine Rd.
Denver, CO 80221
(303) 477-9139

Regis Retreats
3450 W. 53rd Ave.
Denver, CO 80221-6568
(303) 458-4100

Sacred Heart Jesuit Retreat House
P.O. Box 185
Sedalia, CO 80135-0185
(303) 688-4198

CONNECTICUT

Abbey of Regina Laudis
Box 273, Flanders Rd.
Bethlehem, CT 06751
(203) 266-7724

Edmundite Apostolate Center
Enders Island
Mystic, CT 06355
(203) 536-0565

Episcopal Camp
and Conference Center
Bushy Hill Rd., P.O. Box 577
Ivoryton, CT 06442
(203) 767-0848

Holy Family Retreat House
303 Tunxis Rd.
West Hartford, CT 06107
(203) 521-0440

Mercy Center at Madison
167 Neck Road, Box 191
Madison, CT 06443-0191
(203) 245-0401

Montfort Retreat Center
P.O. Box 667
Litchfield, CT 06759
(203) 567-8434

Visitation Center
223 West Mountain Rd.
Ridgefield, CT 06877
(203) 438-9071

FLORIDA

Dominican Retreat House
7275 SW 124 St.
Miami, FL 33156
(305) 238-2711

Franciscan Center
3010 Perry Ave.
Tampa, FL 33603
(813) 229-2695

Holy Name Priory
PO Drawer H
St. Leo, FL 33574
(904) 588-8320

St. John Neumann Renewal Center
685 Miccosukee Rd.
Tallahassee, FL 32303
(904) 224-2971

HAWAII

Spiritual Life Center
2717 Pamoa Rd.
Honolulu, HI 96822
(808) 988-7800

ILLINOIS

Bellarmine Hall
P.O. Box 268
Barrington, IL 60010
(708) 381-1261

Cenacle Retreat House
P.O. Box 797
Warrenville, IL 60555
(708) 393-1231

Cardinal Stritch Retreat House
P.O. Box 455
Mundelein, IL 60060
(312) 566-6060

King's House of Retreats
700 N. 66th St.
Belleville, IL 62223
(618) 397-0584

Resurrection Center
2710 S. Country Club Rd.
Woodstock, IL 60098
(815) 338-1032

St. Mary's Retreat House
1400 Main St., Box 608
Lemont, IL 60439
(708) 257-5102

Tolentine Center
20300 Governors Hwy.
Olympia Fields, IL 60461
(708) 748-9500

Villa Redeemer Redemptorist Center
1111 N. Milwaukee Ave.
Glenview, IL 60025
(708) 724-7804

INDIANA

Beech Grove Benedictine Center
1402 Southern Ave.
Beech Grove, IN 46107
(317) 788-7581

Kordes Enrichment Center
841 E. 14th St.
Ferdinand, IN 47532-9216
(812) 367-2777

Lindenwood Retreat Center
Convent Ancilla Domini, P.O. Box 1
Donaldson, IN 46513
(219) 935-1780

Open Spaces
115 W. Cleveland Ave.
Elkhart, IN 46516
(219) 522-5350

Our Lady of Fatima Retreat House
Notre Dame, IN 46556
(219) 234-1067

Quaker Hill Conference Center
10 Quaker Hill Dr.
Richmond, IN 47374-1925
(317) 962-5741

Sarto Retreat House
P.O. Box 4169
Evansville, IN 47724-0169
(812) 424-5536

Yorkfellow Institute
920 Earlham Dr.
Richmond, IN 47374
(317) 983-1575

IOWA

American Martyrs Retreat House
P.O. Box 605
Cedar Falls, IA 50613
(319) 266-3543

Christian Conference Center
Route 3, Box 70
Newton, IA 50208
(515) 792-1266

Shalom Retreat Center
1001 Davis Ave.
Dubuque, IA 52001
(319) 582-3592

KANSAS

Acuto Center
1165 Southwest Blvd.
Wichita, KS 67213
(316) 945-2542

KENTUCKY

Catherine Spalding Center
P.O. Box 24
Nazareth, KY 40048
(502) 348-1515

Knobs Haven
Loretto Motherhouse
Nerinx, KY 40049-9999
(502) 865-2621

Marydale Retreat Center
945 Donaldson Hwy. (Erlanger)
Covington, KY 41018-1093
(606) 371-4224

Moye Spiritual Life Center
St. Anne Convent
Melbourne, KY 41059
(606) 441-0679

LOUISIANA

Abbey Christian Life Center
Saint Joseph Abbey
Saint Benedict, LA 70457
(504) 892-1800

Archdiocesan Spirituality Center
12951 Morrison Road
New Orleans, LA 70128
(504) 242-1155

Cenacle Retreat House
5500 St. Mary St., P.O. Box 8115
Metairie, LA 70011
(504) 887-1420

Dominican Conference Center
540 Broadway
New Orleans, LA 70118
(504) 861-8711

Manresa House of Retreats
P.O. Box 89
Convent, LA 70723
(504) 562-3596

Our Lady of the Oaks Retreat House
P.O. Box D
Grand Coteau, LA 70541-1004
(318) 662-5410

Rosaryville Spirit-Life Center
400 Rosaryville Rd.
Ponchatoula, LA 70454
(800) 627-9183

MAINE

Marie Joseph Spiritual Center
RFD 2
Biddeford, ME 04005
(207) 284-5671

Notre Dame Spiritual Center
Alfred, ME 04002
(207) 324-6160
(207) 324-6612

MARYLAND

All Saints Convent
P.O. Box 3106
Catonsville, MD 21228
(301) 747-6767

Seton Retreat Center
333 S. Seton Ave.
Emmitsburg, MD 21727-9297
(301) 447-3121

Villa Cortona Apostolic Center
7007 Bradley Blvd.
Bethesda, MD 20817
(301) 365-0612

MASSACHUSETTS

Craigville Conference Center
Craigville, MA 02636
(508) 775-1265

Espousal Shrine & Retreat House
554 Lexington St.
Waltham, MA 02154
(617) 893-3465

La Salette Center for Christian Living
947 Park St.
Attleboro, MA 02703
(508) 222-8530

The Marist House
518 Pleasant St.
Framingham, MA 01701
(508) 879-1620

Miramar Retreat Center
P.O. Box M
Duxbury, MA 02331
(617) 585-2460

Mount Carmel Retreat House
Oblong Rd., Box 613
Williamstown, MA 01267
(413) 458-3164

Passionist Retreat
and Conference Center
110 Monastery Ave.
West Springfield, MA 01089
(413) 736-5458

Retreat Center—Sisters of St. Joseph
339 Jerusalem Rd.
Cohasset, MA 02025
(617) 383-6029

Retreat House
490 Washington St.
North Easton, MA 02356-1294
(508) 238-2051

St. Basil's Salvatorian Center
30 East St.
Methuen, MA 01844
(508) 683-2959

MICHIGAN

Augustine Center
P.O. Box 84
Conway, MI 49722-0084
(616) 347-3657

Capuchin Retreat
62460 Mt. Vernon Rd., Box 188
Washington, MI 48094
(313) 651-4826

Colombiere Retreat/
Conference Center
9075 Big Lake Rd., P.O. Box 139
Clarkston, MI 48347-0139
(313) 625-5611

Manresa Retreat House
1390 Quarton Rd.
Bloomfield Hills, MI 48304
(313) 564-6455

Marygrove Retreat Center
P.O. Box 38
Garden, MI 49835
(906) 644-2771

St. Gregory's Abbey
56500 Abbey Rd.
Three Rivers, MI 49093

St. Paul of the Cross Retreat Center
23333 Schoolcraft
Detroit, MI 48223
(313) 535-9563

Weber Center
1257 E. Siena Heights Dr.
Adrian, MI 49221
(517) 263-7088

MINNESOTA

Assissi Community Center
Assissi Heights, Box 4900
Rochester, MN 55903
(507) 289-0821

The Cenacle
1221 Wayzata Blvd.
Wayzata, MN 55391
(612) 473-7308

Christ the King Retreat Center
621 S. 1st Ave.
Buffalo, MN 55313
(612) 682-1394

Maryhill Renewal Center
260 Summit Ave.
St. Paul, MN 55102
(612) 224-3615

McCabe Renewal Center
2125 Abbotsford Ave.
Duluth, MN 55803
(218) 724-5266

Villa Maria
Frontenac, MN 55026
(612) 345-4582

MISSISSIPPI

The Dwelling Place
HC-01 Box 126
Brooksville, MS 39739
(601) 738-5348

Renewal Center Diocese of Jackson
2225 Boling St.
Jackson, MS 39213
(601) 366-4452

St. Mary of the Pines
P.O. Box 38
Chatawa, MS 39632
(601) 783-3494

MISSOURI

Cenacle
3820 W. Pine Blvd.
St. Louis, MO 63108
(314) 535-2461

Marianist Retreat
and Conference Center
1280 Hwy. 109, Box 718
Eureka, MO 63025-0718
(314) 938-5390

Mercy Center
2039 N. Geyer Rd.
St. Louis, MO 63131
(314) 966-4686

Our Lady's Retreat House
3036 Bellerive Dr.
St. Louis, MO 63121-4622
(314) 389-5100

Pallottine Renewal Center
15270 Old Halls Ferry Rd.
Florissant, MO 63034
(314) 837-7100

Retreat and Conference Center
Conception Seminary College
Conception, MO 64433
(816) 944-2218

White House Retreats
7400 Christopher Dr.
St. Louis, MO 63129
(314) 533-8903

NEW HAMPSHIRE

Durham Retreat Center
33 Demeritt Rd.
Durham, NH 03824
(603) 659-6708

Hundred Acres Monastery
New Boston, NH 03070
(603) 487-2638

Oblate Retreat House
200 Lowell Rd.
Hudson, NH 03051-4934
(603) 882-8141

Star Island
P.O. Box 178, Isle of Shoals
Portsmouth, NH 03801
(603) 964-7252
Winter: 110 Arlington St.
Boston, MA 02116
(617) 426-7988

St. Francis Retreat Center
860 Central Rd., P.O. Box 514
Rye Beach, NH 03871
(603) 964-5559

NEW JERSEY

Good Shepherd Center
74 Kahdena Rd.
Morristown, NJ 07960
(201) 538-4233

Marianist Family Retreat House
Cape & Yale Aves., Box D-2
Cape May Point, NJ 08212
(609) 884-3829

St. Mary's Abbey—Delbarton
270 Mendham Rd.
Morristown, NJ 07960
(201) 538-3231

St. Paul's Abbey
Queen of Peace Retreat House
Newton, NJ 07860
(201) 383-2470 *(monastery)*
(201) 383-0660 *(house)*

San Alfonso Retreat House
755 Ocean Ave., P.O. Box 3098
Long Branch, NJ 07740
(908) 222-2731

St. Pius X Spiritual Life Center
P.O. Box 216
Blackwood, NJ 08012
(609) 227-1436

Stella Maris Retreat House
981 Ocean Ave.
Elberon, NJ 07740
(908) 229-0602

Villa Pauline
Hilltop Rd.
Mendham, NJ 07945
(201) 543-9058

NEW MEXICO

Holy Cross Retreat
P.O. Box 158
Mesilla Park, NM 88047
(505) 524-3688

Our Lady Queen of Peace
5825 Coors Rd. SW
Albuquerque, NM 87121
(505) 877-4211

Sacred Heart Retreat Center
P.O. Box 1989
Gallup, NM 87301
(505) 722-6755

Tres Rios Christian Growth Center
1159 Black River Village Rd.
Carlsbad, NM 88220
(505) 785-2361

NEW YORK

Cenacle Center for Spiritual Renewal
693 East Ave.
Rochester, NY 14607
(716) 271-8755

Chautauqua Institution
P.O. Box 1095
Chautauqua, NY 14722
(716) 357-6200

Christ the King Retreat House
500 Brookford Rd.
Syracuse, NY 13224
(315) 446-2680

Christ the King Seminary
711 Knox Rd., Box 670
East Aurora, NY 14052-0670
(716) 652-7976

Chrysalis House
235 Lake-Bellvale Rd.
Warwick, NY 10990
(914) 986-8050

Diocesan Cursillos Center
118 Congress St.
Brooklyn, NY 11201
(212) 624-5670

Don Bosco Retreat Center
Box 9000, Filor's Lane
West Haverstraw, NY 10993
(914) 947-2201

Franciscan Center
Jackson Avenue
Hastings-on-Hudson, NY 10706
(914) 478-3696

Linwood Spiritual Center
139 South Mill Rd.
Rhinebeck, NY 12572
(914) 876-4178

Mount Alverna Retreat House
P.O. Box 858
Wappingers Falls, NY 12590
(914) 297-5706

Mount Irenaeus
   Franciscan Mountain Retreat
West Clarksville, NY
Write to or call·
St. Bonaventure University
St. Bonaventure, NY 14778
(716) 973-2470

Mount Manresa
239 Fingerboard Rd.
Staten Island, NY 10305
(718) 727-3844

Mount St. Alphonsus
   Spiritcare Center
Rte. 9W, Esopus, NY 12429
(914) 384-6550

New Skete Communities
P.O. Box 128
Cambridge, NY 12816
(518) 677-3928

Notre Dame Retreat House
5151 Foster Rd., P.O. Box 342
Canandaigua, NY 14424
(716) 394-5700

Our Lady's Guest and Retreat House
Graymoor
Rte. 9
Garrison, NY 10524
(914) 424-3300 (Our Lady)
(914) 424-3671 (Friary)

The Priory
P.O. Box 336
Chestertown, NY 12817
(518) 494-3733

Regina Maria Retreat House
77 Brinkerhoff St.
Plattsburgh, NY 12901
(518) 561-3421

St. Columban Center
6892 Lake Shore Rd., Box 816
Derby, NY 14047
(716) 947-4708

St. Ignatius Retreat House
Searingtown Rd.
Manhasset, NY 11030
(516) 621-8300

St. Josaphat Retreat House
East Beach Rd.
Glen Cove, NY 11542
(516) 671-8980

St. Mary's Villa
RR 1, Box 59
Sloatsburg, NY 10974-9617
(914) 753-5100

St. Ursula Center
Middle Rd., P.O. Box 86
Blue Point, NY 11715-0086
(516) 363-2422

Tagaste Monastery
Route 59
Suffern, NY 10901
(914) 357-0067

NORTH CAROLINA

Camp Carolwood & Retreat Center
Rt. 5, P.O. Box 428
Lenoir, NC 28645
(704) 758-1467

Living Waters Reflection Center
1420 Soco Rd.
Maggie Valley, NC 28751
(704) 926-3833

St. Luke's House
322 E. McBee St.
Lincolnton, NC 28092
(704) 735-0929

NORTH DAKOTA

Presentation Prayer Center
1101 32nd Ave. S.
Fargo, ND 58103
(701) 237-4857

OHIO

Bergamo Center for Lifelong Learning
4400 Shakertown Rd.
Dayton, OH 45430
(513) 426-2363

Grailville
932 O'Bannonville Rd.
Loveland, OH 45140
(513) 683-2340

Jesuit Renewal Center/
  Loyola Retreat House
5361 S. Milford Rd.
Milford, OH 45150
(513) 831-6010

Jesuit Retreat House
5629 State Rd.
Cleveland, OH 44134-2292
(216) 884-9300

Loyola of the Lake
  Jesuit Retreat House
700 Killinger Rd.
Clinton, OH 44216
(216) 896-2315

Our Lady of Pines
  Retreat/Renewal Center
1250 Tiffin St.
Fremont, OH 43420
(419) 332-6522

St. Joseph Christian Life Center
18485 Lake Shore Blvd.
Cleveland, OH 44119
(216) 531-7370

St. Mary of the Springs
Conference Center
2320 Airport Dr.
Columbus, OH 43219
(614) 252-0380

St. Therese's Retreat Center
5277 E. Broad St.
Columbus, OH 43213
(614) 866-1611

Spirituality Center/Sisters of Charity
5900 Delhi Rd.
Mt. Saint Joseph, OH 45051-1500
(513) 347-5453

OKLAHOMA

Office of Worship & Spiritual Life
7501 NW Expressway
Oklahoma City, OK 73123
(405) 721-5651

OREGON

Alton L. Collins Retreat Center
32867 SE Highway 211
Eagle Creek, OR 97022
(503) 637-6411

Christian Renewal Center
22444 North Fork Rd. SE
Silverton, OR 97381
(503) 873 6743

Franciscan Renewal Center
0858 SW Palatine Hill Rd.
Portland, OR 97219
(503) 636-1590

St. Rita's Retreat Center
P.O. Box 310
Gold Hill, OR 97525
(503) 855-1333

PENNSYLVANIA

Ciotti Manor
P.O. Box 25, Herman Rd.
Herman, PA 16039
(412) 287-4794

Daylesford Abbey
220 S. Valley Rd.
Paoli, PA 19301
(215) 647-2530

Dominican Retreat House
750 Ashbourne Rd.
Elkins Park, PA 19117
(215) 224-0945

Green Hills Methodist Camp
Barree, PA 16615
(814) 669-4212

IHM Spiritual Renewal Center
Box 568, RR 1
Cresco, PA 18326
(717) 595-7548

Jesuit Center for Spiritual Growth
Church Rd., Box 223
Wernersville, PA 19565
(215) 678-8085

Precious Blood Spirituality Center
3950 Columbia Ave.
Columbia, PA 17515-9714
(717) 285-2215

San Damiano Center
609 S. Convent
Aston, PA 19014
(215) 459-4125

St. Joseph Center
2900 Seminary Dr., US Rt. 30
Greensburg, PA 15601
(412) 834-7350

St. Joseph's-in-the-Hills
Retreat House
2nd and Warren Ave.
Malvern, PA 19355
(215) 473-6500

St. Vincent Retreat Program
St. Vincent Archabbey
Latrobe, PA 15650
(412) 532-6600

Spruce Lake Retreat
RD 1, P.O. Box 605
Canadensis, PA 18325
(717) 595-7505

Villa Maria Community Center
Box 424
Villa Maria, PA 16155
(412) 964-8861

147

PUERTO RICO

Centro Capuchino
P.O. Box 1865
Trujillo Alto PR 00760-1865
(809) 761-8410

RHODE ISLAND

Mercy Lodge
P.O. Box 7651
Cumberland, RI 02864
(401) 333-2801

Our Lady of Peace
Spiritual Life Center
Box 507, Ocean Rd.
Narragansett, RI 02882-0507
(401) 783-2871

Portsmouth Abbey
Portsmouth, RI 02871
(401) 683-2000

SOUTH CAROLINA

Holy Saviour Priory
P.O. Box 40
Pineville, SC 29468
(803) 351-4356

Oratory Center for Spirituality
P.O. Box 11586
Rock Hill, SC 29731-1586
(803) 327-2097

Springbank Dominican Retreat Center
Rt. 2, Box 180
Kingstree, SC 29556
(803) 382-3426

SOUTH DAKOTA

Blue Cloud Abbey
P.O. Box 98
Marvin, SD 57251
(605) 432-5528

Manna Retreat Center
RR 3, Box 105
Sioux Falls, SD 57106
(605) 743-2228

TEXAS

Bishop Thomas J. Drury
Retreat House
1200 Lantana
Corpus Christi, TX 78407
(512) 289-6501

Cedarbrake Renewal Center
P.O. Box 58
Belton, TX 76513
(817) 780-2436

Cenacle Retreat House
420 N. Kirkwood
Houston, TX 77079
(713) 497-3131

Christ the King Retreat Center
802 Ford St., P.O. Box 3745
San Angelo, TX 76902
(915) 658-3900

Holy Family Retreat Center
9920 N. Major Dr.
Beaumont, TX 77713-9316
(409) 899-5617

Mt. Carmel Center
4600 W. Davis St.
Dallas, TX 75211-3498
(214) 331-6224

Mt. Carmel House of Prayer
9600 Deer Trail Dr.
Houston, TX 77038
(713) 445-8830

Mt. Tabor Retreat House
12940 Upper River Rd.
Corpus Christi, TX 78410
(512) 241-1955

Omega Center
P.O. Box 268
216 W. Highland
Boerne, TX 78006
(512) 249-3894

Our Lady of the Pillar
Marianist Retreat Center
2507 NW 36th St.
San Antonio, TX 78228
(512) 433-1408

San Juan Retreat House
P.O. Box 998
San Juan, TX 78589
(512) 787-3852

Schoenstatt Training Center
Star Rt. 1, P.O. Box 100
Rockport, TX 78382
(512) 729-2771

Spiritual Renewal Center
Route 3, Box 238
Victoria, TX 77901
(512) 572-0836

UTAH

Desert Light
2775 Nuevo
Moab, UT 84532
(801) 259-6056

Our Lady of the Mountain
Retreat House
1794 Lake St.
Ogden, UT 84401
(801) 392-9231

VERMONT

Mount St. Mary Convent
100 Mansfield Ave.
Burlington, VT 05401
(802) 863-6835

Weston Priory
RR1, Box 50
Weston, VT 05161
(802) 824-5409

VIRGINIA

Dominican Retreat
7103 Old Dominion Dr.
McLean, VA 22101-2799
(703) 356-4243

The Well Retreat Center
18047 Quiet Way
Smithfield, VA 23430
(804) 255-2366

WASHINGTON, D.C.

Washington Retreat House
4000 Harewood Rd. NE
Washington, DC 20017
(202) 529-1111

WASHINGTON

Houston Conference Center
Box 140
Gold Bar, WA 98251
(206) 793-0441

Redemptorist Palisades Retreat
P.O. Box 3739
Federal Way, WA 98063
(206) 927-9621

WEST VIRGINIA

John XXIII Retreat Center
100 Hodges Rd.
Charleston, WV 25314
(304) 342-0507

WISCONSIN

The Bridge-Between Retreat Center
4471 Flaherty Dr.
Denmark, WI 54208
(414) 864-7230

Byron Center —
United Methodist Retreat Center
Rt. 1, Box 78
Brownsville, WI 53006
(414) 583-3633

De Koven Center
600 21st St.
Racine, WI 53403
(414) 633-1650

Dwelling Place
528 N. 31st St.
Milwaukee, WI 53208
(414) 933-1100

Franciscan Spirituality Center
920 Market St.
LaCrosse, WI 54601-4782
(608) 782-8899

Holy Name Retreat-Chambers Island
P.O. Box 23825
Green Bay, WI 54305-3825
(414) 437-7531

Marynook Inc.
Ecumenical Retreat Center
500 S. 12th St., Box 9
Galesville, WI 54630
(608) 582-2789

Perpetual Help Retreat Center
1800 N. Timber Trail Lane
Oconomowoc, WI 53066
(414) 567-6900

St. Anthony Retreat Center
300 E. 4th St.

Marathon, WI 54448-9602
(715) 443-2236

St. Clare Center for Spirituality
7381 Church St. (Polonia)
Custer, WI 54423
(715) 592-4680

St. Francis Retreat Center
503 S. Browns Lake Dr.
Burlington, WI 53105
(414) 763-3600

St. Joseph Retreat Center
3035 Logerquist Rd.
Bailey's Harbor, WI 54202
(414) 839-2391

Schoenstatt Center
W. 284 N. 698 Cherry Lane
Waukesha, WI 53188
(414) 547-7733

Canada

ALBERTA

Mount St. Francis Retreat
P.O. Box 340
Cochrane, AB, Canada T0L 0W0
(403) 932-2012

BRITISH COLUMBIA

Bethlehem Retreat Centre
2371 Arbot Rd.
Nanaimo, BC, Canada V9R 5K3
(604) 754-3254

St. Elizabeth Seton House of Prayer
RR 4, Site 20, Box 9
Kelowna, BC, Canada V1Y 7R3
(604) 764-4333

MANITOBA

Missionary Oblate Renewal Centre
601 Rue Aulneau
Winnipeg, MB, Canada R2H 2V5
(204) 233-7287

Our Lady of the Prairies
Box 37
Elie, MB, Canada R0H 0H0
(204) 353-2440

St. Benedict's Educational Centre
225 Masters Ave., R.R. 1B ·
Winnipeg, MB, Canada R3C 4A3
(204) 339-1705

Villa Maria Retreat House
100 Place Villa Maria
St. Norbert, MB, Canada R3V 1A9
(204) 269-2114

NOVA SCOTIA

Bethany Centre
Motherhouse of Sisters of St. Martha
Antigonish, NS, Canada B2G 2G6
(902) 863-4726

ONTARIO

Adult Spirituality Centre
3600 Curry Ave.
Windsor, ON, Canada N9E 2T6
(519) 969-7379

Cedar Glen
P.O. Box 345
Bolton, ON, Canada L7E 5T3
(416) 859-0220

CSJ Centre of Spirituality
P.O. Box 155, Station A
Hamilton, ON, Canada L8N 3A2
(416) 528-0138

Holy Cross Centre
for Ecology & Spirituality
RR 1
Port Burwell, ON, Canada N0J 1T0
(519) 874-4502

Holy Cross Priory
204 High Park Ave.
Toronto, ON, Canada M6P 2S6
(416) 767-9081

Manresa Retreat House
2325 Liverpool Rd.
Pickering, ON, Canada L1X 1V4
(416) 839-2864

Marylake Augustinian Retreat House
P.O. Box 550
King City, ON L0G 1K0
(416) 833-5368

Mount Carmel Spiritual Centre
7021 Stanley Ave.
Niagara Falls, ON, Canada L2G 7B7
(416) 356-4113

QUEBEC

Laval Residence Centre
CP 2208 Terminal Postal
Quebec City, PQ, Canada G1K 7P4
(418) 656-5632

SASKATCHEWAN

Madonna House
P.O. Box 928
Gravelbourg, SK, Canada S0H 1X0
(306) 648-3393

Queen's House
Retreat and Renewal Centre
601 Taylor St. W.
Saskatoon, SK, Canada S7M 0C9
(306) 242-1916

St. Michael's Retreat
P.O. Box 220
Lumsden, SK, Canada S0G 3C0
(306) 731-3316

France

Monastère de l'Adoration-Réparatrice
39, rue Gay-Lussac
75005 Paris
43 26 75 75

Monastère de Bethléem
Notre-Dame-de-la-Présence-de-Dieu
2, rue Mesnil
75116 Paris
45 01 24 48

Carmel Notre-Dame-de-Lourdes
17, route de Pau
65100 Lourdes
62 94 26 67
(in southern France, near the
Pyrenees, 80 mi. SW of Toulouse)

Communauté de l'Abbaye
B.P. 3
50116 Le Mont-Saint-Michel
33 60 14 47
(in NW France, 160 mi. W of Paris, 1
mile off the coast of the English
Channel)

Carmel de Notre-Dame-de-Pitié
1164, route d'Auxerre
Saint-Germain
10120 Saint-André-les-Vergers
25 82 20 19
(in NE France on the Seine River, 92
mi. SE of Paris)

Abbaye Sainte-Marie-de-Maumont
Juignac
16190 Montmoreau-Saint-Cybard
45 60 34 38
(in western France,
35 mi. E of Bordeaux)

Monastère Sainte-Claire
2, rue de la Berque
12600 Mur-de-Barrez
65 66 00 46
(in southern France,
75 mi. S of Clermont-Ferrand)

Dompierre-sur-Besbre
Abbaye de Sept-Fons
03290 Dompierre-sur-Besbre
70 34 50 92
(in southern France,
95 mi. SW of Dijon)

Abbaye de Lérins
B.P. 157
06406 Cannes Cedex
93 48 68 68
(in southern France on the
French Riviera, 10 mi. S of Nice)

Abbaye Sainte-Marie-du-Désert
Bellegarde-Sainte-Marie
31530 Lévignac
61 85 61 32
(in southern France,
10 mi. W of Toulouse)

Abbaye Notre-Dame-
de-Bonne-Espérance
Échourgnac
24410 Saint-Aulaye
53 80 36 43
(in southwestern France,
30 mi. NE of Bordeaux)

Abbaye de Notre-Dame-des-Neiges
07590 Saint-Étienne-de-Lugdarès
66 46 00 68
(in southeastern France,
35 mi. SE of Lyon)

Abbaye Notre-Dame-d'Igny
Arcis-le-Ponsart
51170 Fismes
26 78 08 40
(in northeastern France, 80 mi. NE of
Paris, near Reims on the Vesle River)

Abbaye Notre-Dame-de-Timadeuc
Bréhan
56580 Rohan
97 51 50 29
(in western France on the Oust River,
45 mi. W of Rennes)

Abbaye d'Oriocourt
57590 Delme
87 05 31 67 *or* 87 01 31 67
(in northeastern France,
7 mi. W of Chateau-Salins
in the Nancy/Strasbourg region)

Monastère des Carmélites
51, avenue Clemenceau
14000 Caen
31 93 66 63
(a port city in northwestern France
on the Orne-Odon River,
125 mi. WNW of Paris)

Abbaye Notre-Dame-de-Bonneval
12500 Espalion
68 91 40 24
(in southern France, 15 mi. NE of
Rodez and 90 mi. NE of Toulouse)

Carmel
Flavignerot
21160 Marsannay-la-Côte
80 42 92 38
(in east-central France, on the
eastern slopes of Côte D'Or,
a few miles S of Dijon)

Carmel
6, rue du Puits-Noir
18000 Bourges
48 24 34 04
(in central France, 126 mi.
directly S of Paris)

Abbaye Notre-Dame
65190 Tournay
62 35 70 21
(in southern France, 9 mi. ESE of
Tarbes and 70 mi. SW of Toulouse)

Abbaye Notre-Dame-de-Fidélité
13490 Jouques
42 57 80 17
(in southeastern France in Provence;
35 mi. NE of Marseilles)

Monastère de la Visitation
192, rue Lorthiois
59420 Mouvaux
20 26 94 34
*(in the far northern tip of France,
between the cities of Lille and Roubaix)*

Prieuré Saint-Dodon
Moustier-en-Fagne
59132 Trelon
27 61 81 28
*(in northern France,
9 mi. SE of Avesnes)*

Abbaye Notre-Dame
2, rue de L'Abbaye
B.P. 8
61201 Argentan Cedex
33 67 12 01
*(in northwestern France, on the
Orne River, 110 mi. W of Paris)*

Carmel
59, boulevard du Luxembourg
50300 Avranches
33 58 23 66
*(in northwestern France, on the Gulf
of St. Malo, 60 mi. S of Cherbourg)*

Carmel
213, route de Lézeaux
50380 Saint-Pair-sur-Mer
33 50 12 00
*(in northwestern France on the
English Channel, 20 mi. N of
Avranches and Mont. St. Michel)*

Prieuré Saint-Jacques
50240 Saint-James
33 48 31 39
*(in northwestern France,
12 mi. S of Avranches)*

Monastère des Bénédictines
du Saint-Sacrement
1, rue Saint-Benoît
67560 Rosheim
88 50 41 67
*(in eastern France,
at foot of Vosges mountains,
3 mi. SSW of Molsheim)*

Hungary

Reformàtus Kollégium
H-4404 Debrecen
Kàlvin tér 16., Hungary
(36-52) 18-412

The House of Reconciliation
H-5309 Berekfürdò
Berek tér 19., Hungary
(36-59) 12-805

Magyarorszàgi Reformàtus Egyhàz
Soli Deo Gloria Konferenciatelepe
H-1146 Budapest
Abonyi u. 21., Hungary
(36-1) 122-2022

Protestant Study Center
H-9730 Kòszeg
Tàncsics u. 7., Hungary
(36-94) 61-808

153

Appendix C
More Retreat Center Listings in England, Scotland, Ireland
(country code 44; Ireland, 353)

Warm hospitality awaits you at the following Retreat Centers. Since reservations must usually be made in advance, you may want to contact 3 or 4 centers in the area of your choice to assure space availability. Since telephone numbers are constantly changing, you may have to use directory assistance to contact some centers. When writing, include a self-addressed stamped envelope if in the country of origin; otherwise enclose a small sum (a dollar bill would suffice) to cover postage costs. The affiliation of the orders are indicated by the following letters: C, A, Q, I for Catholic, Anglican, Quaker, and Interdenominational. **Guests of all faiths are welcome at every Center.** *(See page 95 for international call dialing.)*

The Hospice of our Lady (A)
Walsingham, Norfolk NR22 6ED
England
Telephone: 0328 820239

Bishop Woodford House (A)
Barton Road, Ely
Cambridgeshire CB7 4DX, England
Telephone: 0353 663 039

Buckden Towers (C)
Buckden, Cambridgeshire PE18 9TA
England
Telephone: 0480 811647

Hengrave Hall Centre (C)
Bury St. Edmunds, Suffolk IP28 6LZ
England
Telephone: 0284 701561

Shalom (I)
Flixton Rd., Bungay
Suffolk NR35 1PD, England
Telephone: 0986 3201

Ealing Abbey Prayer Centre (C)
2 Montpelier Ave., Ealing
London W5, England
Telephone: 081-998-2158

The Royal Foundation
of St. Katherine (A)
2 Butcher Row
London E14 8DS, England
Telephone: 071-790-3540

Damascus House Retreat and
Conference Centre (C)
The Ridgeway, Mill Hill
London NW7 1HH, England
Telephone: 081-959-8971

Community of the
Resurrection of Our Lord (A)
St. Peter's Bourne
40 Oakleigh Park South
London N20 9JN, England
Telephone: 081-445-5585

St. Paul's Retreat Centre (C)
252 Kingston Rd., Teddington
Middlesex TW11 9JQ, England
Telephone: 01-997 4034

Claridge House (Q)
Dormansland, Lingfield
Surrey RH7 6QH, England
Telephone: 0342 832150

St. Columba's House (A)
Maybury Hill, Woking
Surrey GU22 8AB, England
Telephone: 0483-766498

House of Bethany (A)
Tilford Rd., Hindhead
Surrey GU26 6RB, England
Telephone: 042 873 4578

Cenacle Retreat House (C)
Headley Rd., Grayshott, Hindhead
Surrey GU26 6DN, England
Telephone: 042 873 4412

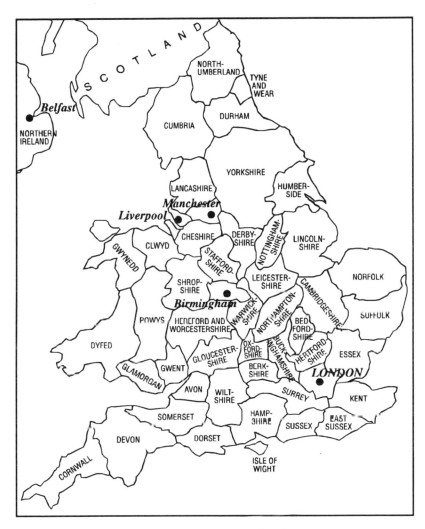

Counties of England and Wales

Hildenborough Hall (I)
Otford Hills, Sevenoaks
Kent TN15 6XL, England
Telephone: 0732 61030

St. Mary's Abbey (C)
West Malling, Kent ME19 6JX
England
Telephone: 0732 843309

Canterbury Diocesan Retreat House (A)
St. Gabriel's House, Elm Grove
Westgate-on-Sea
Kent CT8 8LB, England
Telephone: 0843 32033

Centre Space (I)
Coakham Farm, Crockham Hill
Edenbridge, Kent, England
Telephone: 0732 866338

Neale House
  Retreat and Conference Centre (A)
Moat Rd., East Grinstead
West Sussex RH19 3LB, England
Telephone: 0342 312552

Community of the Holy Family (A)
Holmhurst St. Mary, Baldslow
St. Leonards-on-Sea, East Sussex
TN37 7PU, England
Telephone: 0424 754000

Catherington House (A)
Catherington, Portsmouth
Hampshire PO8 0TD, England
Telephone: 0705 593251

Park Place Centre (C)
Wickham, Fareham
Hampshire PO17 5HA, England
Telephone: 0329 833043

Orthona Community
Coast Rd., Burton Bradstock
Bridport, Dorset DT6 4RN, England
Telephone: 0308 897130

Friary of St. Francis (A)
Hilfield, Dorchester
Dorset DT2 7BE, England
Telephone: 0300 341345

Mercer House (A)
Exwick Rd., Exeter
Devon EX4 2AT, England
Telephone: 0392 219609

Franciscan Servants
  of Jesus and Mary (A)
Posbury St. Francis, Crediton
Devon EX17 3QG, England
Telephone: 03632 2304

The Convent (A)
West Ogwell, Newton Abbot
South Devon TQ12 6EN, England
Telephone: 0626 65337

Brunel Manor Christian Centre (I)
Watcombe Park, Torquay
Devon TQ1 4SF, England
Telephone: 0803 37421

Lee Abbey (A)
Lynton, North Devon EX35 6JJ
England
Telephone: 0598 52621/52622

Copeland Court (A)
Kenwyn, Truro, Cornwall TR1 3DX
England

Ivy House (A)
3 Church St., Warminster
Wiltshire BA12 8PG, England
Telephone: 0985 214824

St. Agnes Retreat House (A)
St. Agnes Ave., Knowle
Bristol BS4 2HH, England
Telephone: 0272 776806/775863

Emmaus House (C)
Clifton Hill, Clifton
Bristol BS8 4PD, England
Telephone: 0272 738056

Almondsbury Conference House (A)
5 Sundays Hill, Almondsbury
Bristol BS12 4DS, England
Telephone: 0454 613041

Convent of St. John Baptist (A)
Hatch Lane, Clewer, Windsor
Berkshire SL4 3QR, England
Telephone: 0753 850618

St. Cassian's Centre (C)
Wallington Rd., Kintbury, Newbury
Berkshire RG15 0SR, England
Telephone: 0488 58 267

Cold Ash Centre (C)
The Ridge, Cold Ash
Berkshire RG16 9HU, England
Telephone: 0635 65353

Cherwell Centre (C)
14-16 Norham Gardens
Oxford OX2 6QB, England
Telephone: 0865 52106

Charney Manor (Q)
Charney Bassett, Wantage
Oxfordshire, OX12 0EJ, England
Telephone: 0235-868206

St. Mary's Convent (A)
Wantage, Oxfordshire OX12 9DJ
England
Telephone: 02357 60171

Bridgettine Convent (C)
Fulmer Common Rd., Iver Heath
Buckinghamshire SL0 0NR, England
Telephone: 75366 2073

Verulam House (A)
Verulam Rd., St. Albans
Hertfordshire AL3 4DH, England
Telephone: 0727 53991

All Saints Pastoral Centre (C)
Shenley Lane, London Colney
St. Albans, Hertfordshire AL2 1AF
England
Telephone: 0727 22010

Ecton House (I)
Ecton, Northamptonshire NN6 0QE
England
Telephone: 0604 406442

La Retraite (C)
Harborne Hall, Old Church Road
Harborne, Birmingham B17 0BD
England
Telephone: 021 427 1044

Coventry Diocesan Retreat House (I)
Offchurch, near Leamington Spa
Warwickshire CV33 9AS, England
Telephone: 0926 423309

Holland House (I)
Cropthorne, Pershore
Worcestershire WR10 3NB, England
Telephone: 0386 860330

St. Philomena's Guest House (C)
Caldey Abbey, Isle of Caldey, Tenby
Dyfed SA70 7UH, Wales

Bishop Mascall Centre (I)
Lower Galdeford, Ludlow
Shropshire SY8 2RU, England
Telephone: 0584 3882

Foxhill (I)
Tarvin Rd., Frodsham
Cheshire WA6 6XB, England
Telephone: 0928 33777

Shallowford House (A)
Norton Bridge, Stone
Staffordshire, England
Telephone: 0785 760233

Spode Conference Centre (C)
Hawkesyard, Rugeley
Staffordshire WS15 1PT, England
Telephone: 0543 490112

Oulton Abbey (C)
Stone, Staffordshire ST15 8UP
England
Telephone: 0785 812 049

Wistaston Hall (C)
89 Broughton Lane, Crewe
Cheshire CW2 8JS, England
Telephone: 0270 68653

Morley Rectory (A)
Church Lane, Morley
Derbyshire DE7 6DE, England
Telephone: 0332 831 293

The Briars (C)
Crich, Matlock
Derbyshire DE4 5BW, England
Telephone: 077 385 2044

Edward King House (A)
The Old Palace, Lincoln
Lincolnshire LN2 1PU, England
Telephone: 0522 528778

Barrowby (A)
Kirkby Overblow, Harrogate
North Yorkshire HG3 1HY, England
Telephone: 0532 886240

The Grange (C)
Ampleforth, Yorkshire YO6 4EN
England
Telephone: 043 93 440

St. Peter's Convent (A)
Dovecote Lane, Horbury, Wakefield
Yorkshire WF4 6BB, England
Telephone: 0924 272181

Wydale Hall (I)
Brompton-on-Sawdon, Scarborough
North Yorkshire YO13 9DG, England
Telephone: 0723 85270

The Briery (C)
38 Victoria Ave., Ilkley
West Yorkshire LS29 9BW, England
Telephone: 0943 607287

Scargill House (I)
Kettlewell, Skipton
Yorkshire BD23 5HU, England
Telephone: 075 676 234

St. Oswald's Pastoral Centre (A)
Woodlands Dr., Sleights, Whitby,
North Yorkshire YO21 1RY, England
Telephone: 0947 810496

Crawshawbooth
  Conference Centre (A)
Burnley Rd., Crawshawbooth
Rossendale, Lancashire BB4 8LZ
England
Telephone: 0706 215120

Cenacle Retreat
  and Conference Centre (C)
7 Lance Lane, Wavertree
Liverpool L15 6TW, England
Telephone: 051 722 2271/2

St. Bernard's Priory (C)
Hyning Hall, Warton, Carnforth
Lancashire LA5 9SE, England
Telephone: 0524 732684

Brettargh Holt (C)
Kendal, Cumbria LA8 8EA, England
Telephone: 0448 60340

Rydal Hall (I)
Rydal, Ambleside
Cumbria LA22 9LX, England
Telephone: 0539 432050

Jennywell Ecumenical
  Retreat House (A)
Crosby Ravensworth, Penrith
Cumbria CA10 3JP, England
Telephone: 093 15 288

Lattendales (Q)
Greystoke, Penrith
Cumbria CA11 0UE, England
Telephone: 085 33 229

Minsteracres (C)
Consett, County Durham DH8 9RT
England
Telephone: 043 473 248

Alnmouth Friary (A)
Alwick, Northumbria NE66 3NJ
England
Telephone: 0665-830213

Fatima House (C))
Coodham, Kilmarnock KA1 5PJ
Scotland
Telephone: 0563 830296

Cenacle Retreat House (C)
Military Rd., Killiney
Co. Dublin, Ireland
Telephone: 01823411

Retreat and Conference Centre (C)
Killeshandra, Co. Cavan, Ireland
Telephone: 049 34140

Appendix D
Methodist Retreat Houses in Britain

Methodist Holiday Hotels welcome everyone to a Christian atmosphere, young or old, families or singles, regardless of denomination. If you want the security and luxury of hotel accommodation, or self-catering apartments, both are available. Single rooms are offered at no additional cost. Guests can find warmth of welcome, peace of mind, fellowship, renewal, educational seminars, and leisure pursuits at all of the Retreat Hotels. Rates for overnight, a hearty breakfast, lunch, and 5-course dinner range from £26.50 per person to £35.50 (includes VAT @ 17-1/2%). Weekly charges per self-catering flat (with completely equipped kitchen), up to 4 occupants (adults and/or children) range from £160 to deluxe @ £275. If you desire a brochure describing all of the Centers, write to: Methodist Holiday Hotels, 212 Kettering Rd., Northampton NN1 4BN, England, or call 011-0604-32792. Smoking in designated areas only and bars are alcohol-free. Payment can be made by credit card.

Palm Court, 166 Queen's Promenade, Bispham
Blackpool, Lancashire FY2 9JP
Telephone and Fax: (0253) 354370 ❖ **Guests:** (0253) 351378
Points of Interest: Bispham's cliffs and beaches, Lake District, Lancaster Castle, Fleetwood Market, cinema, parks, zoo.

Roysdean, 5 Derby Rd., Bournemouth, Dorset BH1 3PT
Telephone and Fax: (0202) 554933 ❖ **Guests:** (0202) 290610
Points of Interest: Only 7 minutes' walk to Bournemouth's golden sands. Christchurch Priory, Corfe Castle, Beaulieu Motor Museum, symphony and live theatre.

The Adelphi, Warrior Square, St.-Leonard's-on-Sea, East Sussex TN37 6BH
Telephone and Fax: (0424) 437622 ❖ **Guests:** (0424) 429750
Points of Interest: Warrior Square Gardens are 150 yards from the sea. Leeds Castle, live butterfly farms, Shire Horse Center, Old Town and leisure centre.

Bodlondeb Castle
Church Walks
Llandudno
Gwynedd LL30 2HH
Telephone and Fax: (0492) 877187
Guests: (0492) 877170
Points of Interest: Bodlondeb is a Victorian castle with a magnificent marble staircase, balcony, and exquisite stained glass. Narrow-gauge railway, dry skiing, toboggan run, copper mines, Bodnant Gardens.

Roysdean, Bournemouth, Dorset, England

159

The Park, Esplanade Rd., Paignton, Devon TQ4 6BQ
Telephone and Fax: (0803) 557856 ❖ **Guests:** (0803) 551532
Points of Interest: The Park is on the "English Riviera" with panoramic views of Torbay's sandy beaches. Kingswear Steam Train, the Donkey Sanctuary, Buckfast Abbey, and Dartington Glass Works.

The Cliff, 63 Esplanade, Scarborough, North Yorkshire YO11 2UZ
Telephone and Fax: (0723) 360581 ❖ **Guests:** (0723) 364067
Points of Interest: The Cliff, on Scarborough's beautiful Esplanade, has views of South Bay, harbor and castle. Access to beach, spa concert rooms and sun terraces. Robin Hood's Bay, Castle Howard, theatre in-the-round.

Highbury, Atlantic Rd., Weston-super-Mare, Avon BS23 2DL
Telephone and Fax: (0934) 621585 ❖ **Guests:** (0934) 621936
Points of Interest: Highbury, with an impressive bay view, has a large concert lounge, most rooms with views. Bath, Glastonbury, wild fowl refuge, Cheddar Gorge, and international helicopter centre.

Damson Dene Hotel, Crosthwaite
Nr. Bowness-on-Windermere, South Lakeland LA8 8JE
Telephone: (05935) 68676 ❖ **Fax:** (05935) 68227
Points of Interest: Damson Dene is at the southern end of Lake District National Park. It is equipped with a fitness center, squash court, jacuzzi, and heated indoor pool. Lakeland Chapel, an important part of the hotel, is open for private meditation.

Bodnant, Cwlach St., Llandudno, Gwynedd LL30 2HH
Telephone and Fax: (0492) 877187 ❖ **Guests:** (0492) 877170
Points of Interest: Bodnant, an annex of Bodlondeb Castle, is for guests who desire self-catering flats. All flats are Grade 4 (next to highest) as rated by the Welsh Tourist Board. Gateway to Snowdonia and beauty of North Wales.

Damson Dene, Crosthwaite, South Lakeland, England

Appendix E

Methodist Retreat Houses in Europe

Following is a list of Methodist Retreat Houses in Austria, France, Germany and Switzerland. They range from small to large, inexpensive to moderate, rustic to plush. Ideal locations, from seaside to the Alps, the Black Forest to the cities. Be sure to call or write ahead for confirmation on price and reservations.

AUSTRIA *(country code 43)*

Chandlerhaus
Dorf 21
A-4853 Steinbach a. Attersee, Austria
07663 306
(35 miles east of Salzburg)

FRANCE *(country code 33)*

Ferienzentrum Landersen
Sondernach
F-68380 Metzeral, France
(89) 776069
(70 miles SW of Strasbourg)

GERMANY *(country code 49)*

Begegnungsstaette der EmK
Seilerstrasse 5
3392 Clausthal-Zellerfield, Germany
(05323) 2570
(Harz Mountains, 50 miles NE of Kassel)

Erholungsheim Martha-Maria
Pöllatweg 5
8959 Hohenschwangau, Germany
(08362) 81142
(70 miles SW of Munich)

Haus Bethanien
Licthentaler Allee 64
7570 Baden-Baden, Germany
(07221) 24881
(60 miles west of Stuttgart)

Haus der Sieben Brüder
Am Nesselberg 1
6384 Schmitten 8 (Hunoldstal),
Germany
(6084) 2631
(30 miles north of Frankfurt)

Haus Hohenblick
Friederike-Fliedner-Strasse 9
6333 Braunfels/Lahn, Germany
(06442) 6087
(West of Giessen, 30 miles NE of Frankfurt)

Jakob-Albrecht Haus
Silversterwerg 11
1000 Berlin 28, Germany
(030) 4043052

Kurhaus Teuchelwald
Schomberger Strasse 9
7290 Freudenstadt, Germany
(07441) 532112
(Black Forest, 50 miles SW of Stuttgart)

Pension Wesleyheim
Ferien und Begegnungstaette
7156 Wuestenrot, Germany
(07945) 2024
(East of Heilbronn, 35 miles NE of Stuttgart)

Schwesternerholungsheim Bethanien
Howingsbrook 3
2400 Luebeck-Travemuende
Germany
(04502) 2796
(On the Ostsee, 40 miles NE of Hamburg)

Katechetisches Zentrum
"John L. Nuelsen"
Bahnhofstrasse 33
6532 Bad Klosterlausnitz, Germany
(75 miles SW of Leipzig)

Hotel Am Spatzenwald
Ferien und Rustzeitenheim
Wesleystrasse 11
6821 Rudolstadt-Schaala, Germany
Rudolstadt 222 57
(50 miles east of Hamburg)

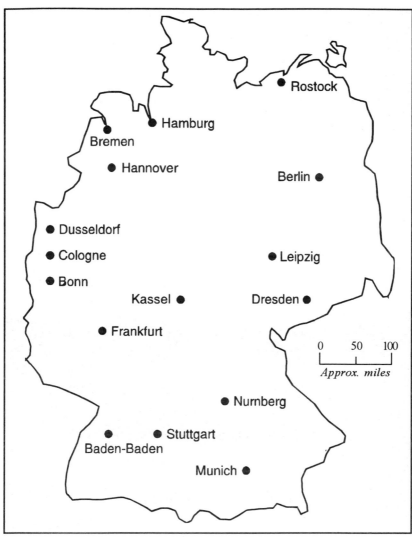

Germany — Major Cities

SWITZERLAND *(country code 41)*

The "Alpina"
CH-3715 Adelboden, Switzerland
(004133) 732235
(65 miles SE of Bern, 20 miles south of Interlaken)

Hotel Bethanien
7270 Davos Platz, Davos, Switzerland

(004133) 21101
(80 miles SE of Zurich, 30 miles north of St. Moritz)

Erholungsheim und
Familienhotel "Artos"
Alpenstrasse 45
3800 Interlaken, Switzerland
(004136) 22 69 16
(35 miles SE of Bern)

Hotel "Alfa" Garni
Laupenstrasse 15
3008 Bern, Switzerland
(004131) 25 38 66

Ferienheim "Sonneblick"
Hohenweg 45
4102 Binningen, Switzerland
(004133) 751240
(5 miles south of Basle)

Ferienhaus Lenz
Pardi 93
7083 Lausch/Lenz, Switzerland
(85 miles SE of Zurich)

Ferienheim "Rechberg"
Im Birchdorfli 16
8050 Zurich, Switzerland

Heidelberg, Germany

163

Appendix F
Italian Monasteries and Convents
(country code 39)

The following is a list of hospitable Italian Retreat Houses which offer excellent possibilities. Many of the convents and monasteries are restored, but remain in a medieval setting, with 15th century courtyards and cloisters, Gothic marble facades, mosaic pavements, and wall-length frescoes. Many have private museums with Roman and Renaissance artifacts; are located within ancient walled cities, along the seacoast with spectacular views, or in valleys surrounded by rolling hills. Rates vary from $20.00 to $30.00 a day, including food. (Map numbers correspond to listing numbers.)

1. Abbazia di Novalesa
   Monaci Benedettini Sublacensi
   Novalesa (TO)
   Telephone: 0122/5210

2. Certosa de Pesio
   Missionari della Consolata
   San Bartolomeo (CN)
   Telephone: 0171/73.81.23

3. Santuario di Vicoforte
   ex Monastero Cistercense
   ora Casa Diocesena di Spiritualità
   Vicoforte-Mondovi (CN)
   Telephone: 0174/63.605 - 63.105

4. Abbazia di
   Santa Maria della Castagna
   Monaci Benedettini Sublacensi
   via Romana della Castagna 17
   Genova Quarto
   Telephone: 010/33.62.92

5. Monastero di S. Croce del Corvo
   Padri Carmelitani Scalzi
   Bocca di Magra (SP)
   Telephone: 0187/65.791 - 65.258

6. Convento di San Pietro Apostolo
   Frati Francescani Minori
   Rezzato (BS)
   Telephone: 030/27.91.474

7. Convento di Cermenate
   Frati Francescani Minori
   Cermenate (CO)
   Telephone: 031/77.17.36

8. Eremo di
   S. Domenica di Montericco
   Frati Minori Conventuali
   Monselice (PD)
   Telephone: 0429/72.114

9. Convento de la Verna
   Frati Francescani Minori
   Chiusi della Verna (AR)
   Telephone: 0575/59.93.56

10. Monastero di Camaldoli
    Monaci Benedettini Camaldolesi
    Camaldoli (AR)
    Telephone: 0575/55.60.12

11. Abbazia di
    Monte Oliveto Maggiore
    Monaci Benedettini Olivetani
    Chiusure (SI)
    Telephone: 0577/70.70.17

12. Abbazia di S. Maria di Farfa
    Monaci Benedettini Cassinesi
    Farfa (RI)
    Telephone: 0765/27.065

13. Eremo di Monte Giove
    Monaci Benedettini Camaldolesi
    Fano (PS)
    Telephone: 0721/805136

14. Santuario del Volto Santo
    Frati Francescani Cappuccini
    Manoppello (CH)
    Telephone: 085/85.91.18

Italy

15. Abbazia di Montevergine
    Monaci Benedettini Sublacensi
    Mercogliano (AV)
    Telephone: 0825/72.294

16. Abbazia di Viboldone
    Monache Benedettine
    San Giuliano Milanese (MI)
    Telephone: 02/984.003

17. Monastero di S. Maria del Monte
    Monache Benedettine
    Bevagna (PG)
    Telephone: 0742/36.01.33

18. Monastero di San Antonio Abate
    Monache Benedettine
    Norcia (PG)
    Telephone: 0743/81.257

Also . . .
Ananda Church of Self-Realization
Ananda Europa, Casella Postale 48, 1-06088 Santa Maria degli Angeli (PG)
Telephone: 0742 / 811 212; Fax 0742 / 811 124
(75 mi. NE of Rome, near Perugia and Assissi)
Write to The Ananda Church, 14618 Tyler Foote Road, Nevada City, CA 95959 for
brochures that describe the centers in Italy, California, Washington, Oregon and
Texas. Room and board included in price.

Notes

Notes

Stay current with the latest edition of the *U.S. and Worldwide Guide to Retreat Center Guest Houses*. New Guest House listings in the U.S., Canada, and overseas added annually.

Your Guide will be sent within 7 days from the time we receive your order.

please tear along perforation

ORDER FORM

MAKE CHECK PAYABLE TO: CTS PUBLICATIONS
P.O. BOX 8355, NEWPORT BEACH, CA 92660

SINGLE COPY...$15.95 (ADD $2.00 for 1st CLASS MAIL)

ENCLOSED IS $_____ FOR _____ COPIES OF THE NEW *U.S. AND WORLDWIDE GUIDE TO RETREAT CENTER GUEST HOUSES*

WE SHIP YOUR ORDER IMMEDIATELY--

NAME _____

ADDRESS _____

CITY _____

STATE _____ ZIP _____